# COLONIAL SUBJECTS

## An African Intelligentsia and Atlantic Ideas

# COLONIAL SUBJECTS

## An African Intelligentsia and Atlantic Ideas

Philip S. Zachernuk

**University Press of Virginia**
Charlottesville and London

The University Press of Virginia
© 2000 by the Rector and Visitors of the University of Virginia
All rights reserved
Printed in the United States of America

*First published in 2000*

∞ The paper used in this publication meets the minimum requirements of the
American National Standard for Information Sciences—Permanence of Paper
for Printed Library Materials, ANSI Z39.48-1984.

Library of Congress Cataloging-in-Publication Data

Zachernuk, Philip Serge.
    Colonial subjects : an African intelligentsia and Atlantic ideas /
Philip S. Zachernuk.
       p.     cm.
    Based on the author's thesis
    Includes bibliographical references and index.
    ISBN 0-8139-1907-X (cloth: alk. paper) — ISBN 0-8139-1908-8 (paper: alk. paper)
    1. Nigeria, Southern—Intellectual life—19th century. 2. Nigeria, Southern—
Intellectual life—20th century. 3. Nigeria, Southern—Relations—Great Britain.
4. Nigeria, Southern—Relations—America. 5. Nigeria, Southern—Relations—
United States. 6. Great Britain—Relations—Nigeria, Southern. 7. America—
Relations—Nigeria, Southern. 8. United States—Relations—Nigeria, Southern.
I. Title.

DT515.9.S63 Z34   2000                                         99-038408
966.9—dc21

For Carol

# Contents

# Illustrations

# Acknowledgments

THIS PROJECT PROBABLY has tried the patience of at least as many people as it has been years in the making. I am certainly indebted to more people than there is space here for adequate acknowledgment. Martin Klein supervised the dissertation behind the present book, but far beyond that he kept the faith over many years. Toyin Falola has been a frequent source of support and encouragement in both Nigeria and North America, not least with his generous undertaking to chase down some elusive last-minute information on my behalf. Leroy Vail provided encouragement that was much appreciated. The staffs of various libraries and archives made my research realizable and indeed enjoyable: E. O. Adeniyan at Sopolu; Terry Barringer at the Royal Commonwealth Society; Sam Odularu at the University of Ibadan; Clare Brown at Rhodes House. The support, friendship, and assistance of Axel Harneit-Sievers, Georg Deutsch, LaRay Denzer, and many others made my work in Nigeria truly enjoyable. Richard Roberts' s advice on the present version proved particularly valuable. Daniel Abriel and Una Cooke helped make the illustrations possible. Figures 2 through 6 were taken from microfilm copies of the original books provided by the Cooperative Africana Microfilm Project (CAMP). François Manchuelle, tragically, died before he could see the inspiration our many conversations had on this work and before our studies of colonial intellectuals in both French and British colonial West Africa could be combined. In ways they might not even realize, my friends and colleagues at both the University of Toronto and Dalhousie University helped shape this study. I must thank John Bingham, Stephen Brooke, Barbara Clow, Jane Parpart, and Gary Kynoch in particular for their attempts (often successful) to reconfigure the prose of various drafts. Dick Holway, my acquisitions editor at the University Press of Virginia, has combined understanding, support, and discipline in ways I have found most congenial, and which played no small part in getting this project completed.

Funds received at the doctoral and postdoctoral stage from the Social Sciences and Research Council of Canada helped finance the foundation of this project and some further work. Fellowships at the University of Calgary Institute for the Humanities and the Institute for Advanced Study and Research in the African Humanities at Northwestern University allowed me to develop some of the ideas in the present work.

My parents and siblings deserve many thanks for supporting me in ways that go far beyond the work on this book; Alexander Kassamali injected both relief and reality with the many "books" he produced while waiting—at times patiently—for this one to be finished. Finally, this book would never have been if not for Carol, who created the space, time, and imperatives that moved me through almost endless stages of near completion.

# Abbreviations

| | |
|---|---|
| AG | Action Group |
| CAMP | Cooperative Africana Microfilm Project |
| *CJAS* | *Canadian Journal of African Studies* |
| CMS | Church Missionary Society |
| CO | Colonial Office |
| C.U.P. | Cambridge University Press |
| *DS* | *Daily Service* |
| FCB | Fabian Colonial Bureau |
| FCP | Fabian Colonial Papers |
| HMP | Herbert Macaulay Papers |
| IAI | International African Institute |
| *IJAHS* | *International Journal of African Historical Studies* |
| I.U.P. | Ibadan University Press |
| *JAH* | *Journal of African History* |
| *JHSN* | *Journal of the Historical Society of Nigeria* |
| *JICH* | *Journal of Imperial and Commonwealth History* |
| *JMAS* | *Journal of Modern African Studies* |
| *JNH* | *Journal of Negro History* |
| LCP | League of Coloured Peoples |
| *LDN* | *Lagos Daily News* |
| *LS* | *Lagos Standard* |
| *LWR* | *Lagos Weekly Record* |
| NCBWA | National Congress of British West Africa |
| NCNC | National Council of Nigeria and the Cameroons |

## Abbreviations

NNAI   Nigerian National Archives, Ibadan
NNDP   Nigerian National Democratic Party
NUT   Nigerian Union of Teachers
NYM   Nigerian Youth Movement
OAP   Obafemi Awolowo Papers
O.U.P.   Oxford University Press
*ROAPE*   *Review of African Political Economy*
*SLWN*   *Sierra Leone Weekly News*
UAC   United Africa Company
UCI   University College Ibadan
UNIA   Universal Negro Improvement Association
*WAP*   *West African Pilot*
*WAR*   *West African Review*
WASU   West African Students' Union

# COLONIAL SUBJECTS

## An African Intelligentsia and Atlantic Ideas

# 1

# The Invented and
# the Inventive

THE BAREST OUTLINE of modern West African history excites interest: societies conquered by European empires through the last century achieved independence in this one as newly configured nation-states. Many elements of this story—imperial conquest, nationalist resistance, capitalist transformation—provide the stuff of great history. So too does the intellectual history, tracing the ideas that Africans engaged and deployed through these grand transformations. Located in African societies being opened to the commercial ambitions, missionary projects, and ethnographic curiosity of Europeans in particular, African thinkers responded not only with their own resources but also with the resources of the modern Atlantic world. This included the culture of the African diaspora, formed by the Atlantic slave trade.

The connections between the intellectual histories of West Africa and the Atlantic world are evident in the lives of some of its more notable figures. Samuel Ajayi Crowther's life began amid the Yoruba wars reshaping western Nigeria in the early nineteenth century. Falling victim to the final phase of the Atlantic slave trade, he was liberated by British antislavery forces in 1822 and then drawn into the evangelical fervor flowing out of England to Sierra Leone. The first African made a bishop in the Anglican Church—in 1864—he not only served his faith but also provided the rapidly growing ethnographic library of his time with unique material about the West Africans among whom he worked. By his death in 1891, however, his position had become unlivable under the forces of colonial conquest and resurgent racism that overwhelmed the earlier atmosphere of missionary fraternity.

Edward Wilmot Blyden's life reveals even wider links. Shunning American racism to make his career in West Africa in 1850, his brilliant mind confronted there the imposing problem of locating Africa in the Victorian worldview. His response—proposing an "African personality" resonant with romantic nationalist ideas from Europe—inspired the Pan-African consciousness emerging across the African diaspora. Along with his colleague Alexander Crummell, Blyden's writings informed the vibrant race consciousness proclaimed by W. E. B. Du Bois at the end of the nineteenth century and elaborated during the Harlem Renaissance of the 1920s. Blyden's declaration of African difference also helped remake British attitudes to Africa. The African Society founded in Britain in 1901—with Blyden himself as a vice president—undertook its ethnographic mission partly in search of Africa's hidden cultural integrity, which Blyden had proclaimed.

Paul Gilroy has argued that the Black Atlantic—the cultural web between diasporan Africans spread around Atlantic shores—has been a crucible for modern sensibilities in the twentieth century.[1] West African intellectuals, although marginal in his analysis, formed an important filament around the Black Atlantic in these years. In Britain they received not only support but also inspiration from such towering figures in Black Atlantic cultural and political life as Marcus Garvey, Paul Robeson, and Alain Locke. In Harlem during the 1940s the African Academy of Arts and Research presented "authentic" African culture to African-American audiences. But West Africans' contacts were not restricted by color. British Fabians developed critiques of imperial policy in conjunction with the West African Students Union. In America, Nigerian students were celebrated by Eleanor Roosevelt and supported as spokespeople for Africa. African attacks on colonial racism appropriated the Allied campaign against Nazi race theories.

If it is clear that West African intellectual history involved complex exchanges with contemporary Atlantic societies, it is not immediately clear how these exchanges worked. In Britain, Crowther became a "household word" denoting the impending triumph of the Victorian civilizing mission;[2] in West Africa he became a herald of African independence and remains a hero of African achievement. Blyden has

2

long been celebrated in Pan-African circles for his assertion of African pride, but he was also celebrated by Lord Lugard—in his bible on colonial administration—in order to endorse British policies that threatened educated Africans' ambitions. After Blyden's death in 1912, Lugard even unveiled a portrait of him in Lagos. Yet a later generation of West Africans cited Blyden not in support of racial difference but as proof of African ability to match universal standards. African-American plans to return to Africa before World War I were welcomed by many West Africans; after World War II African students urged African-Americans to offer support from their own side of the Atlantic. Fabian plans for Africa were adopted virtually whole in the 1940s, while in the 1950s Nigerians roundly condemned even Fabian attempts to devise Africa's future. Throughout the colonial period colonized Africans contributed to metropolitan libraries about colonized Africans.

A history which attempts to explain in this dramatic setting the Atlantic currents that produced such shifting relations and multiple meanings promises to be as intriguing as the intellectual history of any modern community. To date, however, this story has been approached in ways that hide rather than highlight its richness. We have been offered, instead, a misleadingly simple story of the "West" confronting a distinct and distinctive "Africa" and obliging it to absorb—or repel— the forces and ideas of the modern world. Early studies of African intellectual history equated it with the rise of nationalism and focused on the inevitable migration of modern European ideas to Africa.[3] At its most sanguine, this approach saw the triumph of African nationalism as the "capstone to the growing edifice of humanity" under construction since the Enlightenment. This was a one-directional—if still incomplete—development from traditional to modern, resulting in societies divided between "two worlds of superstition and science, separated by centuries of progress, yet geographically united" in an emergent modern Africa. Following Frantz Fanon's criticisms of African leaders in the 1960s and the rise of Marxist approaches to Africa's postcolonial crises in the 1970s, celebration of nationalists gave way to stern condemnation. But the distinction between the African and the European, the indigenous and the imported, remained fundamental. African leaders were attacked for having betrayed Africa by trading African values for ill-suited Western ones. Much of

3

the small body of work on cultural and intellectual history since has continued to see the story in terms of two alternatives. In Robert July's 1980 account of the Bellagio conference on the "condition and direction of the humanities in Africa," "the main issue remained. . . . Was modern Africa to be cast in the mould of the West or would she emerge unmistakably African, an ancient culture reborn in modern idiom?"[4] In various ways, then, the study of modern African intellectual history has been cast as an ongoing struggle between opposed choices: conserving African difference or converting Africa to modern, "Western" ways.

### Rethinking the Colonial Intelligentsia

The flood of studies that have followed Edward Said's *Orientalism* helps to challenge this construction. They have made it clear that European knowledge of Africa, as of many other parts of the colonial world, was very much "invented" and "imagined" according to European needs. Further, the Africa thus invented served as one of Europe's "others," as a contrasting image against which Europe could be defined. In light of this, can we continue to accept that modern African intellectual history is best conceived, in terms used by Rupert Emerson and Martin Kilson almost thirty-five years ago, simply as a "confrontation of the indigenous-traditional and the alien-new"?[5] Should we not, rather, suspect that it is this model of change itself—reflecting the modern European insistence on African difference—which imposes the need to see African intellectuals moving out of "traditional Africa" to join the "modern European" world?

Certainly the premise of posed opposites—sometimes explicit, but often unspoken—has generated unsatisfactory accounts of the African intelligentsia. In the scholarship enthused about and focused on the rise of nationalism, virtually all political and intellectual activity through the colonial period is treated as part of the inevitable growth of nationalist consciousness and modern political awareness that reaches a climax with nationalism and decolonization. Intellectual activity that does not fit the model is left aside, and many questions about it remained unasked. The radical critique that followed tended to dismiss even these activities as unimaginative mimicry. In the popular form of the critique, the intelligentsia are characterized as various types of "bourgeoisie." They are treated as brainwashed actors (or simple mannequins) in the political economy of imperialism and neocolonialism, with little appreciation of their actual situation or cultural reality. At its most blunt, their ideas are reduced to an effect of imperial power: "In the end, imperialism determined culture for the colonized peoples, and the colonized mind was shaped to serve the purposes and intentions of capitalist imperialism."[6] Many recent treatments of colonial culture (by Africanists and others) continue with similar categories, arguing that imperial control negated colonial cultures, forcing at least Western-educated subjects to replace their African identity with a foreign one. Modern African cultural and literary work is criticized as a product shaped by imported values, meant often for foreign audiences rather than African ones.

E. A. Ayandele's singular study of the Nigerian intelligentsia through the whole colonial period is marked by this implicit incompatibility of Africa and Europe. Ayandele sees the intelligentsia as "deluded hybrids" who remained "mentally enslaved" to foreign ideas. Writing deep in the shadow of the Nigerian civil war with much illuminating passion, he remains intent on enumerating the historical failures of the educated, especially as political leaders, to steer Nigeria away from its postcolonial crises. Basil Davidson adopts Ayandele's approach in his more recent argument that a "poverty of speculative thought" led Africa's modern intelligentsia to accept the European nation-state as appropriate for Africa. Moreover, this impulse to convert rather than to conserve "became ever more vulgarized and narrowed into an unthinking truism." Ayandele and Davidson admit that there were exceptions, people like Attoh Ahuma of Ghana and Blyden who were "spasmodically aware" of the vulgarity of this agenda.[7] But their treatment dismisses these as minor, largely forgotten instances within the larger pattern. Both authors adopt attitudes more condemnatory than exploratory toward the intellectual efforts of the colonial intelligentsia. Most scholars continue to judge the intelligentsia either for converting or for failing to convert effectively from the African to the Western, caught by a dualist model which accepts only two basic categories for describing patterns in modern African thought. Studies of modern African intellectual history, constructed around these posed opposites, are too inflexible either to see or to express the intricacies involved.

A second insight can be drawn from the scholarship in Said's wake to suggest a new approach. If European intellectuals invented Africa, so too, we should presume, did African intellectuals. The latter, like Europeans, and notwithstanding their colonized status, had particular interests to serve—not least a need to define their place in the world. They too were driven by the need to express what power they held—even if it was the limited power of colonial subjects—through culture and representation. In this light, what had been seen as a story of Africans accepting or rejecting foreign ideas becomes instead a complex world of inventions—mutual, antithetical, and unconnected—in which African intellectuals engage with others' ideas of Africa to invent their own. It is a world in which paired opposites might not be found, a fluctuating field of inventiveness such as Terence Ranger evoked in examining and especially in revisiting the invention of tradition in colonial Africa.[8] By not accepting that African intellectuals in fact were caught between African and European realities but seeking instead to discern their engagement in a world of competing interests and ideas, this approach makes possible a flexibility in the construction of modern African thought unattainable with just two pillars. The choice between conversion and conservation—posed both by African intellectuals themselves and by those commenting on them—thus becomes a historical artifact to be understood and set in context, not the fundamental reality or necessary dynamic of modern African intellectual life.

African intellectual history, it needs to be said, is not inherently less involved than, say, modern European intellectual history; neither is usefully reduced to simple formulas. To suggest that African thought can be explained by saying it was colonized overlooks the question of what, exactly, it was colonized by. If the African intelligentsia sometimes did accept European constructions of Africa—if they played the part of the "other" in the colonial system—this observation should not close the discussion. European ideas of empire were far from static or monolithic, and just as there were many faces of colonial rule, so were there many faces of its "others."[9] There was also, of course, the imagery of Africa generated by Black Atlantic intellectuals concerned with locating and describing Africa in the world. Both African-

American and British attitudes and ideas about Africa were diffuse, with many minor themes and divergent traditions. Given the diversity among British colonial critics and diasporan Africans, it is not clear what exactly African colonial subjects would have mimicked. Further, the confusion of currents within the colonial period obliges careful consideration of historical periods, despite the basic continuity in the questions faced by the colonial intelligentsia. Imperial penetration complicated rather than resolved many dynamic tensions within African societies. Over the course of West Africa's colonial century before 1960, the nature of the colonial order and the context in which Africans responded to it underwent some very significant changes. The colonial economy and government penetrated farther into the hinterland, completing the connection to the export economy and transforming social relations among Africans. But it did this through the upheavals of two great depressions and two world wars, with significant regional variations as well. The construction of the colonial state ended the Victorian golden age for the West African commercial elite but also offered extensive low-level government jobs to their heirs. This situation changed again with policies of Africanization from the late 1940s. The ideology of empire also changed. Beginning as a commercial and evangelical mission to potential equals, it became a mandate to develop and protect an inferior race, then assumed the task of rapidly engineering "modern" societies. Nor was the common understanding of the nature of human society static: it resisted, then advocated, then repudiated the notion of innate differences between the "races." If a debate between conservation and conversion has endured in modern African thought, it was pursued by a group whose material fortunes and location within society were continually being altered, in ideational contexts no less mutable.

Intellectual life is more diverse, accidental, tentative, and complex than simplified characterizations can reveal. Davidson, with many others, claims that colonial schools conveyed "an invisible but always insistent directive" to their students: "ABANDON AFRICA, ALL YE WHO ENTER HERE."[10] But the education system and European discourse on Africa in general also conveyed a romantic orientalist appreciation of Africa and its cultures. Even schooled Africans could not wholly abandon Africa; family and other ties kept them there. Also, it is not clear that the nation-state ideal swept in so quickly, so early, and so easily.

7

There was a mad rush after World War II both to create African nation-states and to invent national histories to buttress these claims. But this rush emerged from a more varied political tradition which entailed precolonial, racial, and continental identities. Further, assessments of the intelligentsia that treat them as a unified group with a single tradition often conflate the "elite" with the intelligentsia. But especially after World War II, the intelligentsia in many colonies were drawn from a group increasingly divided along ethnic, status, and other lines, producing an increasingly splintered intellectual life.

The various treatments of intellectual history as a unilinear development also have led scholars to overlook the possibilities of other patterns of movement within this tradition. Blyden, with his ideas of racial conservation, is treated in many studies as a precursor of nationalism.[11] He does not fit the overall trend in favor of conversion presented by Ayandele and others; rather, his ideas have been revived in the postcolonial period as remedies for the avid appetite for conversion of the late colonial period. The real historical question, however, is not to remark at Blyden's prescience but to understand why his ideas were once popular, why they faded in the early twentieth century, and why they returned to prominence. There are similar movements back and forth between Pan-African and specifically African identities, shaped by such conditions as ideas about race and the relations of the intelligentsia to the state. We must also ask about which groups within the intelligentsia were attracted to these ideas at different times. Recognizing repeated patterns, rather than straight lines, in the colonial century of African thought opens new questions concerning how it has developed, and where it may next lead.

If the educated Africans were all nationalists, their understanding of *nation* developed over time, as did their sense of the mission of nationalism. Moreover, their nationalist faith developed not in isolation from other intellectual concerns but along with their changing understanding of history and society. If they were, alternately, merely dependent collaborators or decultured compradors within the imperial system, they fulfilled these roles neither thoughtlessly nor faultlessly. These were roles which had to be discovered through experience, and which allowed certain choices to be made. If the intelligentsia have failed to provide intellectual guidance since 1960, this needs to be explained rather than condemned. Certainly their economic position affected their ideas, but these had to be shaped in the context of African material conditions, not in some abstract and predetermined colonial realm. The choices made by the intelligentsia were influenced by their understanding and misunderstanding of their economy, society, and the African past.

This work, then, shares the spirit of diverse other attempts to restore heterogeneity to representations of colonial subjects, to refuse to reduce them to essences. I hope, in the spirit of recent scholarship, to help reorient current approaches to modern African intellectual history by framing it in a way that does not trap the story between two fabrications but rather seeks to recover its complexity and provoke fresh understanding. I ask what *Africa* meant to different people at different times rather than assume some essential or enduring meaning for the term. My wider hope is to provide some substance to a new understanding of postcolonial history which has been called for from various quarters—the need to recognize that the modern African intellectual tradition which has so often been construed in dual terms is somehow neither "traditional African" nor "modern European" but is itself a modern African creation which has to be grasped on its own terms. As the authors of *The Empire Writes Back* argue, the literary history of colonial and postcolonial societies has not been about defining or discovering a traditional essence (although understanding why some have searched for such an essence at certain times is important); rather it has been about interrogating European discourse and power from a location "within and between two worlds" and moving forward from a legacy which includes the West. Asad has suggested that anthropologists (and other scholars) of Africa need to rethink their notion of "real tradition," to recognize not only that much African "tradition" was in fact created, often in the colonial context, but also that African traditions should be seen to include argued, innovative incorporations of African and Western ideas, the very kind of tradition created by the colonial intelligentsia. Hountondji sees little sense in setting African intellectual history in terms of an enduring "African civilization" confronting a "European civilization," preferring instead to see that a plurality of African traditions have long been engaged in an ongoing interrogation of the world.[12] While the colonial intelligentsia may not belong to the "traditional Africa" of colonial discourse, they clearly are part of the plurality of African traditions, a part which cannot be overlooked. This study is about grounding our understanding of this modern African tradition in historical specificity.

A more adequate understanding of African intellectual history would seem to be not only desirable but also necessary. As the fourth postcolonial decade closes with a cloud of pessimism over the transmutation of the nationalists' victory into the "Black Man's Burden," inquiries into the development of modern African ideas are perhaps more relevant than ever before. In literary and cultural criticism, philosophy, theology, and political thought, scholars search through the past and present efforts of African thinkers and writers for insight and guidance. The appeals—by V. Y. Mudimbe, Kwame Appiah, Davidson, and others—to rethink the invention of Africa reveal the need to reevaluate the role of the African intelligentsia both in the processes of this invention and in modern African history generally. One place to start is with a clear sense of what shaped the interests and receptivity of the colonial intelligentsia, and how these changed over time. We must also realize that the colonial years were neither simply vacant nor misspent. There were voices there of value, even if they did not always carry the day. If there were harmful ideas, they also continue to exist as part of the current crises. Cultural imperialism involved both domination and dialogue. As Gyan Prakash suggests, many colonial responses are possible within the constraints of "Orientalist" or colonial discourse.[13] More has gone on than has met most historians' eyes; the struggle to "decolonize" African minds began long before the postcolonial era. Tracing these dialogues will help restore to the colonial intelligentsia the full richness of their endeavors. In any case, their ideas should be understood within the conditions in which they arose.

## The Nigerian Intelligentsia in the Atlantic World

To describe the program of this book in more specific terms, it focuses on colonial southern Nigeria, located within a broader West African setting. It is about who the intelligentsia were within southern Nigerian society, and about the social and intellectual contexts in which they thought and wrote about the pressing questions of the day. It is about how the intelligentsia were situated in Nigerian society at different times, and about connecting phases in their thought to changes in their context. It is also about revising simple ideas about the phases of Nigerian thought through careful attention to its diversity. I attempt not only to trace how Nigerian colonial subjects faced their options of conservation and conversion over a full century but also to illuminate how these options were understood at different times, and how they related to other problems. This study provides a framework within which much existing scholarship about the Nigerian intelligentsia can be connected, in which general characteristics and patterns might become apparent, and in which the tentative and accidental nature of this history can be revealed. My central intent is to provide—for my own future work and that of others—a footing for more confident inquiry into the colonial intellectual tradition in southern Nigeria. For scholars approaching Nigerian intellectual history—and indeed African and colonial intellectual history more broadly—from various disciplines, it provides the means for sharpening their insights both by illuminating the nature of the world in which colonial intellectuals functioned and by highlighting the need to attend to specific contexts within the colonial situation in which particular authors worked.

Nigeria is a rich field for this study, as the many existing studies touching on its modern intellectual history attest. There are a number of excellent works on the nineteenth century and some valuable scattered studies for periods since.[14] Autobiographies and biographies of the colonial elite continue to appear. However, beyond sharing in the generic weaknesses already outlined, most of these touch on intellectual history and the intelligentsia as part of other concerns, such as the history of literature, the press, or elite politics. Two important volumes by Robert July illustrate this. His study of early West African nationalism in *The Origins of Modern African Thought* is invaluable, but its biographical structure is episodic rather than systematic. His more recent study of "the role of the humanities in African independence" is also insightful but focused on the push for cultural independence rather than on intellectual life in general. Despite July's claim that the second volume is a sequel to the first, the interwar period falls largely unnoticed between the two.[15] His selected themes therefore are examined without adequate attention either to issues beyond political and cultural nationalism or to historical continuity. Although the present study does not pretend to be in any sense a comprehensive survey of

Nigerian thought, it does attempt to provide a historical framework which can connect patterns over southern Nigeria's colonial century.

This study both starts from and defends the notion that there is a modern intellectual tradition in southern Nigeria, initiated through the modern period by men and women who contemplated, criticized, and wrote about questions pertinent to Nigerian society and its future. It concentrates its attention on those Nigerians who stand at the core of this intellectual tradition, a group I have called the colonial intelligentsia. The intelligentsia are defined as those men and women born in Nigeria or of African descent who concerned themselves with the past, present, and future problems of Nigeria as an appendage first of the Atlantic economy and latterly of the British Empire. Membership in the intelligentsia is difficult to determine objectively or finally. A large number of Nigerians actively contributed, in public meetings and organizations or through the newspaper press and other publications, to discussions of Nigeria's past, present, and future problems. It is this participation which I use to define the intelligentsia here. The intelligentsia were in fact an amorphous group with an implicit rather than explicit sense of who belonged and who did not. Certain figures, notably journalists, figure large in this story. Later a few historians and social critics appear who set intellectual pursuits as a more central concern. But the bulk of the intelligentsia were those who followed the questions of the day, occasionally criticizing or endorsing the leading figures, without being primarily occupied with intellectual life. Thus while the broad definition adopted here allows a fluctuating and indefinite membership, it also reflects the characteristics of this group. This loose definition also captures many of the interesting but lesser-known figures.

Membership in the intelligentsia studied here is also effectively restricted to those who left a record of their thoughts. Although the colonial impact was contemplated and assessed by men and women with traditional educations in both northern and southern Nigeria, it was the intelligentsia, educated in the European mode and literate in English, who were both intimately connected to the colonial order and equipped to articulate their response to it. It was the intelligentsia who first conceived of Nigeria as an imperial dependency and later as an emergent state and who developed the intellectual tradition that addresses questions about these polities and incorporates or supersedes other traditions. This approach largely excludes two aspects of the complete story of the Nigerian intellectual response to the colonial impact: the northern response generated not by mission school graduates but by writers in the medium of Arabic and the realm of Islam and the response of unlettered Nigerians, who must not be assumed to have been passive because they left sparse documentary evidence.[16] I have, however, endeavored at least to illustrate that the intellectual history studied here not only was pursued in specific African contexts but also was shaped by ideas afoot among the unlettered, by highlighting some instances of connection. Nevertheless, this study is surely centered on the group at the core of modern southern Nigerian intellectual history.

This study traces the history of Nigerian thought by setting it within two broad contexts. The first is the situation of the intelligentsia in the society and economy of colonial Nigeria. The social and economic character of the intelligentsia rests fundamentally on their membership in the Western-educated community literate in English, the language of the colonial order. The Nigerian intelligentsia, like their European namesakes, addressed urgent questions of their day. I use the term because it was applied by both the Nigerians themselves and the British from early in the twentieth century, and because it is convenient for referring to that minority among the educated community who wrote about Nigerian problems. In the European context *intelligentsia* has the sense of a group of thinkers detached from any particular class, pursuing political or cultural ends defined by their own perceptions and knowledge. But this definition is misleading for the Nigerian context: the intelligentsia, educated in colonial ways, were set apart from the unlettered bulk of colonial society and had particular characteristics and interests because of this. They were the products of the colonial system, created to provide the clerical and other skills required by the colonial government, missions, and commercial firms. Because the colonial order required their skills, the educated community was able to reach new standards of wealth and prestige. They were an elite in the sense that they possessed certain advantages not available to the unlettered. They could communicate directly with the British and were well placed to adapt to the new opportunities of the colonial era. Over the colonial period the educated were increasingly recognized by other Nigerians as valuable allies in dealing with colonial authorities. The British also were disposed to treat them apart from other Africans. Whatever attitudes the tides of race prejudice might impose, foreign missionaries, merchants, and administrators often were obliged to rely on educated Africans to connect them to African leaders and producers. The educated community also was dependent on the colonial order, in particular on colonial trade. Without the foreign presence the need for a Western-educated community would not have arisen. As the changes wrought under colonial rule were accepted as irrevocable, the special attraction of education was confirmed. Education—and especially higher education overseas—offered this group a new perspective on things African, but it did not sever them from African societies. Marriage, kinship, political affiliation, and—very importantly—economic interdependence, all tied them to their nonliterate compatriots. Without African interests to speak for, without a rural economy supplying exports, without an "Africa" to change, the educated community was without a purpose. In short, the educated community occupied a medial position in colonial Nigeria. The literate, by virtue of their education, in this sense constituted the "middle classes" situated between the peasant producers and laborers on one side and the European presence comprised of government, merchants, and missionaries on the other. This book shows how the nature and composition of the educated community changed in significant ways over time, while this medial quality endured.

Although the ideas of the intelligentsia are examined here in light of their particular needs and interests, this has been cast as a study of a medial community rather than as a study of class and ideology. I am pursuing here what I take to be the spirit of recent work that seeks to overcome the restraints of "foundational" categories such as race and class, to open new, more contingent ways of interpreting the history of colonialism. This approach allows us to ask how ideas and society were related in colonial Nigeria, rather than following the practice of looking at Nigerian ideas in connection with more or less predetermined social and political processes.

The second setting is the broader context of ideas in which the intelligentsia operated. In particular, this is the context of ideas about colonial Africa current among British critics of African affairs and in the African diaspora. Understanding the broader context of ideas in which the intelligentsia operated, and changes therein, is equally essential to understanding the patterns of Nigerian intellectual history. Christopher Miller argues in *Theories of Africans* that French West African writers must be understood as participants in a dialogue with the discourse of colonialism, and especially with colonial anthropology. Paulin Hountondji argues that "nationalism in the colonies has never involved a total rejection of the colonizer's culture; rather, it has always consisted in choosing from the many currents of that culture those which are most favourable." He suggests in particular a "complicity" between colonial nationalists and "'progressive' Western anthropologists." Patrick Williams and Laura Chrisman argue that future analyses of postcolonial discourse should appreciate the way West African intellectuals, for example, were connected beyond European imperial boundaries especially to the African diaspora. I see—and explore—these broader conversations in Nigeria between the intelligentsia and both European and African diasporan discourses. Through trade, education, and mission, the Nigerian intelligentsia were most closely associated with British society. But significant members of the Nigerian educated community came from other parts of West Africa and the African diaspora. Writers in both these communities were concerned with the development of Africa, and it was their ideas on this question that the Nigerian intelligentsia found most accessible and relevant to their own situation. The Nigerian intelligentsia therefore sought answers to the problems they faced in the idioms of the Atlantic world in general and at times especially within the Black Atlantic. As the ideas in this broader context changed, for example, about the meaning of race in human society, they changed in Nigeria as well. But, rooted in their own particular circumstances as a colonial intelligentsia, the Nigerians did not simply mimic these broader trends or follow them unthinkingly. The Nigerian intelligentsia were aware of the variations and contradictions within Atlantic thought. Even when the main thrust of British thought was inimical, they found there ideas congenial to their needs. On the other front, African-American offers of Pan-African solidarity were received selectively and sometimes broken into their component parts. The Nigerians' relations with this broader context were therefore intricate and continually changing. Over the course of a century, the Nigerian intelligentsia exploited, selected, and adapted British and African-

American ideas about Africa as they attempted to work within accepted bounds of thought to construct their own worldview. The Nigerian intelligentsia are best treated as the contemporaries of the intelligentsia in Britain, America, and elsewhere, critically aware of relevant ideas, rather than as an isolated or backward group lagging behind contemporary trends. They are objects of, but also participants (however minor) in, the modern discourse that simultaneously constructed Africa and the West. Nigerian intellectual history consists, then, of the ongoing adaptation and reformulation of ideas current in the broader context in light of the continually shifting situation and interests of the Nigerian intelligentsia. The patterns that emerge from this interaction are neither simple nor consistent. They need to be perceived historically, not just conceived through theory. To trace colonial Nigerian intellectual history is to trace innovators attempting to define their own discourse with material embedded in other discourses — most notably in colonial discourse — using but not always obeying the terms set by those discourses.

This study, by examining in some detail over a century of this many-sided invention in a particular setting, hopes to suggest a more fruitful approach to modern African intellectual history, which might be of wider value for studies of the former colonial world. I am not content with simply adding to the already extensive literature — often more literary and theoretical than historical — on the culture of imperialism and the intricacies of European conceptions about their colonized others. Rather, my intention here is to help shape a much smaller body of literature concerned with what I consider a much more important question for historians of modern Africa and, indeed, for historians of the former colonial world. Knowing that modern European knowledge of the non-European world is shaped through processes of invention is only a small step toward understanding how people outside Europe perceived and received these bodies of knowledge which clearly figure conspicuously in their postcolonial cultures. I am here concerned less with the objects of European imperial observation than with colonial subjects — with the ideas of a particular community as it lived through a context shaped by these ideas.

The chapters mark out a broad chronological framework which highlights moments of important change in southern Nigerian intellectual history. This framework should be taken as tentative, suited to the themes pursued here and perhaps useful as a general guide but not as the final word on the shape of modern Nigerian intellectual history. Future work, concerned with other themes, might well demand revised or alternate schemes. Because I am concerned with broad patterns more than the content and accomplishments of Nigerian writing, my approach stresses concerns common to the intelligentsia rather than individual luminaries and their works. Chapter 2 examines the founding of the Christian educated community from about 1840 to the 1880s in a few southern Nigerian enclaves. It argues that the intelligentsia of this educated community adopted the promise of the civilizing mission expressed in both mission and colonial policies to reinforce their presence in a tenuous colonial project. Their Victorian demeanor armed them against both European racist denigration and often hostile receptions in the coastal hinterland. Chapter 3 examines the first great set of crises they faced from the 1880s to the First World War, involving imperial partition, the rise of a racist colonial state, and increasingly unfavorable economic conditions. Here, inspired by both Black Atlantic notions of racial pride and British ethnographers' celebration of African difference, the intelligentsia endorsed and developed Blyden's search for the "African personality." Although an effective riposte to racist denigration, this search also launched Nigerian thought in contrary directions, involving the need to both assert and deny an essential difference from Europe. Chapter 4 examines the high colonial period between the world wars, suggesting that conditions here allowed the potential of the Nigerian intelligentsia to surface: an ability to adapt ideas from Atlantic discourse about Africa to suit their particular needs. They resolved some of the tensions generated in the late nineteenth century and devised a promising economic program. I do not argue that the ideas developed here represent some secret formula that needs to be rediscovered by future African or Nigerian intellectuals; I suggest only that the efforts of the interwar intelligentsia reveal how, in this moment of the battle of inventions, colonial subjects could develop effective lines of thought. Chapter 5 examines how the fruits of these efforts were put in disarray during the two hectic final colonial decades, marked by rapid movement from war and radical protest to decolonization, elite complacency, and outsiders' discontent. Here the enduring weaknesses of colonial subjects—notably their limited ability to shape the broader discourse about Africa and development—combined with complex new social dynamics to leave them accepting the prize of their anticolonial struggle in a disoriented state. I suggest, however, that a certain legacy of this long century endured, to rise in time out of the confusion: the ability to adapt ideas about Africa and development from others and to rework them to serve specific Nigerian interests. It is this pattern, as much as the specific traditions developed within it, that this study seeks to establish as the legacy of these colonial subjects.

# 2

# The Race to Civilize

## The Roots of Colonial Intellectual Life, 1840–1880s

IN 1839 SOME SIXTY-SEVEN settlers from Sierra Leone arrived in Badagry in search of a better future. These pioneers were Saro, people of Yoruba descent who had been enslaved in southern Nigeria, shipped overseas, liberated by the British antislavery squadron, then settled and perhaps educated in Sierra Leone. Soon followed by others from Sierra Leone as well as European missionaries, they established new communities in Lagos and its hinterland. British expeditions up the Niger in 1841 and 1854, combining exploration, trade, and missionary interests and staffed in part by Sierra Leonean returnees, soon added an eastern wing. This was anchored to a mission station in Calabar from 1846. From the 1840s, then, Western-educated Africans began to establish foundations for the colonial intelligentsia.[1]

However, these dramatic expeditions should not convey the sense that the history of the colonial intelligentsia stems neatly from these implantations in Nigerian soil. First, the Saro colonists arrived in societies undergoing and seeking to understand many momentous changes and quickly became enmeshed in these changes and discussions, especially as the returnees often had ties to their host societies. Further, as among the Efik of Calabar, European education predated the arrival of the Saro. Tied to the Atlantic economy from the sixteenth century, coastal notables hired foreign teachers or sought education overseas to better equip themselves for trade. By the early nineteenth century, one Calabar town had even established a school for English and accountancy. These early pupils of Western ways were not foreigners but often were closely tied to powerful families, whose interests they advanced jointly with their unlettered peers. The pioneer Saro settlements, then, were not planted in barren ground but in dense growth. Second, the educated immigrants themselves had connections through Sierra Leone to diverse parts of Africa and the Atlantic world. Freetown long remained an important nucleus of colonial West African society. Its Krio culture was formed in a context set by the indigenous Mende and Temne, among whom settled a community comprised of England's black poor, free Africans from colonial America via Nova Scotia, and Jamaican Maroons, complemented by liberated slaves from throughout West Africa. The Krio diaspora contained wealthy and poor, missionaries and farmers, literate Moslems and unschooled Christians. In Lagos further contributions came from returning freedmen from Brazil (known as Amaro) and the Caribbean, as well as American blacks concentrated in Liberia but also circulating along the coast.[2] Thus diversity, not least of political and religious traditions, long marked the Nigerian educated community. The ideas of the colonial intelligentsia have roots in discussions that reach beyond the narrow confines of colonial settlements, intertwining with various traditions of thought.

Rather than trace a single elegant stem, then, this study attempts to make some sense of profuse growth derived and nurtured from many sources. It does this by focusing on the colonial intelligentsia as a group within Nigerian society, but not as a group apart. They have strong links to the Saro immigrants but also to other communities involved in the precolonial Atlantic economy. Their local connections—unbroken, new, and renewed—divided and guided them through diverse histories. Yet they are a recognizable group because they share a cluster of attributes. They held the English language, the Christian church, British law, international commerce, and Western education as institutions relevant—but not always necessary—to their lives. By virtue of their Western education they shared a set of opportunities, roles, and dilemmas. In their printing presses, mission organizations, schools, and mercantile ventures, through intermarriage and family connections, they developed an identifiable tradition of engagement with the modern world. From the 1840s until British colonial conquerors swept through southern Nigeria in the 1880s, the intelligentsia established themselves as critical agents of a project to bring

"Western civilization" to "Africa." They were products of the emergent colonial system, but neither simple nor prefigured ones. Constructing a place for themselves necessarily from the cultures around them, they drew on ideas from all sides to pursue their material and intellectual interests. As a still small and insecure community, they found strength in the civilizing project proffered by contemporary European and Black Atlantic thinkers. But if their lives and ideas in the middle nineteenth century stressed Africa's need for foreign inspiration, they never forgot their identity as "Africans," however little they may have inquired into the deeper contours of this still largely geographical category.

### Minor Clerks to Merchant Princes

A central argument of this book is that we must understand Nigerian colonial subjects within their changing historical context. For the mid-nineteenth century, as for later periods, this context is presented here in layers. Salient features of the general political and economic situation first set the scene for a general description of the Western-educated community. Their geographic and demographic dimensions, as well as their social institutions, provide in turn the setting for the lives and ideas of the intelligentsia themselves, that is, for the minority within the Western-educated population who actively engaged the ideas and issues of their time.

The economy of southern Nigeria in the middle decades of the nineteenth century was marked by uncertainty and transition, but also by certain conditions that favored small-scale traders, including many Saro.[3] If conditions were not ideal, they were at least remembered in the later nineteenth century as something of a golden era. Slave exports dominated trade with Europe in the eighteenth and early nineteenth centuries, although never to the total exclusion of other exports. Delta ports like Calabar had long prospered in this trade. Lagos rose to prominence as a slaving port only in the early nineteenth century, exporting victims of the turmoil among Yoruba states. But in the early nineteenth century, changes in the Atlantic economy and British pressures to abolish slaving disrupted this already disruptive trade, displacing it with industrial markets for palm oil and other tropical products such as timber and cotton. These were collected from the farmers in the hinterland and exchanged for European cloth, alcohol, iron, and other manufactures—a pattern which would endure into colonial times. By 1841 Calabar had converted to palm; elsewhere the transition was slower, and often more reluctant. The British forced their preferences on Lagos through bombardment in 1851 and then conquest in 1861. The change from slave to commodity exports occasioned widespread upheavals that are as yet not completely understood. This transition seems to have been unsettling less because established trades collapsed than because new ones expanded, and new dynamics were introduced. Palm oil exports created new labor demands, reordering gender roles and often requiring increased slave labor. New elites, holding plantations or advantageous positions in the new transportation systems, acquired substantial slave populations often in short order. Land was colonized along the Cross River to provide palm oil and food supplies for the cash-cropping workforce. Trading houses in the Niger Delta absorbed slaves to augment their commercial power, while also exploiting large numbers of slaves on plantations. Hierarchies of authority were threatened by wealth concentrated in the hands of entrepreneurs rather than elders. Added to the "bedlam" of "anarchy, confusion, slave-hunting, pillage and political dismemberment" that raged among the Yoruba states,[4] this clearly was a context ripe for crises and for urgent debates about tradition and change. When the quest for export crops threatened the food supply in the Cross River area in 1828, local prophets warned of disaster if more traditional ways were not resumed. From the 1850s to the 1870s, slaves and ex-slaves in the Delta organized to establish their rights in the new context of abolition and palm production. In Ibadan and Abeokuta, Yoruba political traditions were remolded in the crucible of war, at the behest of war leaders who could not be lightly ignored. Even among the Ijebu, who avoided many of the rampages of war, the younger men acquired new power through trade and began to enforce their will on the established authority of their elders. In this time of marked economic and political rivalry, those seeking advantage would find new ideas attractive. The emergent colonial intelligentsia confronted these issues not only as purveyors of new ideas; they were also soon involved in the competition for advantage themselves.

There were fortunes to be made in this uncertainty and disruption. As Brazilian and other slavers were replaced by largely British palm oil exporters, others also found a place in the new patterns of exchange. Various African middlemen along the coast began organizing labor to collect and bulk goods for export, guarding their role jealously. The Ijebu resolutely refused entry to foreigners from nearby Lagos; others spread false intelligence of the hostile reception awaiting anyone who tried to penetrate the hinterland. Ibadan, at the center of the Yoruba wars, grew rapidly within a vibrant interior trade network. In the east the Aro trade system continued through economic transition, in part by supplying labor to the palm oil complex. Saro and Amaro immigrants joined the system at all levels, but especially as traders, exploiting their advantages to compete with middlemen and exporters. Their relations with established African and European participants combined competition for commercial advantage and pursuit of common interests. The educated returnees had certain advantages over unlettered Africans in expanding exchange with Europe, not least the advantages that literacy allowed in dealing with European suppliers and creditors or in conducting trade through extended networks. Some returnees also could exploit family connections and local knowledge in their relations with the hinterland, advantages most European traders lacked. Amaro exploited their contacts with Brazil. Probably most importantly, the advent of regular steamship service from 1852 created market and technological conditions that favored small-scale traders over large European firms. Operating on small profit margins but taking advantage of quick turnaround times and low capital costs, African traders spread widely along the Nigerian coast and up the Niger, as independent merchants in their own right or as agents of larger Krio, Gold Coast, or European firms. Efik middlemen in Calabar, taking advantage of the Saro traders' better terms, allied with them to challenge the dominant position of larger European firms, evoking the latter's malice. Although prices and alliances remained unpredictable, and European hostility endured, these conditions for prosperity lasted until the mid-1870s.[5]

Trade became the pith of Krio economic life, not least because luck and good management could lead to considerable success. In 1880 over half the population of Lagos was involved in trade, including the upper elite. Some pursued it only temporarily or in addition to other interests. A few "merchant princes" established considerable fortunes in these years. Perhaps most famous was R. B. Blaize of Lagos, whose fortune surpassed those of all but a few European merchants by the century's end. Those who were not merchants relied indirectly on trade. The colonial government in Lagos required clerks, including senior ones, to administer this trade. Although distinguished careers in government service were not numerous, neither were they yet obstructed by a color bar. Every nineteenth-century newspaper editor was also somehow involved in trade. African evangelists—also often traders—saw commerce as Christianity's handmaiden. Clerical jobs expanded beyond Lagos with the steam-powered trade boom; trade and mission stations spread hand in hand up the Niger in the 1860s and 1870s.[6] However difficult and uncertain, the mid-nineteenth century was a period of expansion and promise for the Saro and other Africans engaged in the emergent colonial system.

The Western-educated community was dynamic, spreading geographically as it grew in size, thus gradually altering its significance and position within Nigerian society. But up to the 1880s it remained small, even in Lagos, and more closely connected to communities abroad than within Nigeria. Lagos in 1861 had a total population of about 25,000. This included perhaps 3,000, and no more than 5,000, "native foreigners"—comprised mostly of Saro and Amaro in about equal numbers augmented by West Indians and Liberians—and a few educated indigenes. By 1891 some 5,200 Lagosians were deemed able to read and write and another 3,500 able to read, totaling perhaps 8,700 literates in a township of under 33,000. Although none of the census categories correspond exactly to the educated community, they suggest that it had grown by the 1880s to at most one-quarter of the urban Lagos population. Despite a doubling of Christians in Lagos Township during the 1870s, traditionalists still outnumbered them six to one by 1881, and Moslems by four to three. If literacy in English was on the rise, so was literacy in Yoruba, while Portuguese remained popular among Amaro. The educated communities outside Lagos taken together did not equal it in numbers or significance. Abeokuta was another important center, with perhaps 600 Saro in 1842 and at most 6,000 Christians (not all educated) by the 1880s. There were less than 100 educated Africans in Old Calabar in 1862. Perhaps 400 Krio and

Gold Coast commercial staff worked in both the Niger Delta and up-river in the 1870s.[7] Literacy is not an exact measure of the bounds of the colonial intelligentsia, but it is a skill central to the development of the community. Nigerians not literate in English were not necessarily excluded: the printed word could be spoken, and the spoken word inscribed. But literacy in English made direct participation possible and allowed membership in a group with special opportunities within the colonial order. Even those with only minimal education could both express their views in print and provide a readership for others.

Mission schools appeared quickly to start Nigerian roots for these communities. The first was founded at Badagry in 1843; others soon followed in Abeokuta, Lagos, and other southwestern towns. From the 1850s mission schools in the east spread from centers such as Calabar, Bonny, Qua Iboe, and Onitsha. Antecedent institutions in Sierra Leone, Ghana, and the West Indies provided their teaching staff for some time. Nigerian schools only slowly developed the ability to expand under their own power, even though many graduates became teachers. Missionaries founded schools as tools of evangelism; the colonial government needed them to train clerks. But growth depended above all on African interest. Sierra Leonean repatriates were keen, supplying most of the 3,000 primary students in Lagos by 1891 and sending others to Freetown. For most Nigerians the benefits of Western education remained less than obvious. The protection offered by the mission house first attracted ex-slaves and outcasts; missionaries among the Yoruba redeemed children who had been pawned. Some were drawn by the commercial value of literacy and accounting skills. School attendance dropped in Calabar when missionaries began to offer Scripture lessons in Efik instead of English, the language of commerce. Even so, family heads often sent slaves or dependents to acquire new skills, not their own children. Only as the colonial order became ensconced and the opportunities opened by Western education became obvious did interest in schools expand rapidly. First in places like Lagos and Calabar, but only after the 1880s in towns more protected from the colonial impact, the problem of education gradually shifted from finding recruits to finding space for them. Women were by no means treated equally; their curriculum tended toward domestic rather than literary training. But in relative proportions at least they fared better in these years than they would until the end of the colonial period, in part because the early missionaries and Saro held that educated women were integral to successful Christian families. An all girls' school opened in Onitsha as early as 1858. Early Lagos primary schools had three male students for every two females; as primary education spread to rural communities, the ratio rose to five to one.[8]

These schools offered little more than basic education in Christian and European ways. Secondary schools, following the curriculum and structure of British grammar schools, were much less common or widespread. The first secondary school appeared in Freetown in 1845; Lagos had one by 1859 and four by 1880, one of which was for girls. Secondary education abroad was expensive. The training offered West African elite girls by a London institute in the 1860s approximately equaled the annual salary of a lower-class government clerk or three months' salary for a first-class clerk.[9] Although this meant perhaps only one in twelve primary graduates in western Nigeria might find a place in secondary school, the road would narrow even more sharply for future cohorts, as primary education expanded far faster than secondary in the early colonial period.

Very few Africans had postsecondary education in mid-nineteenth-century Nigeria, especially women. Only those with wealthy families or generous mission sponsors could afford the travel abroad this required. For men, careers in the church were both more popular and more accessible than in law or medicine, not least because Fourah Bay College in Sierra Leone offered training. Founded in 1827 primarily to train African workers for the Church Missionary Society and affiliated with the University of Durham in 1876, it attracted many Saro. Perhaps 180 students from Yoruba families were admitted to Fourah Bay before 1900. It is not clear, however, how many graduated or pursued careers in Nigeria. The early clergy, doctors, and lawyers were from the Gold Coast or the African diaspora, slowly joined first by Sierra Leoneans and then Saro. The first medical doctors—Sierra Leoneans Africanus Horton and W. B. Davies—qualified in London with CMS and British government support in 1858. Of the seven who qualified in the quarter century following 1874, six were born in Sierra Leone and one in Lagos; six also had Yoruba family backgrounds. C. Sapara Williams, the first Yoruba and Nigerian lawyer, returned from the Gold Coast in 1886. Sir Kitoyi Ajasa, the first Lagos-born lawyer, returned only in 1894.[10] Up to the 1880s, then, "native foreigners" commanded the heights of the educational pyramid. Their links to the culture of the Black Atlantic also dominated colonial intellectual life.

The elite few who did sojourn in Britain in the mid-nineteenth century entered a society in which people of African descent were found in a variety of circumstances.[11] After slavery was abolished at the turn of the nineteenth century, many of those who had been domestic slaves continued as servants. The less fortunate formed the black poor; black musicians, especially in military bands, enjoyed a higher status. A few had risen from slavery to active roles in the abolitionist movement, in the manner of Olaudah Equiano and Ottobah Cugoano. Such men could associate with other abolitionist leaders among the middle classes. In the mid-nineteenth century black American abolitionists joined these circles. Already Britain was a meeting place within the African diaspora. Racial prejudices existed; but for blacks with education and social connections, barriers were more permeable than they would become through the period of Britain's imperial dominance in Africa. Educated Africans were still objects of curiosity rather than contempt and were evaluated more by class than by color. Early university students clustered at London and Edinburgh, expanding later to Oxford and Cambridge. When men such as Horton came to study with government and CMS support, or when others came with personal or family funding, they therefore found a relatively congenial setting. The West African elite of the later nineteenth century could holiday in Britain, marry there, and carry some of their status with them. Queen Victoria was godmother to the first child of Saro merchant J. P. L. Davies and his wife Sarah. Self-proclaimed friends of Africa, such as Ferdinand Fitzgerald of the African Aid Association and the *African Times* or Thomas Hodgkin, a founder of the Aborigines Protection Society, were also part of Africans' social network, in addition to their commercial relationships. Some twenty-three West Africans visited Britain under CMS auspices between 1840 and 1883. A long-standing pattern was established early on. Britons interested in African affairs, for commercial, scholarly, or philanthropic reasons, linked up through such figures as Hodgkin and Fitzgerald with Africans on the coast and in Britain to pursue these interests. Interests often overlapped, as in the project to spread the gospel and promote trade. Through such exchanges the West African

intelligentsia kept themselves abreast of current British thought pertinent to their situation. Nigeria's missionary and commercial contacts
with America were much weaker than with Britain, but not absent.
Few West Africans traveled to America until late in the century, but
connections were established from the early decades through back-to-
Africa movements in Liberia, and members of both communities
intersected in England. The most direct evidence of connection was
the tour of the American Martin Delany and the Jamaican Robert
Campbell among the Yoruba in 1859-60, undertaken with an eye to
promoting African-American settlement. Campbell returned in 1862
to establish a newspaper in Lagos.

## Uncertain Victorians

Life in Lagos in these decades was precarious. This was especially true
for the educated immigrants attached to the nascent colonial order.
The cession of Lagos in 1861 promised to strengthen the colonial presence, but the immediate effect was to provoke local suspicion of
British power, with which the educated Africans were associated.
Britain's commitment to the colony seemed hesitant, as British politicians discussed reducing their West African possessions, and the official seat of administration rested from 1866 to 1874 in Sierra Leone,
then until 1886 in the Gold Coast. Trade conditions fluctuated frequently, often sharply. Citizens of property were plagued by both
criminal and accidental fires; chronically underfunded public hygiene
left noxious odors and threatened worse. The judicial system, according to Adewoye, long remained "characterized by improvisation."
The Saro missionary James Johnson was unimpressed with the architecture and amenities when he arrived in Lagos from Freetown in
1874. Inland the threats were even more direct. Typically, the early returnees were treated with suspicion or disdain in their areas of origin,
which they had often left as slaves. British antislavery policies in particular aroused the resentment of interior slaveholding notables and
inspired a group of Lagos Saro to petition the government in 1864 for
more tolerance of the way "the natives look upon and hold their domestic slaves in the same light and manner as civilized nations [do]
their real and personal property." Anti-British feeling, they made clear,
was threatening Saro interests. "During the protectorate the British

name was venerated, confidence placed to an unlimited extent, so much so that then the dress of an Englishman was a sufficient passport to any man to travel through these parts inland, as far as the banks of the Niger . . . but since the cession of Lagos the interior is closed against us, either for commerce or exploration. We are looked upon as spies and deceivers, the British name has become odious, our lives are not even safe among the natives."[12] At Brass in 1873 the killing of a totem animal led to assaults on church property and Christian converts, indicative of a persistent antipathy. Abeokuta, a town recently founded by the Egba in the midst of the Yoruba wars, was something of an exception. There were many Egba among the Saro, and many were welcomed back to Abeokuta as a means of strengthening the fledgling city against its rivals. But even here Egba disagreement with the British antislavery agenda and their sense that the Lagos government favored British over African traders inspired the violent expulsion of colonial agents in 1867. Some returnees chose to confine themselves to Lagos rather than face such hostility. But hostility was balanced with the recognition that the educated community could play an invaluable role mediating between hinterland states and British authorities, especially for Yoruba leaders facing the simultaneous problems of civil war and British penetration. Even isolationist Ijebu maintained contact with Ijebu Saro in Lagos in spite of distaste at seeing compatriots adopt European ways.

This insecurity was not relieved by the divisions of class, ethnicity, and politics within the educated community itself. Economic fortunes among the Sierra Leoneans varied widely. Saro also faced competition for elite status from educated Amaro, wealthy Muslims, and non-Yoruba educated Christian repatriates. Cultural distinctions were maintained between the Saro, the educated "natives," and the uneducated. Amaro, especially after the abolition of slavery in Brazil in 1888, crossed the Atlantic in both directions in pursuit of marriage, education, and employment, reinforcing their special identity. Lagosians formed a variety of ethnic associations to promote the interests of specific polities and to strengthen their own commercial relations with them. Ijesha and Ekiti in Lagos formed the Ijesha Association in the 1850s, and later the Ekitiparapo. A specifically Brazilian group later emerged from the more inclusive Ijesha Association. Egba formed a mercantile association in 1860 and an Egba National Club in 1892. As early as 1865 Saro and Amaro with Ibadan connections founded a Yoruba National Association. Many of the early leaders were returnees with very little European education, but some notable members of the intelligentsia were also involved. For example, James Johnson and J. A. O. Payne, an almanac writer and historian, were prominent in the Ijesha Association.[13] If these associations forged connections with Yoruba states in the interior, they also divided Lagos along the battle lines of the continuing Yoruba wars.

These divisions were overlaid by a thick covering of Victorian culture, a feature which struck European observers most forcefully. In Calabar wealthy chiefs imported prefabricated houses from Liverpool and stuffed them with foreign furnishings. In frock coats and elaborate dresses, the Lagos elite organized and attended music recitals, soirées, levees, cricket matches, elaborate church weddings, the Queen's Birthday Ball, and jubilees. High street fashions from England shaped high style on the marina. Lagos even sported a musical merry-go-round in the early 1880s. Fraternal societies, such as the Masonic lodge founded in 1868, rounded out the picture. Their connections to Europe and even America were close in timing as well as spirit. J. A. O. Payne was the first African member of a civil servants' Prayer Union which had been founded in Britain in 1872. In 1887 he helped form a similar union in Lagos. The Independent Order of Good Templars, established in the United States in 1851, opened a Lagos chapter in 1868 with African members. At least some of the 100 or so Europeans in Lagos shared parts of their social life with the elite. Prominent families like the Coleses, Moores, Randles, and Williamses dined at Government House and exchanged social calls among their intertwined families. A scattering of debating, literary, and scientific societies appeared bespeaking Victorian middle-class interest in science and improvement. An Old Calabar Literary Society was active in Duke Town in 1864 and 1865. Another early effort was the Lagos Academy proposed by prominent merchants in 1866 to foster the study of arts and science. Bishop Samuel Ajayi Crowther, the famous CMS missionary, was the patron; Payne was a member. The academy seems to have had at best a short life. But its vice president, Robert Campbell, who became "one of the leading intellectuals of Lagos" in these decades, organized the Lagos Science Society in the 1860s which at least hosted some lectures.[14] Campbell, with Nathaniel King, was again active in the Lagos Mutual Improvement Society established in 1879. It had 150 members by 1884, including a European president, and lasted until at least 1890. Churches and schoolrooms were popular venues for public meetings and lectures; Glover Memorial Hall, founded in 1887, quickly became a favorite site.

They also made efforts to secure contemporary books and journals. The evangelical and educational literature that arrived with the early missionaries was complemented by a wider selection of English books by the 1860s. The CMS bookstore and press established in 1869 soon proved reliably profitable, dealing in some secular texts along with its religious publications. It quickly faced competition from a book section in J. P. Haastrup's retail establishment. By the 1880s Lagosians could order books with relative ease, from America as well as from Britain. Libraries reveal less steady growth. At least three attempts were made to found lending libraries in the 1860s, by among others the academy and Governor Glover. The Young Men's Christian Association, which also sponsored lectures and debates, had some success with a lending library around 1874, but public libraries seem to have remained only proposals until at least the end of the century. Efforts to produce printed material were more successful. The first presses came with the Presbyterian mission to Calabar in 1846 and the CMS outpost in Abeokuta in 1854. Both were used to train printers while producing educational and religious material. The earliest newspaper, printed mostly in Yoruba, came from the CMS Abeokuta mission between 1859 and 1867. Robert Campbell used his press to train apprentices and produce the *Anglo-African* newspaper in Lagos from 1863 to 1865; the *Lagos Times* in 1880 initiated the continuous history of the Lagos newspaper press. The wealthy merchant Blaize opened a commercial printing press in 1875; by 1880 there were at least five printing establishments in Lagos alone.[15]

But these Victorian social habits are only part of the story. As Kopytoff observes, the Sierra Leoneans early on made clear that they did not "look upon the new and the old cultural practices as mutually exclusive alternatives."[16] The Catholic Brazilians and Muslim Yoruba among the social elite did not fit British Victorian norms; neither did Saro family trees. As Mann's research shows, economic change and kinship structures in Lagos inspired a variety of marriage practices, combining Christian and Yoruba patterns, which better suited contemporary reality than Yoruba or Victorian forms. The extended family remained central to social relations. The bride and groom of a high society wedding in 1886 graciously received both a silver teapot and locally woven cloth as gifts. While some merchants imported prefabricated houses, others devised styles of housing drawing variously upon British, local, and Brazilian models, adapted to the climate and materials of the coast. Mission converts in Abeokuta joined the Ogboni Society by 1861, a traditional Egba body of considerable secular authority. Challenged by European missionaries, the Ogboni members refused to accept that they were in any way repudiating their Christian faith. Returnees and converts in Abeokuta acquired titles and pawns in traditional ways. So too, Saro merchants could conspire with Abeokuta chiefs to attack European merchants threatening their trade or harass British expeditions harboring their escaped slaves. There was no clean opposition here between Victorian and African ways.

Why this incomplete reproduction of Victorian society? The conventional explanation has been that the educated community was a transitional group moving from the "African" world toward the "modern." They supposedly aspired to become "Western" instead of "traditional." Thus Mahmud Tukur can argue that this group was becoming "fundamentally and essentially Anglo-Saxon." In the meantime they remained "suspended . . . between two possible world views," neither here nor there.[17] Ultimately, of course, they are held to have failed to bridge the chasm. But posing this kind of opposition obscures historical understanding. The educated community was situated in societies in flux, not resting in tradition, and never would move along Western lines. It did exist at the interface between the European colonial presence and African society. The culture that developed in this space did include elements from both worlds. As Baker sees them, the Saro stood "between the two worlds of European and African culture . . . collectively distinguished from other Lagosians by their unique cultural background. They emulated English behaviour and mannerisms, rejected native authority, and adopted Christianity; but most Saros were also fully conscious of their Yoruba origins."[18] The mistake is to see this as a culture suspended between two possible realities, with no possibilities of its own. The educated community was not moving from the African to the European but rather was seeking to define itself within an emergent Nigerian society. This was not an unstable transitional society waiting to find order by absorbing Western norms but an admittedly changeable society engaged in an ongoing—and unending—process of living through problems as it met them. As their culture developed it did not become more modern but rather more Nigerian, more profoundly a product of its own history. It used elements of both not to construct a bridge between them but to create a habitat distinct from both. There were many degrees of attraction to British culture within the educated community, but very few members sought full assimilation. Even if they did, few Europeans in Nigeria or abroad were willing wholly to accept them. Nor were many of the educated inclined simply to join their illiterate compatriots. Rather, they sought the unique advantages that came with the territory between. Western acculturation opened opportunities unavailable to the mass of the population and established an elite status. Connections to African societies gave them leverage with colonial authorities and advantages in trade. Remaining in this medial position, not getting beyond it, made the educated a special and increasingly enviable group.

It is more useful to think of invented identities here than of cultural transitions, of innovative fluidity rather than inevitable flow. The educated clearly were not intent on reproducing Victorian society but on using it. They were operating in a very competitive trading economy, where variable identities could be very useful. When politicking in Lagos or London, an elite Lagosian might be very English. When settling family disputes or politicking in the village, the same person might be very Yoruba. Yoruba in Brazil dressed in Yoruba fashions to stress their distinct identity but adopted a Brazilian style in Lagos to set themselves apart from the Saro.[19] The garden parties and the Victorian parlors so prominent in mid-nineteenth-century Lagos were important expressions of ambition and status. They projected attributes that set the educated community apart from other Africans and closer to European merchants and administrators. But they were not the essence of this group or foretokens of their future. These Victorian performances were one part of a much more diverse repertoire. If Victorian material played better in the middle of the nineteenth century than it would at the end, the simple explanation is that this identity allied them with the burgeoning power of Britain at a time when it promised much against their insecurities and uncertainties.

## Civilizing Schemes

What kinds of ideas occupied the intelligentsia situated in this society? By virtue of their Western education, the intelligentsia were introduced to contemporary European ideas about Africa. The circulation of ideas and people in the African diaspora introduced similar notions. Africa was more central to the latter than the former, but when it was discussed, questions of its present condition and future prospects were foremost. In general, judgments about its condition were not flattering. Africa was seen as benighted. Isolated, backward, and weak in itself, it had been further degraded by the Atlantic slave trade. Some thought this condition was more or less permanent; Africans were simply destined to be an inferior "race." Most, however, believed that great change was imminent. Various interested parties competed to promote their preferred future; this competition would not end with partition. Merchants tried to maximize their trade profits; administrators sought limited and inexpensive changes that would improve trade more generally and end slaving. Abolitionists and missionaries in particular had more potent plans to lighten Africa's burden, involving nothing less than remodeling tropical civilization. For them Africa might be suffering, but it had the potential to be redeemed. The core of this "civilizing mission" was set forth most coherently by Thomas Fowell Buxton in *The African Slave Trade and Its Remedy*. Slavery had to be eradicated within Africa through the joint agency of Christian enlightenment and trade in the produce of free African labor. Under British protection, connected to foreign commerce, and reformed through missionary efforts, West Africa would develop a class of industrious and progressive farmers, traders, and teachers to be the vanguard of a new progressive civilization. Because Europeans could not thrive in the West African climate, educated West Indian blacks and slaves liberated at Freetown were recommended as the willing and available agents for this project. Christianity loomed large in this proposal. It was further developed in numerous missionary programs, most extensively by Henry Venn, lay secretary of the CMS from 1841 to 1872. Accepting the necessity of Christianity and African agency, Venn argued that Africans should assume control of their own church as soon as possible. This not only would facilitate the growth of a truly African church adapted to "national peculiarities" but also would afford them valuable experience in managing their own affairs. In time this independence would extend to the secular realm, as mission schools spawned a skilled middle class. The Sierra Leone "Native Pastorate" from 1861 and the consecration of Samuel Crowther as bishop for West Africa in 1864 were widely proclaimed applications of these ideals.[20]

This civilizing mission had a more secular version as well. Generally, British administrative policies in West Africa were the product of expedience rather than any long-term strategy. But as their West African commitments formed, the British resorted to imperial precedent and, from the 1840s, established crown colonies with executive and legislative councils to assist governors in their tasks. Lagos was thus constituted after its annexation in 1861. While official policy avoided predicting the distant future, for some such arrangements were seeds from which full-scale parliaments might someday grow. The third Earl Grey, colonial secretary from 1846 to 1852, clearly connected the "rude Negro Parliament" he had promoted in the Gold Coast with this vision. A legislative assembly including local chiefs, he believed, had "converted a number of barbarous tribes . . . into a nation, with a regularly organized authority." Britain's duty, Grey argued, was "gradually to train the inhabitants of this part of Africa in the arts of civilization and government, until they shall grow into a nation capable of protecting themselves and of managing their own affairs, so that the interference and assistance of the British authorities may by degrees be less and less required."[21] When a British Parliamentary Select Committee in 1865 endorsed a gradual withdrawal from West African commitments, it evoked the spirit of this dream, recommending that Africans be encouraged to acquire the skills required for running their own governments.

Similar ideas informed the attitudes of African Americans, evident among the settlers in Liberia or the expedition to Nigeria undertaken by Delany and Campbell in 1859. Africa's great potential needed the enlightened leadership of their black Christian brethren who had been exposed to civilization in America. At the very least Africa needed spiritual and industrial missionaries; a minority favored the return of black Americans en masse as agents uniquely suited by race, sentiment, and sympathy to "introduce, in an effective manner, all the well-regulated pursuits of civilized life."[22]

These ideas from the Atlantic world painted, at least in broad strokes, a West African future in which a native elite would create and control a new outpost of British civilization. They were focused and propagated from London by the African Aid Society, which was established in 1860 by prominent philanthropists inspired by Delany's expedition and backed by industrial interests hoping to promote West African cotton production. The *African Times*, the society's organ, acted as "the public advocate in England" of the "educated African." It was clear that "educated natives . . . are and will be indispensable as a vanguard of the great army of civilization that must be projected upon the ignorant barbarism of heathen Africa."[23] Of all the proponents of this future, the West African educated community had the most obvious reasons to promote it; not surprisingly they quickly adopted the civilizing mission as their own. Its elements were not yet worked out in detail, let alone universally accepted. Elaborating and defending the civilizing mission were the central problems of the mid-nineteenth-century intelligentsia.

### Toward "The Future Rise of Africa"

"On What Depends the Future Rise of Africa?" Finding the answers to this question, posed at the Lagos Mutual Improvement Society, began by accepting some fundamental tenets of prevailing ideas about Africa. The intelligentsia did not question that Africa was behind and benighted. In the stern words of Bishop Crowther, the Niger expeditions had found Africans "still in the darkness of superstition, ignorance, and vice, in a most servile and abject degradation and slavery, and in a state of spiritual death." It was above all "for want of Christian enlightenment" that Africa suffered; the spread of Christianity henceforth would remain a central tenet of the intelligentsia's project. It offered a more inclusive intellectual framework than did African religions, one suited to the widening context of southern Nigerian life. Christianity, in particular, helped explain the cultural context of the new economy. As the simultaneous growth of Islam in southern Nigeria generally suggests, the need for new intellectual frameworks was spreading. Other kinds of external aid were also required. The early Saro emigrants, on departing Sierra Leone for their Yoruba homeland, hoped vaguely "that the Gospel of God our Saviour may be preached unto her, that schools may be established, that Bibles may be sent, that the British flag may be hoisted, and that she might rank among the civilized nations of the earth." Clearly, as Horton asserted, "civilization must come from abroad."[24]

The intelligentsia avidly committed themselves to the fundamental institutions they felt West Africa required, joining the missionary endeavor as teachers and ministers, exercising their power on the Legislative Council, and taking on diplomatic assignments for the British government. They also adopted and elaborated upon the rather congenial economic prescription of the civilizing mission, notwithstanding their enduring preference for commerce. With European mercantile interests, they pushed the Lagos government to secure their freedom to trade with the hinterland. Agricultural produce was seen as the essential resource of West Africa and the basis of its future prosperity. Horton, reinforcing a favorite theme of the *African Times*, stressed that "the great wealth of a country depends upon the amount of its agricultural products." As Crowther observed in the 1860s, "The country abounds with produce; labor is cheap: if the youths are only taught to prepare them for European markets our work is done. . . . Let us improve the country from its own resources." In keeping with the ambition of the civilizing mission to create a skilled middle class and inspired by the obvious hazards of depending solely on the fluctuating prices of palm produce for prosperity, there were also recommendations and efforts to move beyond agriculture alone. Often promoting schemes in which they had an interest, Africans along the coast sought support for a variety of industrial schemes to exploit natural resources, such as Horton's gold mine and railway scheme in Ghana, or to process agricultural produce, such as cotton ginning and sugar refining. In Lagos similar diversification, involving sawmills, brickmaking, and other light industrial ventures, was both recommended and pursued with the hope of reducing dependency on agricultural exports and imported manufactured goods.[25]

The West African intelligentsia adopted this scheme actively rather than passively, vociferously defending the positions it awarded them. They supported the Native Pastorate scheme in Sierra Leone and the Niger Delta, though not as keenly as some hoped they would. Newspapers promised to "always endeavour to assist, in all matters of public policy, in pointing out the means by which admitted evils may be remedied." They requested that the seat of government be moved from the Gold Coast to Lagos, to become better apprised of local opinion. The *Lagos Observer* demanded "a Legislature composed of European and Native merchants, men whose interests are thoroughly identical with the country and people, men whose 'un-officialism' would permit them to denounce openly and fearlessly those acts of misrule, abuse of power, official terrorism and those nameless annoyances to which we, at present, submit." Long after British policy had drifted away, they remained loyal to the vision once espoused by Earl Grey. The recommendations of the parliamentary committee of 1865 were not followed; but in preparation for British withdrawal, Horton devised detailed proposals for the governance of the West African settlements. These states would be strengthened by applying forms of European government appropriate to their different histories and conditions. The *Lagos Times* asked in 1881 why the

> recommendations of the Select Committee of 1865 . . . are still a dead letter. . . . We are not clamouring for immediate independence, for the sufficient reason that we are *not* prepared for it; but it should always be borne in mind that the present order of things *will not* last forever. A time will come when the British Colonies on the West Coast of Africa, Lagos included, will be left to regulate their own internal and external affairs. . . . It is time for us boldly to ask England to associate us with themselves in the matter of regulating and superintending our own affairs.[26]

Further, these ideas were applied in local political struggles, as part of the ideological arsenal of African states. When the Henshaw Town section of old Calabar sought greater independence from Duke Town in the 1870s, it explicitly adopted the civilizing mission to define its distinct identity. The Young Calabar Movement espoused the adoption of Christianity and European dress and the eradication of certain Efik ways as part of its declaration of independence and search for allies. It won the endorsement of local European missionaries and the pro-missionary British consul but lost its bid for secession in the face of Duke Town authority effected through the voice of the established elite's Ekpe Society. By the end of the century, however, most Efik had effectively adopted these new ideals, seeking fortune in colonial careers.[27]

But merely adopting, defending, and applying the civilizing mission could not meet the needs of the intelligentsia, seeking as they were to understand their new role in an emergent social order. They also shaped it along more congenial lines. Venn of the CMS and others spoke of the need to adapt Christian ways to African life, but European missionaries were not well equipped—and often not inclined— to disentangle the essentials of their faith from the trappings of their culture or to view African societies with empathy. African missionaries were both more equipped and more inclined. Crowther argued that African polygamy would have to be replaced by European monogamy but also held fast to the policy that the role of Christianity was only "to abolish and supersede all false religions," not "to destroy national assimilations." "Heathen" aspects of African societies that were "not immoral or indecent" should be "improved upon and enriched from foreign stocks as civilization advances." Crowther and his European and African colleagues devised written texts for six southern Nigerian languages by the 1880s and made careful studies of the history and culture of their prospective flocks, including Muslim communities, hoping to generate a Christian culture with some African forms.[28]

One of the most striking cases of adapting the civilizing mission was the Egba United Board of Management, which operated in Abeokuta between 1865 and 1874. It was the inspiration of G. W. Johnson, an Egba Saro. Suspicions about British expansion had soured early Egba eagerness to strengthen themselves through missionary connections. Johnson, leading a faction of the Saro community, sought to strengthen Abeokuta against British and other threats by having African leaders adapt European ideas of government without European aid. The Board of Management tried to unite the notoriously fractious political structure of Abeokuta under a single authority and for a time succeeded in implementing postal services and bureaucratic revenue collection. Plagued by British and internal opposition, its power faded, to be revived in the 1890s. Johnson, apparently undaunted, continued to propagate his ideas of independent African modernization in the West African press.[29]

The intelligentsia not only reshaped European ideas of the civiliz-ing mission, injecting them with concern for African realities and at-tempting to situate local facts in European forms. They also moved beyond them, engaging ideas provided not by European and Ameri-can discourse about Africa but rather by the African societies to which they were connected. The discourse of the colonial intelligentsia was not born afresh from the colonial situation and the mission school; it had roots beyond these institutions, as it would have through colonial times. The intelligentsia sometimes were introduced to these problems as they settled into local situations, for example, as missionaries or diplomats sent forth into the Yoruba wars. They also, as it were, grew up with them. Local recruits, even more than Krio returnees, brought their domestic or local intellectual problems with them through the schoolyard gate to address in the light of their new education. Often, ideas that engaged them most were those which intersected issues raised by the civilizing mission, but this is not to say that these issues were important only because foreigners made them so. The ideational links between the early colonial intelligentsia and their mid-nine-teenth-century peers are faintly registered in the historical record and difficult to reconstruct. We can, however, recognize a few points of connection.

Clearly the generic African improvement envisioned by the civiliz-ing mission was reshaped from the start by the intelligentsia's more particular agendas, which rose from their engagement in the political and economic rivalries of the mid-nineteenth century. The ethnic asso-ciations of Lagos formed in part to serve these rivalries often did so at the expense of the general good of trade. Identities as Egba and Ijebu cut across others as agents of "civilization." In playing these roles they sometimes adopted ideas and ideological positions embedded in these interstate rivalries. Thus Samuel Johnson's bias toward Oyo was rein-forced by citing traditions of origin of various Yoruba states that fa-vored Oyo, a practice much repeated by later local historians. J. P. Haastrup, closely related to the Ijebu Remo royal house, espoused the Ijebu view that Ibadan was the principal threat to peace.[30]

European declarations of the civilizing mission confronted many important institutions of Nigerian life: polygamy was un-Christian; slavery had to end; pawnship—only a disguised form of slavery—was immoral. External prescriptions clearly shaped attitudes toward these institutions among many of the intelligentsia. James Johnson, notoriously, took a hard line on pawnship in 1879 (and a softer line later). Crowther opposed polygamy on Christian grounds. But even without this external challenge, social relations were being unsettled by the new palm oil economy and, among the Yoruba, by war. The reexamination of these institutions arising from these changes also informed members of the colonial intelligentsia. Discussions about pawnship and domestic slavery illustrate this. British administrators admitted a distinction between Yoruba slavery and domestic slavery and accepted that the latter would have to be tolerated until it could be displaced by wage labor and enlightenment, but they nonetheless thought it evil. Robert Campbell, similarly, allowed some distinctions between slaves and pawns but insisted both were unacceptable. In contrast, numerous Yoruba missionaries and converts joined with interior leaders to defend domestic slavery especially. Crowther presented the objections of Egba leaders to the Lagos government concerning the asylum Lagos offered fugitive slaves in 1872. Yoruba converts also used their deeper knowledge of Yoruba society to offer a more informed and subtle distinction between slavery and *iwofa*, or pawnship. Crowther defended pawning as a means for families to raise money to avoid the enslavement of its members. It was a means of obtaining credit and of putting children in the care of families that might provide more security or better training. Samuel Johnson argued that *iwofa* did not have an exact "foreign analogue" but that it combined the functions of European systems for "banking, apprenticeship and domestic service," and that it would be important for future economic development. This benign view of pawnship, which persisted in Nigerian writing, seems to represent the views of pawn holders, a group which included Saro as well as local elites. As in early colonial times, chiefs and well-to-do men probably spoke of pawnship not only as useful to them but as contributing to the public good. Further, it seems that they had occasion to voice this defense. Pawnship had expanded and been abused under the pressures of war in the mid-nineteenth century. War chiefs in Ibadan had gone so far as to assemble fighting units from young male pawns. Severe casualties in 1880 inspired a reaction against this innovation and, presumably, led to clarification of the limitations and rules governing pawnship. Thus when various prominent educated Yoruba argued at a CMS conference in Lagos in 1880 that the rules governing *iwofa* were clear and not exploitative, they were possibly reiterating in missionary circles arguments first essayed in Ibadan for another debate. Discussions on marriage, before independent African churches arose in the late 1880s, also incorporated African lines of argument, as the intelligentsia resisted missionary interdictions against the combination of Christian faith and polygamy so popular in Lagos and elsewhere. If Bishop Crowther invoked a Yoruba women's proverb in his scriptural and social case against polygamy, others argued that African marriage institutions were proper and good when not "misunderstood by strangers." Although the evidence here is perforce circumstantial, it suggests that on these issues at least, the intelligentsia's version of the civilizing mission had input from more than European and African-American sources. Another line of continuity, narrower but more direct, is suggested by J. D. Y. Peel's examination of the engagement between missionaries and Yoruba *babalawo,* priests of Ifa divination. Singular records from Badagry in the 1860s and 1870s relate the conversion of three *babalawo* to Christianity; the intellectual complexity here entailed not conversion and discontinuity but rather a rethinking on both sides. At the very least this is evidence of colonial intellectuals emerging from a Yoruba intellectual tradition. In some cases, such as that of Philip Jose Meffre, they continued in their Christian lives as intellectuals, writing on Ifa and other issues.[31]

### "Black Englishmen," Africa's Advocates

Both the cultural and intellectual lives of the intelligentsia up to the 1880s are aptly encapsulated in the title "black Englishmen," a new breed drawing on diverse sources but aspiring to be neither wholly black nor wholly English. In certain contexts they saw themselves as outsiders, like the British, bringing illumination to Africa and Africa to illumination. One Lagos paper, for example, promised to save space especially "for the insertion of any reliable information of the Interior countries . . . which may throw some light into the degree of civilization and religion they had attained to, before the light of Christian civilization began to dawn upon them."[32] The intelligentsia were the elite vanguard of a foreign civilization. This elitism was founded on their education in and emulation of European ways. At the same time, clear distinctions were maintained between Africans and Europeans, a difference which becoming "civilized" would not erase. If African agency had initially been required by a climate inhospitable for Europeans, it was soon raised to the status of prescription. As one Krio clergyman wrote in 1844, "If Africa could be raised from its present degraded state . . . Africans themselves must be the principal harbingers of peace." Merchant Henry Robbin declined becoming a commercial agent for Lagos in 1857 because as government dependents "intelligent Africans will continue to be servants and the spirit for promoting our country's and our own interest with independent authority will lie dormant and still."[33] Further, many among the intelligentsia saw themselves as "Africans," as a vanguard of the race now spread around the Atlantic. This promised role, which must have seemed doubly enticing to the ex-slaves and outcasts among them, reflected their often direct ties to Sierra Leone and the diaspora, where the specific cultural divisions of Africa were swept aside by the grand notion of "Africa" as a geographical and racial category, accepting the grand European division of the world by continent and somatic type.

This was an identity rich in ambiguity. As Michael Echeruo has remarked, the *Anglo-African* used "us" to refer to both Africans and to the "civilizing" British, even in a single editorial. It also pointed out that "we in Africa . . . do not hold ourselves amenable to all the formalities and exactions of fashionable life in Europe" but rather recognize "our veritable gentlemen" in either African or European dress.[34] But it was always anchored in a clear sense of the medial position and mediating role of the intelligentsia. As one Sierra Leonean told a missionary in 1865, "We have always considered ourselves as Middlemen between you and the Egbas." J. A. O. Payne, writing against the CMS policy on polygamy, stood firmly in this middle ground in 1887: "We are here on behalf of the heathen, for it is for us to speak on their behalf." It made sense to sustain both identities as part of their medial role. They did not intend to efface Africa but to refashion it. They were the agents of improvement, racially allied to but culturally distinct from the people to be elevated. Africa, it was understood, someday would be for the Africans. Martin Delany urged this in 1860; G. W. Johnson affirmed it in Abeokuta. Crowther, familiar with both the Egba United Board of Management and Delany, cautioned that "to claim Africa for the Africans alone, is to claim for her the right of a continued ignorance." But he was equally insistent that Africans had their special role in the redemption of their continent. Although African culture would be subordinate to European—and especially Christian—standards, the principle was adaptation, not displacement. European aid was necessary, but not European domination. The poles, then, were between a minority seeking African improvement along foreign lines under African guidance and the mainstream, seeking African improvement with variable amounts of European aid.[35]

This opposition of "European" against "African" was not altogether convenient for an educated community that was clearly neither, but these were the poles offered to it by the Atlantic community in which they were embedded. The intelligentsia was obliged to deal with these terms—in the mid-nineteenth century as through the colonial period —because they were colonial subjects, beholden to a British presence backed by commerce and cannonry. This limitation on Nigerian intellectual life must not be forgotten; it is not a tradition of thought developed under the range of choice that obtained, for example, within European discourse about Europe. Ideas about Africa were imposed. To ignore them was to be severed from the civilizing mission itself; to accept them was to receive premises that set the task of understanding Nigerian societies profoundly askew. The Africa imposed here was primitive and benighted, undeniably different from "civilized" societies, housing false gods. Midcentury Victorian thought did not hold Africa to be mysteriously different—it was after all subject to redemption and liable to civilization—but neither did Victorian categories always fit African institutions. If pawns were not free, they were slaves; if marriages were not monogamous, they were not civilized. Africa was seen as subordinate, deserving to learn from Europe but not to teach it. The early intelligentsia attempted to adapt European discourse about Africa to their needs, to render from imposed categories something more suited to their medial position between imperial discourse and African realities. These impositions were more congenial now than they would soon become. The barrier between "Africa" and "Europe" was still held to be cultural and historical rather than racial, still surmountable by commerce and Christianity. "African civilization" was not the oxymoron it would later become in racist imperialist discourse based not on mutual commercial development but on blunt imperial control. Cooperation between white and black missionaries—by no means untroubled—bespoke a certain common Christian ideal which rose above race and culture. Yet even later, these impositions were not as debilitating as one might expect. Imperial ideas about civilization, economic development, or morality could be rendered useful for other purposes.

That the intelligentsia did work with these ideas is an eloquent argument against those who would dismiss them as mere colonized copyists, unable to conceive or pursue their own interests. They were, to be sure, strongly inclined toward Victorian culture and ideas in the mid-nineteenth century, but not just because these ideas were entwined with the civilizing mission. They were attracted to Victorian ideas, as to Victorian culture, as a potent source of power within West Africa. They strove to have their input into the foreign institutions they helped build. They also exercised some choice, and effected some changes, in their search for a suitable worldview, built with ill-suited ideas. They always remained "African," always ready to assert a special relation to the continent which diasporan Africans might share, but which Europeans could not. Nevertheless, the early Nigerian intelligentsia were more preoccupied with promoting the civilizing mission than questioning it, and it is not clear that the meaning of being "African" was deeply probed. Their immediate need was to establish a new social order and a place for themselves, to support European expansion while resisting European deviation from the promise of the civilizing mission. Neither understanding exactly how the "black" and the "English" could be joined nor separating the kernel of Christian teachings from its European shell was a pressing question. The intelligentsia's connection to African sources of ideas would become more conscious, active, and direct in the cultural nationalist climate of the approaching decades. But this was not a wholly new orientation for them; Africa was not exactly a new discovery. From the start they had attended to African ideas in their race to civilize. The difference was that in the mid-nineteenth century, for the most part, they looked upon things African with a different attitude. Civilization would come from abroad. Africa was relevant because it marked what had to be improved, and it was not to be discarded wholesale. But it was to be judged according to external standards. As circumstances changed, the civilizing mission was given many different shapes and meanings. The rise of European racism imposed the need to define their "African" identity more explicitly and to ask hard questions about the nature of "black Englishmen" and Christianity in Africa. In the cultural nationalist phase, the interest and connection to things African would continue, but with a sense that Africa might set the standards of what was relevant. Between the wars conditions allowed for more balanced inquiry. In the late colonial rush toward the nation-state, external standards would again be invoked.

# 3

## "The Sphinx Must Solve Her Own Riddle"

New Imperialism and
New Imperatives, 1880s–1920

**F**ROM THE 1880s to World War I, the educated community was incorporated into a formal colonial order constructed on the economic, political, and ideological subordination of Africans. At the same time, the intelligentsia began to deepen their roots inside Nigeria while they remained embedded in the intellectual world of the Atlantic. Challenged by Europe's scientific racism and new imperialism that repudiated the civilizing mission, they sought inspiration and endorsement from certain British colonial critics and African-American intellectuals. A set of luminary figures—Edward Blyden, Mojola Agbebi, John P. Jackson, and James Johnson—articulated a response: African values could guide Africa's progress on lines distinct from Europe's, European claims to superiority notwithstanding. But this externally supported defense contained internal flaws. The African values it defined were part of an Africa invented for European and African-American rather than Nigerian or even West African needs. The use of such material in the foundation of Nigerian cultural nationalist thought set the project askew, constructing a precarious stage for later generations.

### A State of Dependence

The transformations during the four decades straddling 1900 are symbolized in the new modes of British control. Company charter, protectorate, and colony were joined into the Colony of Southern Nigeria in

47

1906 and then amalgamated with the north in 1914. The British established the fundaments of colonial administration beyond Lagos, clarifying the lines of subordination, building the channels for economic exploitation, and naming chiefly allies within subordinated African polities. This expansion of colonial order was punctuated by military expeditions against persistent resistance to both the very idea and the particular forms of British control. Abeokuta, subordinated by treaty in 1893, was finally fully absorbed with protest in 1914. These decades, then, saw the reframing of southern Nigerian society, a dislocation extended by World War I. They also saw a less dramatic but equally important reorganization of the economy, which also subordinated Nigerian to European interests. After about 1880 trade conditions became increasingly less favorable as global competition increased, prices dropped, and credit became more difficult. All merchants suffered, but small traders were especially hard-pressed. A few large foreign concerns with the capital, careful management, and sheer size to succeed in this economic environment began to gain the upper hand. When trade improved in the 1890s and then was promoted by the emergent colonial state, these large firms further consolidated their position at small traders' expense.[1]

As the era of African merchant princes became the era of the United Africa Company, Saro traders began to look back upon their golden age. Effectively barred from reaching the heights of the import and export economy, some retreated to the more manageable import function. Many moved into the vast new fields opened in the interior by the expanding rail and road networks. Acting on their own or as agents for European firms, merchants from Lagos and Calabar worked to expand the exchange of cash crops for imported consumer goods. The decline of commercial opportunities also inspired economic diversification. Amaro and Saro turned to plantations in cocoa and cotton and to investments in real estate. A Lagosian observed in 1918 how onetime African merchants were now acquiring "acres and acres of Farm lands." In Port Harcourt and Calabar, too, Africans had become landlords.[2]

If economic changes reduced the scale of mercantile fortunes, the expansion of the state bureaucracy increased the scope for clerical careers geographically and numerically. Forty-five African civil servants had sufficed for Lagos in 1881; southern Nigeria required some 1,200 by 1908. There were 1,140 civil servants and commercial clerks in Lagos in 1901 and 5,310 in 1921. But official policies of racial discrimination limited vertical movement. Africans could not rise above first-class clerk; African doctors in the West African medical service were subordinated to Europeans in 1902. Henry Carr, starting as an inspector of schools in 1892 and retiring as commissioner of Lagos in 1924, would have been fairly unexceptional in a previous generation but was rare in his. Not only were Africans barred from supervising Europeans, they were consistently paid less, often only half what their European counterparts received. A fortunate few escaped official discrimination by entering private professional careers in medicine and law. Commercial clerkships and diverse careers in education, church, or mission work were other, less prestigious options. In 1880 the majority of elite men studied by Mann were primarily in trade; by 1915 a larger majority were in civil service or professional careers. Some family fortunes survived this transition—and indeed laid the basis for what Folarin Coker has called a "Nigerian aristocracy"—in large part by investing in land and the education of younger generations. Mann's prosopography shows how "elite men with literate fathers were more likely than elite men with illiterate fathers to receive advanced education."[3] The economic bases of the educated community, then, were moving away from their original direct attachment to the missions and trade. But as government employees and commercial clerks, and even as professionals serving urban populations, they remained dependent on colonial trade conditions at one remove. Conditions did allow some security and even prosperity, but at the cost of becoming increasingly dependent on a government hostile to their grand ambitions. The Lagos Standard on 8 September 1897 voiced a popular sentiment of the period: "To many a man, rather should we say, to many an African, the Government Service is often the end of all usefulness and respectability, all manliness and independence."

Over these forty eventful years, the Western-educated community expanded rapidly from its rather precarious start. There was a continued influx of "native foreigners" in search of career opportunities, for example, railway clerks from the Caribbean. By 1921 about 2,500 "native foreigners" from the British Empire counted among the "educated." But the principal source of growth was local recruitment. From the late nineteenth century, the demand for education increased sharply as various communities made the connection between Western education and mobility within the colonial order. The Ijebu, for example, pursued mission education with such alacrity after their defeat in 1892 that by 1898 there were perhaps 4,000 literate Christian converts. Isichei places the crucial decade just after 1900 for many Igbo. Provincial elites, not just marginal people, now sought education for themselves and their children. The children of Ibadan chiefs first attended mission schools in 1894. By 1900 one Egba chief had converted, and a literate Christian had become Obi of Onitsha. The 1921 census classified about 32,000 southern Nigerians as "educated," defining these roughly as primary-school graduates. This is four to six times the 1880s total but still less than 0.5 percent of the total population. There were also some 317,000 southern Nigerians with less than a complete primary education, deemed in the census "imperfectly educated," comprising about 4 percent of the population. In Lagos Township, where the basis for charting growth is more reliable, some 10,000 Africans were "educated" by 1921, double the 1891 figure and about 10 percent of the town's expanding population. The more broadly defined educated community in Lagos amounted to only slightly more than the one-quarter it comprised in the 1880s. Important qualities of the educated community were changing. It had more diffuse roots in Nigerian societies, recruiting more widely and from more elite levels. But for all its growth since the 1880s, the mark of its small, largely external beginnings remained. A small circle of key figures in Lagos and Freetown continued to be recognized as leaders.[4]

The structure of the educated community is suggested by some statistics on education.[5] Basic education expanded swiftly. There were 3,200 students in Lagos in 1891 and four times this number by 1921. There were almost 12,000 students in all of southern Nigeria by 1906 and nearly twelve times this number by 1920. The northern region, where mission schools were restricted, lagged far behind the south. Excluding Koranic schools, primary enrollment was just 2 percent of that in the south in 1912. Among the over 2,200 schools in southern Nigeria by 1921, 90 percent were unassisted by government grant (and thus not government inspected); clearly popular rather than government or mission interest powered this growth. Secondary education grew less quickly. Four secondary schools in 1880 became twelve by 1913 and eighteen by 1926, augmented by teacher-training institutions. Only two of these were girls' schools. The 1926 enrollment of over 500 was more than seven times the 1913 figure. Fees, perhaps ten times higher than for primary school, affected access. Although King's College in Lagos offered a few scholarships, most students had to draw on family resources. There was, however, a reasonable expectation in these years that graduates could secure a clerkship and repay their debts.

Postsecondary education also expanded more slowly than primary education. The few hundreds involved sought their training abroad almost exclusively in Sierra Leone and Britain. By 1904 about thirteen African doctors had appeared in Lagos; various sources list thirty-four professionals in Lagos by 1913 and seventy-three African professionals in all of southern Nigeria by 1921. Further education carried great prestige. Publisher and civil servant J. A. O. Payne welcomed a university graduate to Lagos in 1881 with the confession that "we all envy and feel jealous of you tonight, and would all like to be 'Bachelors of Arts.'"[6] It still frequently meant training for service to the church, not surprising given the mission dominance in education. Of eleven African university graduates named in 1918, five bore the title of reverend.[7] However, professional training in medicine or law was the ultimate achievement, not least because of the increasingly harsh official and unofficial racism administered by colonial Europeans and mission churches. Engineering and education also were attracting some away from church careers. Higher education was still expensive, and possible only for the wealthy few. The rare women who went to England for postsecondary education, such as Mrs. Oyinkan Abayomi (née Ajasa) and Mrs. Charlotte Olajumoke Obasa (née Blaize), were daughters of wealthy Lagos families. Although they often became prominent in Lagos politics, their training tended toward courses in music, dressmaking, and domestic economy.

As approximate as these numbers are, they should sustain some suggestive comparisons of different levels within the educated community. In the 1921 census "illiterates" still outnumbered those with some Western education by twenty-four to one. Thus even those with only a partial primary education could make a claim to special status. But it was easier to get into primary school than beyond it. The "imperfectly educated" outnumbered those with a full primary training by about nine to one. In the late nineteenth century there were perhaps twelve primary students for every secondary student; by 1920 this had increased at least to seventy to one, and perhaps much higher. By an educated guess, around 1920 between twenty and fifty Nigerians attended secondary school for every one who went beyond, and this would seem to be a marked improvement over previous decades. Women had an even harder time moving beyond primary classrooms. The primary-school ratio of about five males to each female student increased to about thirty-five to one in secondary school. Thus primary education—and the clerkships it could garner—was sufficient for educated elite status, especially as this community was too tiny to be exclusive. Beyond this, the more difficult transition was from primary to secondary level. All the men who overcame this barrier through application and access to wealth, not just university graduates, were particularly posed to be an elite among the educated. These expanding statistics also reveal an enduring pyramidal structure in the demographic profile of the educated community, as each generation outnumbered the one preceding. This set the stage for popular resentment against senior cohorts whenever the colonial order did not provide opportunities to satisfy the ever-increasing expectations of each rising generation.

The educated community was spread rather unevenly across southern Nigeria, concentrated among the Yoruba and Niger Delta trading centers. Lagos Township held about 30 percent of the entire southern Nigerian educated community in 1921; Calabar ranked next with 4 percent. By 1913 there were also African lawyers in Onitsha and Warri. The distribution of schools helps explain this. Of the twelve secondary schools established by 1913, eight were in Lagos, including King's College, the most assured route to higher education. Three more were in Yoruba cities; only one, the Hope Waddell Institute of Calabar, was in the east. Saro and other "native foreigners," along with Yoruba and Efik, enjoyed a presence among the educated disproportionate to their overall numbers. In the 1921 census Yoruba accounted for over 40 percent of the "educated" but for only 25 percent of the whole population. The Ibibio (the census included Efik here) accounted for over one-quarter of the former but just a tenth of the latter. "Native foreigners" from British possessions were 8 percent of the "educated" but an infinitesimal fraction of the overall population. In contrast, although the Igbo did supply 15 percent of the "educated," they accounted for almost one-half the population. It is not surprising then that Yoruba were the first to challenge the dominance of immigrant Africans in higher education. Of the seventy-three professionals counted by Coleman in the early 1920s, two-thirds were Yoruba and the rest were "native foreigners." The educated were most concentrated in centers of administration and trade, reflecting their ties to the colonial system. In 1921 the thirteen principal southern Nigerian townships with only 2 percent of the population contained 40 percent of the "educated." But this concentration does not mean that the educated were typically urban: on average 60 percent still lived outside these townships, with higher rates in more remote provinces. Educated Nigerians clearly were not strangers to village life, nor would they become so later.[8]

The Victorian habits of Lagos life continued. Elite Lagos women formed the Ladies Social Club and in 1901 the Lagos Ladies' League. European, Amaro, and Saro men joined the Order of Foresters in 1891 and encouraged "the study of Literature, Science and Art" through the Lagos Institute from 1901.[9] The material of literate culture now proliferated, at least in Lagos. Newspapers sprouted, although many had short and troubled lives. It seems the editors and journalists were moved more by a desire to be read than to secure rewards. Between 1880 and 1920 at least nineteen titles appeared; in 1920 only about five remained in print. Sales of the three main papers amounted to about 1,500 per week in 1897 and almost double that in 1921; perhaps three to ten times as many people actually read these copies or heard them recounted. Among the more important and successful papers were John Payne Jackson's *Lagos Weekly Record* (1891–1930), edited from 1914 by his son Thomas; James Bright Davies's *Nigerian Times* (1910–15); and George Williams's *Lagos Standard* (1894–1920). All were notable for their antigovernment stance, although the *Record* supported Governor Carter's policies in the 1890s. Numerous printing presses made it possible to publish books in Lagos as well as England. A Library Club was active in 1881, but no public lending libraries were operating in 1901.

The educated community continued to circulate through West Africa and travel to both Brazil and England. Relations with the provinces were quite altered from the mid-nineteenth century, not least because all southern Nigerians were now colonial subjects. As lobbyists and spokespeople, also as creditors in trade, the educated became involved as valued mediators with the colonial system. By the early twentieth century, they could be widely found as court advisers and in patron-client relations with provincial kin. Saro dominated African political organizations in Port Harcourt's early years. Barristers, doctors, and churchmen helped formulate a petition with Lagos chiefs and traders about land appropriation in 1907, directing it to London when Governor Egerton's response did not satisfy them. During the fervor over the land question in 1912 and 1913, when such people headed a delegation to London, educated men in Lagos streets could hardly avoid being asked by illiterates about the progress of the case. The new cordiality was also the product of closer social ties as Saro culture extended outwards. Elite families, especially clergy, often took in children from nonelite families to oversee their education. Saro cocoa plantations supplied cultural exposure as well as employment. The immigrants also married into local families. Among the social elite of Lagos examined by Mann, repatriates and "native foreigners" remained in the majority but fell from 92 percent in 1880 to 72 percent by 1915. Contact with Europeans became more common. The 1,200 Europeans counted in Lagos Township by 1921 were ten times more numerous than in 1881. The over 2,700 Europeans in all of southern Nigeria by 1921 were, like the educated community, most concentrated in townships. Although racist attitudes raised barriers between Africans and Europeans, contact continued. Much of it was limited to the office or to political necessity. During World War I, for example, the lieutenant governor met regularly with representatives of the press to address their grievances. But the European colonial elite maintained contact with at least some of their African peers. Governor MacGregor helped establish the Lagos Institute and in 1903 unsuccessfully recommended Saro lawyer Sapara Williams for a knighthood. The Supreme Court feted Chief Registrar Payne on his retirement in 1899. Barrister Kitoyi Ajasa had many European clients. Governor Lugard presided over a ceremonial unveiling of Blyden's portrait in Glover Memorial Hall in 1914.[10]

As in earlier decades, the educated community was riven by factions and disputes. Instead of interior affairs, however, rivalries now featured politics and personalities. John P. Jackson and Richard B. Blaize, in a public quarrel stemming from their joint interests in the *Lagos Times*, strained relations between their two families for many years after the 1890s. Ayandele, with only some exaggeration, has observed that the educated "did not have similar or same views on any single issue, besides the belief that Christianity was the best religion for Nigeria."[11] There were, as ever, differences in wealth. Senior clerks might earn more than double a headmaster's salary, doctors more than triple. But these differences do not necessarily indicate a hierarchy within the elite, as many individuals moved through phases as teachers, clerks, traders, and even newspapermen without or before becoming professionals. The economic profile of individuals within the educated community was fluid rather than set; this justifies Mann's treatment of at least the elite among the educated as a single group with multiple functions rather than as a group usefully divisible into discrete subsections. Even for the "imperfectly educated," upward mobility remained a real possibility.

For many at the turn of the century, Lagos promised to "become the proud Queen of West Africa, the greatest emporium of trade in this part of the continent," even the "Liverpool of Western Africa."[12] By 1920 the place of the educated community in this vision had become more clearly defined and more secure, if not settled. Partition and amalgamation had brought subordination, but also more stability. That the members of the educated community considered themselves the natural leaders of Nigerian society is evident in their sense of both goals they had accomplished and goals they had failed to achieve. Several founding members of the Lagos Institute hoped it would rise above the dismal records of similar past societies. One member proclaimed that "it should be the duty of every educated person to instruct and educate the less favoured ones in everything that concerns their welfare." The Institute itself intended to "bring together all classes of society with a view to promoting among them kindly understanding and intelligent sympathy." A leading intellectual lamented the all-too-common tendency of his peers "to pull to pieces, to reduce to atoms, to break, to tear, to disorganize." Adebesin Folarin reiterated this despair on the eve of World War I. "In short, our cringing tendency, our parasitical partiality, our entire lack of patriotic devotion, our want of aspiration for freedom, our dislike of one another, our disinclination to form definite societies of our own, are the reasons, yea, the justifiable reasons, why we are looked down upon as nonentities, and despised."[13] More interestingly, there were also hints of the intelligentsia becoming aware of themselves as leaders of thought with an established audience. One Nigerian left church employ in 1902 "for the purpose of continuing literary work" in Lagos; another addressed his 1915 pamphlet to "the reading public of Nigeria." They were also becoming aware of belonging to a broader intellectual tradition with its own luminaries. James Johnson in 1903 listed examples of able West Africans, including Bishop Crowther, Alexander Crummell, Horton, and various Liberian and Sierra Leonean leaders. G. W. Johnson marked his faith in "our Mr. Blyden"; the *Lagos Weekly Record* called Fadumah "yet another Blyden."[14] Agbebi, fashioning Horton and Robert Campbell as heroes of Africa, was himself the "uncrowned poet laureate of Lagos" in the 1880s. At his death in 1917, Agbebi was eulogized as a "poet, writer, preacher, lecturer, patriot, supporter of the Press." This emergent intelligentsia—vibrant but not yet substantial, linked with Nigeria but still oriented toward the Atlantic—would be thoroughly tested by the intellectual challenges of this era.

### "The Despair of the Civilized Native"

If the educated community was extending its culture into Nigeria as prophesied in the civilizing mission, little else was going according to plan. The civilizing mission and, indeed, the very self-image of the intelligentsia were being threatened by the new colonial order, which not only reduced heralds of civilization to colonized clerks but also was infused with racist ideas and practices. The idea that humankind was divided by race had long been widely accepted in Europe, but in the civilizing mission these divisions were understood to be superficial, effaceable through religious and cultural conversion. Now, with the advent of evolutionary thought and Europe's global hegemony, these differences acquired a deeper significance. Races were ranked hierarchically, with Africans near the bottom. If racial traits were not immutable, they were subject to only gradual change. The European race had created an unsurpassed civilization which Africans, as an inferior race, were incapable of assimilating. Africans, in short, could not be "civilized." In the judgment of the most hostile racists such as Richard Burton and Winwood Reade, missions were producing not the vanguard of a new African civilization but racially alienated misfits who "at the very best" displayed "imitative faculties, with an utter barrenness of creative power." Certainly educated Africans, as bishops or chief registrars of the Supreme Court, were out of place. Even to more sympathetic racists, who shared and exchanged many ideas with the Nigerian intelligentsia, the educated African was the "curse of the Coast." In Mary Kingsley's celebrated phrase, "A black man is no more an undeveloped white man than a rabbit is an undeveloped hare."[15] West Africans' access to polite society in Britain narrowed as doctrines of race hierarchy intertwined with more exclusive concepts of class, despite the efforts of philanthropists and the Colonial Office to counteract the trend. In 1913 black graduates were barred from the London University Club; black barristers also were refused equal treatment in certain court circuits. Brown detects prejudice rising in Lagos from the 1860s; it boiled over in the 1890s. Crowther was succeeded in 1891 by a long line of European bishops, as the new generation of missionaries questioned African ability to run churches and missions with propriety. Soon after the turn of the century, Europeans in Lagos sought a colonial church and a Freemasons' lodge for whites only. Official residential segregation was added to employment and salary discrimination; during the World War I Port Harcourt was planned on this principle. Racial tension could become taut at times, for example, in 1897 when Africans were excluded from the Chamber of Commerce.

Clearly the West African intelligentsia no longer could simply pursue their civilizing mission while the very possibility of being "black Englishmen" was under attack. Some within the educated community ignored the challenge as best they could and retreated to enjoy the fruits of colonialism. Among the intelligentsia, however, these issues could not be ignored. The force of this challenge is reflected in the "despair of the Civilized Native," voiced by the *Weekly Record* and other papers as their projected self-image was obscured by the tides of racism and pierced by British ridicule. The *Observer* decried "the general idea of civilization on the West Coast" as little better than "a simple copying after or imitation of European excellence; hence . . . the contempt of the European and his low estimate of the race." The *Standard* was more blunt: "The Europeanized African is a geographical, a physiological, and a psychological monstrosity." As Agbebi saw it, "The age of changes is come and we are at the threshold of a grand revolution."[16] The intelligentsia now had to find a means of defending their civilizing mission, of showing that they could be African and civilized. They had to show that they still deserved to control Africa in the long term, and that they had a vital and valuable leadership role now. They had to assert reasons to take pride in their African identity despite Africa's patent weakness against European imperialism. They had long seen themselves as a distinct group but had not asked hard questions about what distinguished them. These investigations could no longer be held in abeyance. But the intelligentsia had to respond by addressing the questions of "race" and "civilization" as they were understood at the time. They had to accept that "Africans" were a distinct race, that "European civilization" was a unique and enviable accomplishment, but also to ascertain what elements of civilization Africans might attain.

What ideas attracted the intelligentsia as their founding charter was betrayed? Their response was complex. Although the new ideas of empire rejected them, the intelligentsia did not reject the ideals of empire. They still needed and pursued the advance of British power, with its concomitant economic and social reordering, because their medial position required it. They could no more repudiate the colonial order than they could function without the newspapers and debating societies of their culture. The press duly supported British imperial power. Despite continuing sympathies with different Yoruba polities, the overall thrust was in favor of intervention against resistance to colonial trade. The *Weekly Record*, for example, vehemently opposed Egba resistance, regarding it simply as "impossible that the progress of development and civilization in Africa should be retarded by the ignorant caprice of native chiefs." Between the alternatives of the status quo or incorporation by another European empire, the intelligentsia remained ardently pro-British. "The Natives of Africa—we venture to say *all* Africa, love the Queen not only for what she is, but for what she represents—the freest and best system of Government the world has ever known."[17] This sentiment would be ardently reiterated during World War I. They also held fast to their rights as full British subjects. Studying medicine at Edinburgh in the footsteps of Horton, Bandele Omoniyi called for the continued adherence to the "true British school" of colonial policy, which admitted the capacity of Africans to enjoy full political and civil rights. In 1905 the Lagos elite established the Aborigines' Protection Society (later the Lagos Auxiliary of the

Anti-Slavery and Aborigines Protection Society) as a "corrective against the imperfections of the Crown Colony System."[18] The People's Union, established in 1908, protested the water rate. Earlier economic principles, notably the faith in free trade, also endured. The decline of merchant princes was lamented, and the growth of the Royal Niger Company monopoly was opposed. Blyden praised "British traders and merchants in West Africa, black and white," as a vital source of civilization and progress. Their gently progressive influence and the measured spread of commerce and cash crop production that Africans could control in their own interests constituted the best hope for development. Ademola II, being crowned as the Alake of Abeokuta in 1920, recommended that "all the nooks and corners of the country should be as free to commerce as the air we breathe; it is the principal mainstay of all progressive states."[19] They also, of course, maintained their faith in Christianity as the means of Africa's advance.

But the intelligentsia were not compelled to respond only in their Victorian manner. If an allegiance to Victorian culture had suited their needs earlier, addressing the new imperial dispensation now required dressing their medial culture in new colors. The substance and function of the educated community endured, but its members' ideas and culture adopted a fashion more suited to the times. They began by asserting that Africa's culture was too substantial to be simply displaced by Europe's, and that in any case their pride in being African would not allow this. It became popular in Lagos, as in British West Africa generally, to promote African dress and names in preference to those derived from Europe. Thus Edward Macaulay became Kitoyi Ajasa, and D. B. Vincent became Mojola Agbebi. In 1889 Lagos teachers resolved to wear only African dress, a reform frequently advocated if not universally practiced during the 1880s. Charlotte Olajumoke Obasa promoted the idea from her house furnished in high European style. As the intelligentsia around Lagos began to explore Yoruba culture especially, they created what Ajayi calls a "minor renaissance."[20] The predominance of Yoruba among the intelligentsia in these years gave this movement a certain cultural core. Yoruba-language publications swelled in number and variety from the 1880s. G. A. Williams established a Native Literature Publishing Bureau as a means of disseminating indigenous knowledge. The Yoruba language was promoted as a spoken, written, and musical medium; collections of

Yoruba proverbs and riddles were published in 1885. G. W. Johnson had favored English-language education in Abeokuta in 1868; at the end of the century, under the name Osokele Tejumade Johnson, he emphasized Yoruba language and history. Doctors asked what West African medicine might offer to improve the modern world and Africa itself. Obadiah Johnson's 1889 M.D. thesis on "West African Therapeutics," for example, explicitly attacked racist arguments linking the reputed ease of African childbirth with supposed evolutionary proximity to lower animals, explaining the superiority of African women's birthing practices. Moses Lijadu in Ondo researched the medicinal properties of Nigerian flora; Joseph Odumosu wrote four volumes in Yoruba on "indigenous therapeutics." There were also studies of African divination.

Their African identity also was given meaning through historical investigation. One of the earliest works is J. O. George's *Historical Notes on the Yoruba Country,* an 1884 lecture revised and published in Lagos in 1895 with the acknowledged assistance of many peers. A principal concern was to show that the "Yoruba people may not be properly called real savages; they are not quite ignorant of the elements and marks of civilization." There was also Payne's 1893 *Table of Principal Events in Yoruba History.* Obadiah Johnson in 1901 presented a historical work built from his brother Samuel's research, before publishing his late brother's voluminous *History of the Yorubas* in 1921. The Johnsons showed that while Yoruba society might still benefit from European, and especially Christian, influence, it still clearly had its own past glories and tragedies. The Egba United Government placed Yoruba history above European history in its school syllabus, and in 1909 its inspector of schools produced "A Chapter in the History of Yoruba Country." In 1916 A. K. Ajisafe (then known as E. O. O. Moore) produced the first edition of his *History of Abeokuta.* Practical concerns also inspired investigations into history and traditional political structures, as the intelligentsia sought to establish the groundwork upon which the colonial administration could best build.[21]

The challenge to the civilizing mission was faced more comprehensively in the independent African churches, which began to separate from European missions in 1888. It was usually in the church, after all, that the intelligentsia had been trained and had first considered the idea of a distinct African Christianity. There was a range of intention within the movement. All African churches were founded to resist European domination in church affairs and to advance Africans' control of their own ecclesiastical and secular lives. But for the more anglophile United African Church, the aim was simply "that a purely Native African Church be founded for the evangelization and amelioration of our race, to be governed by Africans." For the more "nationalist" proponents, African control had to be matched by African content. "The religion must be divested of all foreign admixtures, and be localized, and preached in its purity and simplicity, or the plant will ever remain exotic and all its ramifications dwindle to nothing when the foreign agency for its propagation is withdrawn." For Agbebi and many others, independent African Christianity was still also a means to more complete freedom: "When no bench of foreign bishops, no conclave of cardinals, lord over Christian Africa . . . then there will be an end to Privy Councils, Governors, Colonels, Annexations, Displacements, Partitions, Cessions and Coercions."[22] African churchmen were disproportionately prominent as writers and publishers of nationalist literature. The African church movement spawned numerous early inquiries into the relationship of Africa to Christianity and European civilization. These ranged from debate on the acceptability of polygamy within Christian teachings to numerous inquiries into the common ground between Christianity and African religions. The Christian Ogboni Society (later the Reformed Ogboni Fraternity), first created in 1900, was an explicit and eventually a very popular attempt to combine the power and authority of the traditional Ogboni society with Christian ideals and ceremony. It became "the most dramatic institutional symbol of the impact of traditional society on Christianity in Africa."[23]

In the realm of politics, imperial conquest fostered alliances between chiefly and educated elites in the spirit of African pride. In the turmoil of partition, the intelligentsia defended the rights of chiefs in general against imperialist excesses. As the *Weekly Record* lamented on 6 October 1894, "To the African, anxious for the preservation of his race, there is something despairingly distressing in the spectacle of Native chiefs and tribes being hunted down and made fugitives." They allied more closely with traditional rulers, protecting the interests of the latter as the realm of British power expanded. "All intelligent Africans," the same paper maintained, "would desire that the

Native Potentates should continue to maintain their ancestral position and status under the light and influence of civilized government." The alliance focused on the question of land ownership. As law and precedent began to shape the patterns of tenure, a vocal faction resisted the trend "in which the rights of Natives in the private ownership of their lands are being assailed and the recognition of those inherent and ancestral rights is being denied."[24] The educated and chiefly leaders of the Lagos Aborigines' Protection Society assumed the mandate to protect native interests. This alliance also was forged in Ijebu and other places, where local patriotism infused the mix of political resistance and cultural nationalism. In the initial phase after conquest, Christian and Moslem reformers allied with the British to attempt a wholesale reordering of Ijebu government. The traditional rulers then led a revolt in 1904, reducing the reformists' power. But in 1907, when a British merchant attempted to secure extensive timber rights, the Christian reformers, led by Joseph Odumosu, acted in close patriotic concert with the chiefly elite to resist, using funds raised by popular subscription. Odumosu used his newspaper and the acumen of a leading Lagos lawyer; the new Awujale worked through ritual and sacrifice. Here, as elsewhere, the defense of local interests led to the creative alliance of educated and other groups and the creative synthesis of their ideas and methods.

### Atlantic Affinities

These assertions and explorations of things African were made throughout British West Africa, not only because similar conditions obtained but also because the intelligentsia circulated throughout the region. However, material from Nigeria alone, or even from West Africa, could not be molded into a sufficient response. Although Nigerian-born Yoruba were coming to outnumber other groups in the educated community, the cultural and intellectual horizons of the intelligentsia still stretched around the Atlantic, most directly to the diasporan Africans in America and to colonial critics in Britain. Further, the European attack was on the whole African race, not just on West Africans. Pride in Yoruba dress or accounts of Yoruba history could not in themselves defend the race as a whole or resonate clearly within the entire African diaspora. To form an adequate response, the Nigerian intelligentsia had to speak both to and with the ideas of others concerning Africa, race, and civilization. The powerful support available in this wider setting, however, also set their response askew, because it provided ideas of Africa more suited to communities based outside than within colonial Africa.

Although British ideas about Africa were now in the main inimical to the intelligentsia, they were neither monolithic nor static. In the 1890s a minority among British colonial critics voiced ideas in which West Africans could find material more congenial to their interests. These flowed from a number of sources. The violence of imperial conquest had reawakened humanitarian traditions from earlier in the century. The need now to govern African societies efficiently created an urgent need to get beyond haughty judgments, to understand Africans accurately. Further, growing doubts about the virtues of European industrial society provoked a new interest in an imagined Africa which was a living repository of such qualities as communal harmony and spiritual insight that Europe seemed to lack. Perhaps Europeans had something to learn after all from "primitive" man, uncontaminated by modern industry and ideology. An early voice along these lines was Mary Kingsley, a traveler and amateur ethnographer in West Africa in the 1890s. She stressed that sound African development required that British experts dispense with "the fancy African, the fiend-child planted in the imagination of the British public by unscientific people," and study the African carefully and sympathetically. Accepting that Africans were a distinct race, unsuited to European civilization, Kingsley nevertheless argued that they had qualities worth preserving and the innate ability to improve their own condition with minimal interference from missionaries, merchants, and colonial overlords: "No race can, as a race, advance except in its own line of development."[25] Europeans were superior and rightly placed as colonial overlords, but not right to deny Africans their culture. Similar sentiments found a growing audience from the turn of the century. The British African Society was founded in 1901 to effect the ideals of "Kingsleyism"; these were picked up by E. D. Morel, the organizer of the protest against King Leopold's Congo. The German ethnographer Leo Frobenius praised the beauty of Yoruba art and culture (while also explaining how it had been created initially by foreign invaders). Early British social anthropologists shared a similar cultural relativism. The idea that African pecularities had to be preserved would cause the intelligentsia some unease in later years, when it was used to justify indirect rule and segregation. For the moment, however, it countered attempts to diminish the significance and capacity of Africans as a race.

Similar ideas were being promoted throughout the Black Atlantic, eloquently expressed by African-American intellectuals. The scientific racism of the late nineteenth century added to already well-developed American racial doctrines, resurgent after post–Civil War Reconstruction in disenfranchisement and official discrimination. Lynchings and race riots were widespread; migration to the American North placed African Americans in ghettos subject to new forms of segregation and oppression. At the same time, a middle class was rising conscious of new problems and opportunities, anxious to find solutions. Thus, as in West Africa, the intelligentsia turned to race pride to defend themselves against an increasingly prejudicial power structure. Crummell, an associate of Blyden's in Liberia in the 1860s with very similar ideas about the need to redeem Africans by establishing a sense of dignity as a race, returned to the United States in 1873 to spread this message. This stress on racial pride and solidarity informed the growing Pan-African sentiment that animated the diaspora by the end of the century. The African-American intelligentsia, especially from the appearance of W. E. B. Du Bois at the turn of the century to the Harlem Renaissance of the 1920s, drew on ideas like Blyden's and Crummell's to proclaim a program that many within the African diaspora could share. African Americans were to make their claim to dignity and equality within American society on the basis of their unique and valuable racial heritage. To Du Bois, emerging as one of the towering black American intellectuals, humanity must develop "not as individuals, but as races." "Negroes," he proclaimed, "must strive by race organization, by race solidarity, by race unity" to establish their place among the races of the world.[26]

The Nigerian intelligentsia were of course well aware of both communities of thought. Blyden had met Kingsley in London in 1898 and corresponded with her afterwards. He accepted the invitation to become a vice president of the British African Society established in her memory. Other notable West Africans, such as R. B. Blaize, R. A. Savage, and Agbebi, ranked among the members and contributors to its journal. Blyden was quick to welcome Kingsley's critique of British thinking about Africa. To Blyden, Kingsley was "the prophet of Africa to her people"; her ideas were "like the song of the nightingale after the long and dreary winter of misconception on the part of the foreigner and of woes innumerable on the part of the native."[27] Blyden linked her to other authors in a "new school of thinkers on African and racial questions."

> These writers, most of whom have been conscientious investigators on the spot, have broken through the sinister traditions of hundreds of years, and are teaching their countrymen to judge the Man of Africa by the impartial light of truth, and not from the standpoint of prejudice and preconceived ideas. They have rejected the theories of the noisy and blustering anthropologists of forty and fifty years ago—the Notts and Gliddons, Burtons, Winwood Reade, Hunt, *et id omme genus*—who invented all sorts of arguments . . . to prove the mental and moral inferiority of the Negro.[28]

West Africans' links with diasporan Africans were made in both America and London. Agbebi established a friendship with African-American leader John E. Bruce in New York in 1903 and sent his son Akinbami to stay with Bruce in 1919. J. E. K. Aggrey of Ghana and Orishtukeh Fadumah of Sierra Leone pursued teaching careers in America from around the turn of the century. Moses da Rocha, a Lagosian educated at Edinburgh, became an honorary member of the Negro Society for Historical Research in New York in 1912. The African Association, founded in London in 1897 by Trinidadian Henry Sylvester Williams, organized the 1900 London Pan-African Conference. Williams's circle connected men and women from the United States, Canada, the West Indies, West Africa, and Abyssinia. Here Nigerians such as James Johnson, Payne, and Agbebi met men such as Du Bois and Booker T. Washington. The African Association faded away, but London remained the center of Pan African life, focused during World War I in such associations as the West African Christian Student Union and the West African and West Indian Christian Union. Dusé Mohamed Ali's Pan-African efforts there received financial support from several West Africans long before he first visited West Africa in 1920.[29]

In both cases, the ideas and intellectual debts flowed both ways. Kingsley and Morel both held Blyden and John Mensah Sarbah in high esteem. R. E. Dennett, a trader and amateur ethnographer in West Africa and an admirer of Kingsley's ideas, acknowledged the assistance of many Nigerian writers, including James Johnson and Charles Phillips, E. M. Lijadu, Obadiah Johnson, and J. O. George. Henry Carr corrected the proofs of one of his books. Many of the essays in Blyden's best-known collection, *Christianity, Islam, and the Negro Race*, were first presented as lectures in the United States. Henriksen argues that through his twelve American tours and indirectly, "Blyden was a principal precursor of much of the awakened African consciousness in America." Henriksen also notes that much West African scholarship found a North American audience. The various bibliographies in Alain Locke's 1925 collection *The New Negro* mention Samuel Johnson, Sarbah, Horton, Hayford, and Blyden. Richard Burton and Dennett also appear. There was a sense that an intellectual community existed, connected by a common concern for Africa's future. As Sarbah noted, his study of the *Fanti National Constitution* was principally for "the information and consideration of persons in Africa, Europe and America affected by or interested in African affairs."[30]

It is clear that beyond an interest in Africa, this community also shared several key premises. Its members accepted that racial qualities were both innate and culturally significant. In other words, they accepted the Europeans' assertion of African difference. They also held—racist assertions about primitive Africans notwithstanding—that Africans had a culture, with laws and customs, in which to take pride and by which to guide their future development. Further, they shared the faith that the future of Africa should be (at least partly) in the hands of educated members of the race. African-American writers included West Africans within an inclusive "Negro" world leadership symbolized in their presence at the Pan-African Conference of 1900 and invitations to the 1912 International Conference on the Negro at Tuskegee. Although Kingsley thought African imitation of European culture risible, she nevertheless recognized that Western-educated Africans were the best equipped to both understand and explain problems presumed to be particular to their race. She judged that "there is now in West Africa a handful of Africans who have mastered white culture, who know it too well to misunderstand the inner spirit of it, who are men too true to let it cut them off in either sympathy or spirit or love from Africa." It was their duty, as the unique group "educated in our culture, and who also know African culture," to act "as true ambassadors and peacemakers between the two races and place before the English statesmen the true African, and destroy the fancy African made by exaggeration, that he has now in his mind." Morel suggested that Blyden's "race will regard him some day as its misunderstood prophet" and urged educated West Africans to stop ignoring his message.[31]

## "The Genius of Africa"

The Nigerian intelligentsia adopted these ideas to defend themselves. The vague, unformed sense of being "black Englishmen" was displaced by a sense of being black, of being part of the rising community of diasporan Africans. The members of the educated community could become a genuine elite not by serving as agents of the Western penetration of the African darkness but by combining Western knowledge with their putative racial characteristics, acting in concert with other black elites of similar mind. For West Africans this identity could assume many forms—they could see themselves as Yoruba, West Africans, Africans, or "Negroes"—but in what Echeruo has called the "cosmopolitan black ethos" of the period, all these identities were subsumed under their "common historical and racial identity with the negroes of Black America." Whatever Yoruba or West African qualities they held virtuous were virtues of the race affirmed against claims of European hegemony and superiority. Similarly, accomplishments by any black—West African or not—were taken as evidence of ability that pertained to all. The intelligentsia adopted this racial community for their own in diverse contexts, in the pursuit of what Blyden termed "race organisation and race consolidation."[32] To build an African church in Lagos in 1901 was to "lay the foundation of the church for the black race." Omoniyi personified this wider identity, writing in Britain in defense of African independence in both West and South Africa and later forming a league in Brazil "for the elevation of the Negro Race . . . in his native land and . . . throughout the world." James Johnson greeted the 1900 Pan-African Conference as "the beginning of a union I long hoped for"; the *Standard* appealed "to members of the Race the world over to extend their hearty co-operation" to its "great and noble aspirations." Further, the intelligentsia envisioned a racial leadership spanning the Atlantic. Blyden had long called for the return of the "exiled Negro in the Western hemisphere," in the faith that "the seed of a spiritual, intellectual, industrial life has been planted in his bosom, which, when he is transferred to the land of his fathers, will grow up into beauty, expand into flower." In 1912 Hayford greeted the International Conference on the Negro at Tuskegee as a step toward the joint West African and African-American leadership of the "African Nationality," for the good of the race.[33] They belonged to one race and faced one problem with a joint set of ideas. Hayford suggested to Booker T. Washington that "if leading thinkers and workers of the African race had the opportunity of exchanging thoughts across the Atlantic, the present century would be likely to see the solution of the race problem." This sense of shared identity culminated in the reception awarded Marcus Garvey in 1920 and lingered on through the interwar years, most powerfully among Nigerians abroad. Nnamdi Azikiwe, for example, would call from America in 1934 on "the Negro intellectual" in Africa, the West Indies, and the United States to kindle "a conception of race pride and race consciousness."[34] By then, however, other identities had gained favor within Nigeria.

Blyden was the most well known and energetic writer in West Africa addressing these questions. As one Lagos writer noted, "Both African and European acknowledged him to be one of the wisest and most cultured representatives of African opinion during his lifetime."[35] His proposal for organizing higher education within West Africa was endorsed by an impressive body of Lagos leaders in 1896. In Lagos his ideas were endorsed and popularized most notably by John Payne Jackson, editor of the *Lagos Weekly Record,* James Johnson, and Agbebi. The lives of these men intertwined with Blyden's. Jackson was a fellow Liberian. Johnson had lobbied with Blyden in Sierra Leone for a West African university during the 1870s. Blyden awarded Agbebi an honorary doctorate in the 1890s for his "literary ability and racial fidelity."[36] In a fitting encapsulation of the backgrounds of the early twentieth-century intelligentsia, this group augmented Blyden's rather ubiquitous West African presence with, respectively, a Liberian (married into a Lagos West Indian family), a Saro, and a Nigerian-born son of Saro parents. The ideas of these men diverged on many points. Blyden, for example, could recommend Islam as more appropriate than Christianity for Africa, while Agbebi and Johnson remained unswerving Christians. Agbebi was an active pastor in the independent church movement while Johnson, although sympathetic to the movement, never left the CMS. But they all endorsed Blyden's entreaty that Africans discover the "African personality" and develop in consonance with it. Agbebi warned that "the introduction of the usages and institutions of European life into the African social system has resulted in a disordering and a dislocation of the latter which threatens to overthrow the system altogether and produce a state of social anarchy. . . . Social organizations are the outgrowth of a people's life, and, founded more or less upon innate racial characteristics, are incapable of being transferred from one people of a certain type to another of a different type and condition." Africans not only had to establish a church freed of European trappings and rooted in African culture, they had to develop social and political institutions suited to their race. Africans had to discover their past and present in order to guide them in this work and to refute European claims that Africa had nothing of value to contribute to the world. As Blyden asserted, "We must not suppose that the Anglo-Saxon methods are final, that there is nothing for us to find out for our own guidance, and that we have nothing to teach the world." James Johnson lamented that "in the work of elevating Africans, foreign teachers have always proceeded with their work on the assumption that the Negro or African is in every one of its normal susceptibilities an inferior race, and that it is needful in every thing to give a foreign model to copy; no account has been made of our peculiarities, our languages enriched by the traditions of centuries, our parables many of them the quintessence of family and national histories." For Agbebi, only through discovery of the African personality could West Africans don the "toga of manhood."[37]

These four writers formulated most cogently the southern Nigerian intelligentsia's response to the betrayal of the civilizing mission. Their mission was not simply to accommodate African dress and language within the overriding values of some civilized absolute or to assert that "civilized" Africans could take pride in their African names as well as their British education. Although their arguments were not always clear or consistent, they in effect sought to reverse the onus of the civilizing mission—it was no longer a matter of retaining what was acceptable to the West within Africa but of discovering what was acceptable to Africa within the West. Accepting the premise of innate racial distinctions but proclaiming that African differences were not inferiorities, they sought to establish African standards of civilization by which European contributions might be judged valuable or not. Africa would create a unique civilization on its own terms, learning from the West but not betraying its racial essence. The "inspiration of the race is in the race," Blyden argued. Each race had its own particular genius and future, and "that only way must be found before there can be peace and harmony and progress." Jackson made dire warnings: "Only by following the simple and primitive customs branded 'heathenish' and adopting polygamy and other wholesome institutions obtaining with his people" would the educated community "avert the terrible calamity of utter and complete demoralization which now threatens to engulf him and his people." Agbebi was more concise: "The Sphinx must solve her own riddle. The genius of Africa must unravel its own enigma."[38]

### The Enigma of the "African Personality"

These men all died between 1912 and 1917, but they left a clear set of principles for their followers. In the prevailing atmosphere of racist denigration, this position seemed an effective riposte. It asserted, within the accepted assumption of innate racial differences, grounds for African equality. It did this not just for the Yoruba or for southern Nigerians but for the whole race, with the full weight of the African diaspora behind it. And it did so with the endorsement of a not insignificant group of British colonial critics. Yet it seems neither their identity with the race nor their assertion of the "African personality" assuaged their sense of unease or fully illuminated the path ahead. A correspondent of the *Lagos Times* lamented in 1882 that "Africans, as a race" sorely lacked not only "self respect" but also "the true essence" of both "personal and national dignity," criticisms echoed by J. G. Campbell in 1923. Morel reflected in 1912 that all of the "native papers" in Lagos "ceaselessly lament the Europeanizing of the country, the decay of the national spirit, the decadence of family authority, and the deterioration of the rising generation without, however . . . ever making an attempt to grapple with the problem in a constructive sense."[39] The enigma remained.

Abiola Irele finds that the West African intelligentsia of this period "were afflicted with a profound *malaise.* . . . They knew themselves to be marginal men without any stable cultural links and consequently without a firm sense of identity." Most historians, like Irele, have attributed this confusion and insecurity to the intelligentsia's "marginality." Ayandele presents them as "victims" of their acculturation, caught "betwixt and between" the European and the African worlds.[40] Certainly the medial position of the intelligentsia was not easy to hold, especially through the turbulent changes of this period. The demographic shift under way—pushing up an increasingly indigenous intelligentsia to assume the legacy of a largely foreign one—no doubt also injected confusion. Certainly, too, the problems of meeting African and European ideas of civilization or of understanding the meaning of "African" in the "African personality"—which remain on the agenda of many intellectuals today—are not tractable in any setting. But these explanations are inadequate. The intelligentsia's medial position was an enduring fact of their history, while this malaise was more acute now than at earlier or later periods. If they were victims in the sense of being colonial subjects, they were also part of an established colonial middle class with vested interests to defend. The intelligentsia had not been lifted out of some enduring African world but not yet placed in a discrete European world. Rather, they were actively building their own world, struggling to meet their needs in a location surrounded by diverse African societies and awash in Atlantic currents. The particularly acute malaise of these years was not simply a result of their political and economic subordination. It was also a product of certain ideas at play in a particular historical setting.

The Sphinx could not solve her own riddle because it was posed in terms that were not wholly her own. The West African intelligentsia, as much as any of the three main communities shaping the Atlantic discourse on Africa, had to create a meaning for the idea of "Africa" to answer the challenge posed by the new imperialism. Specific Yoruba or Efik intellectual traditions addressed questions of identity, but the idea of being "African" needed to be addressed in terms of the continental confrontations construed by the Atlantic context. The other two communities provided a meaning composed largely with material external to Africa, addressed primarily not to African needs but to their own. Their "Africa" was largely a symbol pitted against an image of "the West." For the West Africans' idea of Africa to meet their needs, it not only had to confront the idea of the West, it also had to help explain the concrete colonial situation in which they alone lived. The ideas they deployed, however, designed for the common needs of three distinct communities, were ill suited to the task the West Africans alone faced.

For British colonial critics, even in the African Society, Africa was viewed through the lens of empire as a primitive continent in need of paternal tutelage or as an exotic alternative to European civilization. "Africa" was seen less as the total or the essence of the diverse religious ideas, oral literatures, and social relations found among its people than as an exotic place distinct from the West. British writers frequently referred to Africa, or even the tropical empire, as if it formed a single meaningful division in human society. One was "African" not because one believed or did certain things, but because one was clearly neither European nor Asian. Further, as Hammond and Jablow (among others) argue, the British image of Africa was constructed in "reciprocal contrast" to the British self-image. In the British mind "Africa *is* what the British *are not*." Thus in the earlier nineteenth century, the smugly civilized Briton created the savage African, and the Briton intent on imperial expansion created an Africa in need of external control. For malcontents at the end of the century, for whom Victorian civilization seemed "marked more by discontent than satisfaction," Africa became by contrast a place "simple and content, close to nature and the eternal verities."[41] Thus Kingsley came to West Africa "in quest of herself" and took special interest in what she called "fetishism" because of its affinity to her own pantheistic beliefs. P. A. Talbot deemed the primitive West African indigenes "more clearly alive to spiritual conditions and truths than other, more materialistic, races." This attitude continued in the writing of Leonard Barnes, one of the more outspoken critics in the 1930s: whites betrayed an evolutionary "degradation" to which India and Africa possibly held the cure in their "intimate sense of brotherhood and common humanity . . . [their] capacity of social self-sacrifice [and] . . . co-operative communism." For many of the British writers congenial to Nigerians,

Africa was a repository of virtues, and these became part of the African character. Further, the image of the African bound to the soil fed into British dreams of exploiting a productive peasantry. Governor MacGregor echoed the popular idea that "the instincts of the race are clearly in the directions of industries affecting the soil, forest produce, and trade."[42] Morel, supporting Liverpool traders' resistance to the emergent oligopoly in West African trade, incorporated the image of Africans as natural farmers into his economic prescription, which combined indirect rule, merchant participation in government, and free commerce.

The Africa seen by the African-American intelligentsia in the early twentieth century similarly had more to do with American than African reality. African Americans in the nineteenth century tended to share the white American notion that Africa was a dark and savage continent in need of redemption. In the time of rising race pride, the principal value of Africa was as a symbol of black ability and proof of a rich race heritage which could empower African Americans to resist racist attacks on their dignity and worth. This reevaluation of African history drew some inspiration from Kingsley and her ilk. Colonial society was far less interesting to the "New Negro" than the cultural glories of Africa's ancient and medieval past. The African Americans were less interested in creating some kind of amalgam between living African societies and modernity than in finding in Africa refutations of white American claims that their race heritage was either nonexistent or worthless. Arthur Schomburg, for example, observed that the "Negro has been considered a man without a history because he has been considered a man without a culture" and looked to the African past to find "a record of credible group achievement" which could establish the common heritage and pride of the "New Negro." This African-American endeavor to define themselves rested in large part on a critique of Western civilization rather than knowledge of Africa. Kwame Appiah sees Du Bois's views on race as a dialectic response to both European racism and a general African-American denial of racial difference: countering racism meant abandoning notions of universal equality to assert pride in racial peculiarity. Marion Berghahn argues that Du Bois "looks for, and finds, in the African all those virtues which he had seen the West betray." More generally, the "New Negro had no intention of assimilating African ideas, languages, literature or music. What he had in mind was to define his own position *vis-à-vis* Africa."[43] In short, African-American intellectuals were not much concerned with understanding African society under the impact of colonial rule but rather with claiming a lost heritage which could sustain an African claim to respect in the context of American society.

There are hints that some of the West African intelligentsia faintly recognized these divergent perspectives. Blyden acknowledged a debt to Venn and other British writers for developing the basic idea that each race must raise itself, but he resented the "patronizing or apologetic tone" of much of their writing. Hayford thought the "exclusive and provincial" work of Washington and Du Bois compared poorly to Blyden's attempts to address the "entire race problem." Later writers would recognize divergences more clearly, but for now they were less important than the recognition of mutual support. The Nigerian intelligentsia, prone themselves to the kind of dialectic response formulated by Du Bois, could hardly resist this propensity when it was reinforced by ideas from around the Atlantic. In any case, as a minority in this discourse and without an overpowering presence within West Africa, they could not easily defy the trend. The Nigerian image of Africa developed for the "African personality" showed its Atlantic affinities well into the interwar period. The notion that Africans still held the spiritual propensity Europe had lost played into the sense that Africans were essentially religious. This of course meshed neatly with the Christian foundations of the intelligentsia and with the broad significance religion had in nineteenth-century African society. The power of faith would redeem Africa because religion governed their lives. Secular education, James Johnson argued, "however it may commend itself to some people in Europe, is entirely unAfrican, and foreign to the traditions of a people to whom Religion is everything . . . it cannot commend itself to thoughtful Negroes who are anxious to see preserved inviolate the religious instincts of the people, as they know this purely secular Education cannot fail to produce those hybrids of humanity, Atheists, Infidels, and Indifferents which Africa has not yet given birth to." Blyden, with Crummell and others, had long argued that Africa's special role was to "cultivate" the "spiritual elements" of humanity, to become the "spiritual conservatory" of a world in need of renewed faith.[44]

Economic prescriptions also were written for this symbolic Africa, as desired economic patterns were reified as racial destiny. In general, the intelligentsia's economic prescription sought a return to the earlier conditions of small-trader prosperity. But heated protest arose in the face of repeated colonial government attempts to legislate state control of land ownership. Seeking a distinct line of development, the leaders of the race resisted these initiatives by insisting that Africans' proper place was on the land, while manufacturing should be left to Europe. This narrowed the vision of economic diversification prevalent in mid-Victorian times. As Blyden had made clear, the African's talent was not to re-create modern industry but to live close to nature as man in "his perfect state." The Reverend E. E. Ukpabio, an early convert from eastern Nigeria, was confident that "with our soil, the richest in the world, we can supply the wants of traders and sufficiently support an intelligent and growing population."[45] The Ghanaian Kobina Sekyi, elaborating on Blyden's notion that "diseased" European industrial society would disrupt the African social order, advised against emulating European "intellectual and industrial development." This faith in agriculture as the principal source of West African prosperity remained strong despite the severe commodity price fluctuations that followed World War I. Ivanhoe Maye's 1919 appeal to go "Back to the Land," for example, extolled modern methods and cooperative organization but did not look far beyond Nigeria's agricultural sector. Adebesin Folarin was still adamantly Blydenesque on the point in 1931. "Eminent thinkers and writers among whom may be mentioned the late Dr. Blyden have pointed out time without number . . . that the ordained vocation for the native is agriculture, that he must go back to the plough. . . . Not being manufacturers of European goods which are commodities mostly in demand in African markets, to compete with them in their own industry would be as hopeless and absurd as to attempt to fly with the wings of a bird pasted on the arms. The native employing his natural endowments in the proper ways will surely prosper."[46]

More generally, Africa was constructed as an edifying opposite to an imagined Europe, with little reference to available knowledge about specific African qualities or research into African societies. The *Weekly Record* charged Africans to overcome the "pernicious" notion of being European, to recognize that the complex European way of "making, spending, or hoarding money is not ours." Africans, to survive, needed to "go back to the simplicity" of their ancestors. In *African Life and Customs* Blyden defined Africa in large part by contrasting it to Europe. The qualities of "pure and simple" Africa were presented as the positive contrast to the evils of crime, poverty, and prostitution plaguing industrial countries. Enlightened Africans, he noted, were "rapidly arriving at a revision of . . . former immature" praise for European civilization. "They have discovered all the waste places, all the nakedness of the European system" and rejected it. Their aim was "to save Africa from such a fate." Nnamdi Azikiwe, in his 1934 defense of Liberia, was as direct. His Africa was defined not in specific African terms but as "an anti-thesis to the impracticalities of Western civilization, especially in the realm of human relationships." Liberia, he argued in the spirit shared by Barnes, "should emphasize spiritual values, and should apply the African ideal of hospitality, of friendliness, of honesty, of truth, of justice, and of the brotherhood of man."[47]

Promulgating the "African personality" responded effectively to the challenge of the new racism but not to the other challenges faced by the West African intelligentsia. It could serve as a solid foundation for the West African defense of their "race" but was a rather precarious vantage point from which to survey their own society. This task required an outlook open to the full variety and potential of diverse European and African societies. Instead, their ideas offered an understanding of Africa based on oppositions. Jackson, significantly, observed that "under the new order of things introduced into West Africa, two points of view have evolved; the European point of view, and the Native point of view."[48] Challenged as a "black Englishman," Jackson could see no middle ground: if educated Africans were "neither European nor Native," they were merely "chaotic and hybrid."[49] Africans who tried to live in both worlds lived "pseudo-lives" doomed to end in calamity, because "any violation of the indigenous order of life . . . which experience has rendered adapted to the unpropitious conditions, is bound to prove fatal." This filter did more than reduce to black and white a world of many shadings; it projected an image of Africa which bore little necessary resemblance to their actual surroundings. Their ideas led them toward assuming the true Africa had to be distinct from Europe, that, as an "African Doctor" put it in 1933, "the first essential in negro improvement is, obviously, negro purity," not "the Admixture of Black and White."[50] They defined African qualities as the spiritual and pastoral counterpoint to Europe's industrial atheism. The intelligentsia's sense of failure flowed in part from the fact that this ideal image, derived from abstract notions of Africa and Europe, was impossible to realize.

Their unease also stemmed from their failure to grapple with urgent social questions of their day. The intelligentsia, like the educated community from which they arose, needed to know a great deal about their surroundings in order to pursue and protect their place in the unfolding colonial order. The interests of chiefs and traders had to be articulated under British law. African knowledge about medicine, religion, and morality had to be rendered into forms recognizable in imperial discourses. The actual marriage practices of the educated community, which often fit neither polygamous African nor monogamous European patterns, needed defining. Rivalries between former sovereign states, transformed but not extinguished by colonial rule, needed reformulation. These were complex questions, embedded in the historical processes of the time, involving the further integration of West Africa into European imperial and economic systems. The intelligentsia, armed with ideas that construed this process as a clash of irreconcilable races, were poorly equipped for grasping them. Their intellectual charts identified only two shorelines on their horizons, the "European" and the "African." They remained uneasy because their charts said little about their actual location and, indeed, indicated that no one could survive in the waters between, not grounded firmly on either shore.

Finally, their unease may be linked to the way the "African personality" demanded a choice between being of one "race" or the other. As Adeyemo Alakija described his role and that of his predecessors in 1926, "My aim is to act as the bridge connecting the two sections, to understand the white man's view and interpret it to my countrymen and to interpret to Europeans the needs and aspirations of my countrymen."[51] They were a medial community whose situation required flexible identities. European skills empowered them among Nigerians; African connections made them valuable to European rulers and merchants. The atmosphere of intense racism notwithstanding, they had to remain free to play roles as British agents and as African leaders. The idea of being purely African, even if this identity was weakly rooted in the specifics of African cultures, threatened one of the tenets of their existence.

This external orientation was not absolute. The "renaissance" in Lagos has ample evidence of the continuing input of ideas rooted in Nigerian societies into the discussions of the intelligentsia. The urge to establish the substance of African culture in the face of corrosive European commentary led the intelligentsia—and especially the Yoruba intelligentsia with close affinities to the hinterland—to ask questions of intellectuals there. Payne's *Almanacks* and *Principal Events* were largely compendiums of information about the colony of Lagos, but they also gave short accounts of the precolonial histories of Abeokuta, Lagos, and the interior wars, as well as guides to Lagos chiefs and local nonelite organizations that patently required some conversation with local noncolonial intelligentsia. Obadiah Johnson's medical research involved learning from traditional practitioners. James Johnson's *Yoruba Heathenism* was obviously the result of intimate knowledge of the *babalawos'* ways. These explorations, and the many others like them, searched for specific knowledge of African societies in ways that were beyond the broad proclamations about African history and character heard elsewhere around the Atlantic. These writers transcribed Yoruba ways of knowing into print and thus firmly into the realm of the colonial intelligentsia. Connections with Nigerian intellectual traditions beyond the colonial one would endure and, indeed, expand, dissolving some of the enigmatic qualities of the African personality. But at the turn of the century, they remained embedded in the dominant pattern of colonial intellectual life, a pattern based on stark oppositions. J. K. Coker's defense of polygamy was made only with Scripture; African marriage was to be justified in Christian rather than African terms. The specific and detailed knowledge they acquired about Africa was valued, in the main, as ammunition in the battle for racial dignity. The study of Yoruba medicine used specific Yoruba ways to stand in for the case that Africans in general knew of medicine, rather than to develop Yoruba medicine as a corpus of knowledge in itself, distinct from other West African traditions. Abayomi Cole lectured on Ifa not to show how it worked or to investigate it in its own terms but rather to assert that it was as deeply grounded and moral as Christianity. His call was simply to "unearth and refine their time-honoured science and religion and show to the world that we too have something to add to human knowledge." Ifa represented "a source of new life and inspiration to the race possessing it," but Christianity remained the best way forward.[52] The intelligentsia moved between the categories of Yoruba, West African, African, and Negro freely because they subsumed the former in the latter and saw their Nigerian societies as exemplifying their Africa.

The Nigerian intelligentsia were both empowered and weakened by their thorough participation in the intellectual currents of the Atlantic during these years. These connections helped raise an assertion of cultural pride into a more positive and provocative program—the ambition to realize the "African personality." But these connections also supplied an ideal and symbolic Africa better designed for use outside Africa than inside, obscuring their view of the actual colonial society in which they operated. Set askew by their external orientation, the intelligentsia had not, in short, successfully reversed the onus of the civilizing mission. Instead of using African criteria to assess European ones in defining their new society, they defined African values largely by contrasting themselves to Europe. Their investigation of things African was less a dialogue with Africa than with Europe. The Sphinx's riddle remained not only unsolved but insoluble with the materials at hand.

# 4

## "Unity, Self-Help and Co-operation"

### Pragmatic Prescriptions, 1920–1940

IN RETROSPECT, the interwar period marks perhaps the most promising moment of Nigerian intellectual history, at least to 1960. The interwar intelligentsia faced an unfolding series of adverse conditions, encompassing economic depression, challenges by an oligopoly of foreign firms, unemployment for school graduates, and persistent racism. To meet them, as always, they reworked Atlantic discourse about Africa in light of their own situation. Now, however, their greater numbers, deeper local roots (especially among the Yoruba), and more intimate knowledge of both their Black Atlantic and British peers helped provide them with a more substantial sense of their own situation. Drawn increasingly from the burgeoning numbers of traders, transporters, and clerks, the intelligentsia identified the common interests of these groups to devise, under the banner of "Unity, Self-help and Co-operation," a pragmatic economic prescription.[1] The self-proclaimed "youth" of the 1930s, identifying more with a Nigerian nation than with the African race, strove to prove themselves the rational leaders of a modern state. A now substantial number of writers rooted in the provinces explored past and emergent problems of specific Nigerian societies. They did not resolve fundamental issues, remove all inconsistencies, or dissolve their enduring unease. They did, however, fix themselves against the Atlantic tides that had earlier pulled them between Victorian and Black Atlantic perspectives on Africa, to launch their own inquiries with a promising mixture of qualities: they maintained a sense of African difference and Pan-African solidarity but looked past generalized notions of "Africa" to work up from empirical detail, treating sympathetic elements of Atlantic thought selectively. Much of the postwar generation, in their eagerness to board the newly launched ship of state en route to sovereignty and modernization, would again sail into Atlantic waters and lose sight of the Nigerian landscape.

## Diversity in Adversity

Through the interwar years the economic interests, distribution, and social character of the Nigerian medial classes extended along lines set in the nineteenth century, in the face of a deepening sense of crisis. The interwar colonial economy also opened new possibilities and created new problems for Nigerians generally.[2] Severe disruptions early in World War I eventually were controlled, leading to high demand and prices for Nigerian produce into 1920. This boom attracted more producers to cash crops and expanded the roles for middlemen. At the same time, it dulled awareness of impending problems for relatively inefficient African merchants. After 1921 this boom collapsed, introducing over two decades of sharp price and demand fluctuations spread unevenly over different commodities. From the late 1920s to the mid-1930s Nigeria endured a second phase of prolonged depression. The value of trade recovered its 1920 levels only after 1940. However, the volume of exports steadily increased, reflecting growing Nigerian participation in the colonial economy. In these changing conditions a handful of large European firms consolidated both their oligopoly and their reputation as excessively powerful rivals of quondam and aspiring African merchant princes. If the standard of living improved for some, the crises attendant on these fluctuations inspired much discontent—not only among the educated, as palm and cocoa producers' protests of the later 1930s testify. But the medial classes also responded by becoming more diverse and more organized, particularly in the forums provided by the newly consolidated colonial state of Nigeria.

In these troubled times only a few Nigerians continued to succeed as large-scale importers. J. H. Doherty fostered a successful importing firm from the 1890s until his death in 1928 which his son carried on, but this was an exceptional case. Attempts were made to reenter the export trade on a major scale and to compete with the established banks, but the merchant princes were now largely historical figures. Opportunities for men and women remained at other tiers of the trade structure, despite the vagaries of the market, notably in produce buying, merchandise retailing, and transport. As in the nineteenth century, illiterates could still succeed in their own economic ventures. The Onitsha trader Omu Okwei thrived until her death in 1943. Literacy, however, eased arrangements with the European firms at the commanding heights. A number of educated entrepreneurs moved into these openings to build considerable stakes in the system.

Western education became an ever more essential element in attempts to find more diverse and stable economic foundations; demands for education therefore multiplied. Educated Africans took pains to launch their children's careers through Western education. It was rare indeed for the children of educated Lagosians not also to be educated. Those who could afford to do so schooled their children abroad, at secondary if not at primary levels. Doherty's will provided for at least two of his sons to become lawyers, another son a doctor, and a daughter one of the earliest female government clerks. Production of cocoa in the west and palm oil in the east provided illiterate farmers and traders with the means to invest in education, producing an influx of educated Nigerians with direct ties to rural producers. S. L. Akintola's father, a textile trader in Minna during the First World War, had his children educated when business allowed them free time. As one intellectual later reflected on the depression years: "Those who had savings spent them to send the children to schools and colleges, because they saw that only salaried people were secure even in spite of salary cuts and stabilization, and that to get a good salary one had to be educated. It was then that I began to look at education as a commodity that does not fall in price."[3] Even poor rural families made sacrifices to secure at least some of their children a basic education.

To meet this demand schools entered a period of striking expansion in both enrollment and geographic distribution. By 1937 there were over 3,500 primary schools in southern Nigeria, 450 of them government assisted, with over 218,000 students. These numbers are almost 60 percent higher than those for 1921. By 1931 about 13 percent of school-age children were enrolled in southern Nigeria. Secondary ed-

ucation enrollments made dramatic leaps after the early 1920s, growing about eight times (to over 4,000) by 1937. Eastern primary-school
populations caught up to Lagos and the western region by 1930. The
western advantage at postprimary levels faded less quickly: over two-
thirds of the twenty-six secondary and teacher-training institutions established by 1930 were still in the west. Postsecondary enrollments are
more difficult to pin down. They increased but remained on the order
of a few hundred at most. Nigerians attending British universities
probably passed the 100 mark only in the later 1930s; they certainly
did not exceed 200 before World War II. Few if any Nigerians attended
American postsecondary institutions before 1920. By 1938, when a
small exodus was organized, there had been about twenty. Nigerians
continued to attend Fourah Bay, and from 1934 to 1944 Yaba Higher
College in Lagos produced 142 graduates trained for lower, technical
civil service posts. Because schools were spreading so rapidly from
such small beginnings, first-generation school graduates probably
outnumbered those with educated parents. Certainly Nigerian-born
recruits now overwhelmed immigrants in the younger cohorts of students. At the same time, the small circle of highly educated leaders remained prominent within the wider educated community.

Women remained largely excluded from clerkships and higher education, with only slight improvements over the previous generation.
The imbalance in education for women and men remained more or
less unchanged at the primary level, at between four and five to one.
Ratios at the secondary level remained much worse but improved
more markedly, standing at about seventeen to one in 1930 and at
around eight to one by 1937. Ratios were most even in Lagos, least so
outside southwestern Nigeria. The curriculum for women now included some clerical training but was still skewed toward domestic
skills. A few daughters of the elite, however, emerged among the
highly educated. The first Nigerian woman qualified in medicine in
1929. Lady Ademola was perhaps the first Nigerian woman to graduate from Oxford, in 1935. The first African woman lawyer appeared in
1934, the first Nigerian woman lawyer only around 1950.[4]

Some brief comparisons of data on primary, secondary, and tertiary
education are worth making here, however imperfect the data. The
earlier increase in primary schools means that through the interwar
years the ratio of primary to secondary enrollments was never lower

than 50 to 1, and in the late 1920s perhaps as high as 250 to 1. Promotion from secondary to tertiary education seems to have been no higher than about 50 to 1 through these years. Thus the ratio of primary to secondary enrollments was always markedly higher than the ratio of secondary to tertiary enrollments—at its peak perhaps five times higher. This sharply narrowing pyramid suggests secondary and postsecondary graduates were still remarkable in this period, set off from increasingly common primary graduates. But if mere literates and primary graduates were becoming subordinate strata in the hierarchy of the educated, university graduates remained too small in number to form a tier unto themselves.

Economic uncertainty, job retrenchment, and continuing racist practices in government and mercantile firms created a context in which the rising generation often moved through diverse jobs, pulled by the ambition to secure a clerkship. Higher education and a professional career, Louis Mbanefo made clear, were sought as security from economic cycles or dependence on government employment. Soyode's 1921 *Reference Almanack*, for example, reveals Africans working as letter writers, private teachers, importers, medical dispensers, auctioneers, booksellers, and photographers. Many careers involved a period of teaching, but clerkships in government and mercantile firms were widely seen as more prestigious—even by some school headmasters. The Alake of Abeokuta had his eldest son work as a clerk for two years before and after his legal studies abroad. N. A. Fadipe, a contemporary sociologist, suggests that an earlier typical career pattern, from schoolteacher to catechist to minister, was now redirected toward clerkships. Daniel Anirare (later the Ewi of Ado-Ekiti) felt this attraction. He left a secure teaching post to seek a Lagos clerkship in 1929 but, failing to find a job immediately, could not bear to have his friends discover that he had been reduced—even temporarily—to day labor. "In order not to arouse the suspicion of gossiping housewives in my residence I had to dress up like a clerk going to a large office when leaving home in the morning, and that included putting on a tie to match my outfit. As soon as I got to the site I changed to my labour garment. At the end of the day's work I returned home a neat worker with the appearance of a clerk." Lawyers were increasingly conspicuous as clergy (and the church) became less so. Obafemi Awolowo was a journalist, moneylender, transport owner, and cocoa buyer before saving enough to read law in London in 1944; H. O. Davies was a teacher then a clerk before reading economics at the London School of Economics in 1934 and a journalist and government marketing officer before returning to London for law in 1944. Of fifty-six candidates for the Legislative Council from 1923 to 1947, twenty-four were barristers and ten were medical doctors, while only three—all from Calabar—were men of the church. University careers also began to diverge from law and medicine. P. O. Cardoso took a master's degree in agriculture from Cornell in 1927; Eyo Ita took one in education from Columbia in 1933; Nnamdi Azikiwe did graduate work in anthropology at several American universities in the 1930s. Fadipe attained a Ph.D. in sociology from the University of London in 1939. If the elite among the educated were diversifying, they were still exposed to the occupations and preoccupations of the medial classes in general.[5]

Government, railway, and mercantile openings increased from World War I; there were at least 5,300 government and commercial clerkships in 1920 and some 4,600 government clerkships alone in 1939. But the desire for a clerical post was much more easily filled in the 1920s than in the 1930s. Governor Lugard complained in 1920 of the inadequacy of Nigerian grammar-school graduates in both numbers and quality. Many vacancies had to be filled by "native foreigners," leading to a situation in the later 1930s when the handful of senior African posts were largely in their hands. Standards also rose as the pool of educated applicants grew; by the 1930s a mere primary-school certificate no longer served as a ticket to clerical service. CMS Niger Mission schools hired most of their Standard Six graduates in the 1920s; by 1932 they only took in a third. Further, government budget crises during the 1930s depression severely reduced job openings. The Nigerian railway, for example, reduced its workforce by some 20 percent from 1929 to 1933 and had not quite regained its 1929 size by 1938. The cohort of Nigerians who had flooded the secondary schools only to face retrenchment would express their frustration with both the colonial government and the entrenched "native foreigners."[6]

Thus, by the 1930s the complexion of the intelligentsia had changed from the late nineteenth century. The expansion of education—in both numbers and geographical reach—had elicited a new wave of recruits. These recruits were attached to the medial classes much as earlier cohorts had been, but across a much wider base in both cultural and social terms. They were Nigerian rather than foreign-born and the first rather than the second or third generation of their families to be educated. This changing complexion is most clearly revealed by a cohort of intellectuals identifying themselves as "youth" who challenged the nineteenth-century order in the 1930s. This movement receives more extended attention below. For now, a brief analysis of these challengers can help uncover the social forces behind them. The leaders of the main political parties of the 1920s—the Nigerian National Democratic Party, Reform Club, and People's Union—were all of elite Christian, often Saro, families. By contrast, a significant minority of prominent Nigerian Youth Movement leaders in Lagos came from provincial families with only one or two generations of exposure to mission education. Although the NYM leaders tended to be younger in the mid-1930s than the earlier leaders had been in 1920, both leaderships contain similar numbers of lawyers, doctors, journalists, and businessmen. The antagonism between the "youth" and established groups was therefore not clearly a conflict between economic classes or interest groups. Rather, the "youth" were moved to action in part by economic crises and job retrenchment in the 1930s, which upset their ambitions to replicate their seniors' careers. Their recurrent demands for civil service employment, couched in terms of Nigerianization, suggest this. Davies, a very prominent NYM leader, lamented the "deficiencies in the life of the African youth," who "in spite of their growing number, find no place in the Administrative Service. As lawyers and doctors, they have to accept appointments at great disadvantage to themselves."[7] Competition between indigenes and "native foreigners" also seems to have been at play here. The fielding of non-Nigerian candidates was an issue in the 1938 elections. Adeniyi-Jones, an NNDP candidate, accused the Youth Movement of having a "Nigeria for the Nigerians" policy and insisted that his Yoruba ancestry mattered more than his Sierra Leonean birth. Sierra Leonean candidates in Calabar had to be defended as legitimate against a similar sentiment. The NYM argued that electing its indigenous candidates would "assist in shattering once and for all the old myth . . . of the Nigerian's incapacity for leadership." Its charter pressed simply for more "qualified Africans" in the civil service in one passage but elsewhere urged explicitly that "Nigerians" be hired into a service which was "manned today entirely by foreigners." This demographic shift toward a younger, Nigerian-born intelligentsia is not, however, absolute enough to explain the youth era. Ernest Ikoli and several others figured among the leadership of both the old guard and the new. Dr. J. C. Vaughan, the first NYM president, was a forty-two-year-old son of a wealthy merchant once active in the Reform Club. Nor was the competition against "native foreigners" new. Herbert Macaulay, now accused of supporting non-Nigerian candidates, had once leveled the same charge at Henry Carr.[8] The youth era was also a product of a new intellectual climate.

## Lagos Life

Lagos remained the cosmopolitan center of education and of the educated community in the interwar years. In 1936 it held about three-quarters of Nigeria's seventy barristers. Lagos also remained the center of the press as newspapers increased steadily in number, circulation, and frequency. Nineteen papers had been seen in Lagos by 1920. By 1937 twenty-two more had appeared, including the first daily in 1926. Five of these were in Yoruba. Omu estimates that weekly circulation in 1920 was about 3,000; by 1937 three dailies alone had a circulation of almost 18,000, and the nine weeklies had almost 22,000. Of the eleven Nigerian papers publishing in 1937, eight were in Lagos. At least ten printing presses were established in Lagos during the 1920s, widening the flow of books, handbills, and pamphlets. There were also more books on loan: by the late 1930s three public libraries were open.[9]

Lagos also served as center stage for the explicitly political organizations that multiplied after World War I. Marcus Garvey's Universal Negro Improvement Association, based in New York, appeared in Lagos and Calabar in 1920. The Lagos branch boasted 400 members at its height but declined sharply after Garvey's arrest in 1922. The Lagos elite also formed a branch of the National Congress of British West Africa in 1920. The Congress branch was widely supported when it appeared but then fell victim to the factional divisions of Lagos politics. Never as strong as other branches in West Africa, it was moribund by 1930. Elections were held for the Lagos Town Council every three years from 1920. Three Legislative Council members from Lagos and one Calabar member were elected every five years from 1923. These councils stimulated the press and political parties to a more vigorous life, focused on Lagos and Calabar rather than the African diaspora or even British West Africa, giving some substance to the framework of Nigeria created by amalgamation. In Calabar a National League and an Improvement League were inspired to political action under educated leadership. The NNDP, under the guidance of Herbert Macaulay and promoted by his *Lagos Daily News,* represented one of the basic factions in Lagos politics. This camp included Thomas Jackson of the *Weekly Record,* Dr. C. C. Adeniyi-Jones, lawyer Egerton Shyngle, and African church leader the Reverend J. G. Campbell. Through the 1920s it demanded that the Eleko be returned to the throne of Lagos. The Macaulay faction was opposed on the Eleko question and much else by a group which had first formed in 1908 as the People's Union and later organized as the Reform Club to oppose the Congress. Dr. John K. Randle, Dr. O. Obasa, and lawyer Adeyemo Alakija were prominent, supported by Kitoyi Ajasa's *Nigerian Pioneer.* Journalist Ernest Ikoli switched to this camp in the early 1920s. This group tended to be of the established educated elite but also enjoyed support from Lagos Moslems. Henry Carr was also among Macaulay's opponents but as a government servant was less free for political activism. Dusé Mohamed Ali, who had published the *African Times and Orient Review* in London from 1912 to 1920, established the *Comet* in Lagos in 1933 and advanced Pan-African perspectives while staying relatively free of factional disputes. The NYM was formed as the Lagos Youth Movement in 1934, to insist that Yaba Higher College not be created as a second-rate school for colonial subordinates. It successfully challenged the Democratic Party's long-standing domination of both the Lagos Town Council and the Legislative Council in 1938. The views of the Youth Movement were expressed by the *Service* (later a daily) from 1933 and by Azikiwe's *West African Pilot* when he established it in 1937. With extensive provincial membership and strong ties to the growing number of produce traders and transporters, the NYM finally began to realize the ideal of a political party embracing all of southern Nigeria. Many leaders of the nationalist era first appeared in the NYM, including Azikiwe, Samuel Akisanya, Davies, and Awolowo. Party divisions were not clearly tied to ethnicity but were shaped in intricate ways by ethnicity, generational competition, personalities, and policy issues. Personal vitriol was often too harsh to ignore. Carr, for example, once referred to the Democratic Party as "a little clique of ambitious and vainglorious men led by an evil genius." Macaulay regarded Carr as a dangerously conceited man cut off from his African roots.[10] There was an ethic among young intellectuals to rise above ethnic identities. King's College staff and students were inspired to eschew subnational divisions; on many newspaper staffs collaborative friendships took little notice of them. The famous Akisanya crisis of 1941, however, did foreshadow the divisive ethnic politics of later years.

Like political parties, the economic associations formed in these years, with members of the intelligentsia among their leaders, reveal them recognizing and defending the interests of the medial classes. Educated elements formed the Civil Service Union in 1912, the Nigerian Law Association in 1923, and the Nigerian Union of Teachers in 1931 and figured among the leadership of other trade unions and commercial organizations like the Nigerian Motor Transport Union and the Nigerian Association of African Importers and Exporters. Most of these reached into the provinces from bases in Lagos. Within Lagos, ties between the educated elite and other social groups were deepened in this period, with the elite assuming leadership roles. Macaulay stood prominently among the educated who involved themselves with traditional politics and market women in Lagos. The Lagos Women's League lobbied for better conditions for market women, in a relationship which "was always ambivalent and was far more one of patrons and clients than of comrades."[11] Younger men and women worked with the Lagos poor in philanthropic organizations such as the Green Triangle Club.

Relations between educated Nigerians and Europeans were far more extensive, and probably much worse, in the interwar years than in the late nineteenth century. The number of Europeans in Nigeria more than doubled from 1921 to 1938, with a marked increase in the proportion of women. The Victorian age was remembered as a more friendly era by European and Nigerian observers, while charges of racism, especially regarding hiring practices in the civil service, were both frequent and well founded. Both African and European civil servants enjoyed a pay increase in 1920, but while the former received at most 30 percent, the latter received up to 50 percent. Top salaries for the handful of senior African clerks in the mid-1930s were below European officers' starting pay. In cities like Lagos and Port Harcourt, residential segregation cut Europeans off from any easy contact with Africans, beyond those they met officially or at work. Racial segregation was practiced in clubs and at racetracks. To the eyes of Rex Niven, a longtime colonial servant, Europeans might have had African mistresses, but there was little "genuine mixing" between the groups in Lagos between the wars. As in the nineteenth century, colonial administrators might invite elite Nigerians for certain formal occasions, but the reverse seldom happened. Outspoken young teachers like J. I. G. Onyia could befriend some Europeans, but such contacts were poisoned by the atmosphere of colonial racism: British officials repeatedly transferred him as a troublemaker; Nigerian peers suspected him of being an informer. Official contact in delegations to the colonial government were not infrequent but did not necessarily help relations. There were attempts to swim against the current. Among the elite Carr entertained whites and blacks; Governor Cameron was said to be on friendly terms with Macaulay. Missionaries and traders were less segregated than government officials. William Geary, a lawyer who spent some years in Nigeria, had many African clients and many Nigerian admirers for his active opposition to unpopular legislation. James Stuart-Young, a European trader and "author, poet, philosopher" in Onitsha, was much appreciated for his interest in Ibo culture. Mbonu Ojike later described him as "practically Africanized." Governor Bernard Bourdillon and his wife Violet fostered better race relations in the later 1930s, guided by the insight that reasonable accommodation now would forestall more radical nationalism later. As a sort of reward, the governor's preferred style of hat, christened the "Bourdillon," became fashionable Lagos headgear. But their efforts could not change the racist tenor of colonial life.[12] Only after the war, with a fillip from new colonial policies, did race relations seem to improve.

## Rooted Recruits

The reputation of Lagos as Nigeria's cultural and commercial center was already well established in the provinces. To ambitious young men around Enugu in 1920, Lagos appeared as "a wonderful city, all the streets broad and paved with white gravel, and flanked by magnificent storey buildings," where "the inhabitants were literate and held responsible posts in the white man's government."[13] Until this time the Lagos intelligentsia had been tied to Freetown and the Atlantic as much as to the hinterland of Lagos or Calabar. They were now placed in a different orbit as educated Africans, often dominated by Saro and "native foreigners," spread into a widening galaxy of provincial centers without escaping their attachments to Lagos. Emulating the institutions and culture of Lagos life, they disseminated their intellectual legacy across southern Nigeria. But at the same time, this diffusion, recruiting provincial members as it advanced, altered the overall orientation of the educated community. The provincial intelligentsia came to view the problems inherited from Lagos and Calabar—for example, about the civilizing mission or the "African personality"—from new perspectives.

Communities of educated Africans spread to staff the thickening web of colonial commercial and administrative centers as clerks, merchants, and teachers. Immigrants formed a cosmopolitan core in the new colonial enclaves. One woman interviewed by Sylvia Leith-Ross in Onitsha had been born in Nnewi, had married a Sierra Leonean civil servant, and had once lived in Arochuku. Another, the daughter of a Sierra Leone man and an Aboh Igbo woman, had herself married a Ghanaian. They made elite social clubs and lodges of the type established in Lagos available to people in Benin, Onitsha, and Enugu. The eleven fraternal lodges established by 1911 were concentrated in Lagos and Calabar; by 1939 another dozen stretched from Kano to Port Harcourt. Kofo Ademola, daughter of the notable Moore family in Lagos, established a Literary Club in Warri when she was posted there with her African magistrate husband in 1939. The Study Circle established in Lagos in 1927 with Henry Carr as patron found many provincial counterparts, for example, in the Ibadan Reading Circle with the Reverend Canon Akinyele as president or the Onitsha reading circle to which the young Azikiwe belonged. In 1940 a Nigerian federation connected the growing numbers of literary societies. This expanding network now allowed Lagos-based newspapers and political organizations to extend beyond Lagos. The *Daily Times* was available in some thirty provincial centers by 1930, a distribution Azikiwe's *West African Pilot* emulated later that decade. Both papers secured their sales by speaking to the substantial group of clerks and primary-school graduates now spread across the south. The NNDP and NCBWA both tried to establish branches beyond Lagos in the 1920s without much success. By 1940, however, the NYM had a total membership of between 10,000 and 20,000 scattered in some twenty branches. They connected southern immigrants in Zaria and Kano to their counterparts in eastern towns like Sapele and Calabar and throughout Yoruba.

The more intimate connections between the educated in Lagos and in Yoruba towns are well illustrated in Wole Soyinka's literary accounts of Abeokuta in these years, *Ake* and *Isara*. But links extended farther. Several easterners joined the Nigerian delegation to the 1920 NCBWA meeting in Accra. Kusimo Soluade, the first African lawyer in Jos, remained well connected in Lagos circles. Nyong Essien acknowledged the help of many "literary geniuses" from "his fraternity, the Calabar Community in Lagos" in his panegyric to a recently deceased Calabar leader.[14] The Nigerian Reconstruction Group formed in Lagos in 1942 was composed largely of non-Yoruba. The provincial recruits lagged perhaps a generation behind Lagos in producing their own highly educated leaders, especially outside of Yoruba. By 1930, when Lagos had an established professional community, a senior clerk was still considered well educated in Onitsha. In Benin City in the late 1930s, the leaders of the local intelligentsia seem to have been educated at most to the grammar-school level.[15] Efik lawyers began training in the 1920s; the first Igbo doctor and lawyer returned in the mid-1930s. Northerners remained almost wholly excluded, largely because of restrictions on mission schools. Excluding Koranic schools, by 1937 primary enrollment was only 10 percent that of the south; the mere sixty-five secondary pupils amounted to less than 2 percent that of the south. The first northerner arrived at Yaba in 1937; the first graduated from a university only in 1951.

The leadership of the early centers was acknowledged. The NUT elected leaders from either Yoruba or Calabar through the 1930s. Photographs of Macaulay were widely distributed in the 1920s; in the buildup to the Aba riots through 1928, concerned groups in the eastern provinces sent delegations to him in Lagos. More broadly, William Moore declared that "no Itsekiri of average intelligence can boast of any knowledge of procedure, discipline, and etiquette in ecclesiastical, secular, political or any other society today, without first doffing his hat to the Sierra Leone man. We owe him and his immediate colleagues (Gold Coastians and Lagosians) a great debt of sincere gratitude."[16]

But this picture gradually changed, starting in the interwar years. More than mere offshoots, these communities soon developed their own institutions and voices. Provincial newspapers, often short-lived, began to appear during World War I; by 1940 Onitsha had seen four, Port Harcourt, Calabar, and Abeokuta three each; Aba two; Enugu, Ibadan, Ijebu Ode, and Oshogbo each one. The stream of provincial recruits flowing into Lagos and through it to the Atlantic world widened. Further, as the 1930s closed, local recruits began to dominate institutions imported to the provinces. Port Harcourt's Grand Native Club, founded by immigrants in 1920, had an executive by 1935 that was half Igbo. Similarly, Saro led the African Community League that dominated Port Harcourt interwar politics, but by the late 1930s their power relied on an alliance with indigenous interests. Onitsha's Bishop Crowther Memorial Church, built originally for the mission's Sierra Leonean staff, was still under a Sierra Leonean pastor in 1937, but the congregation was largely Igbo. In Calabar incoming Igbo began to assume the senior clerical positions previously held by Efik. Locally recruited intelligentsia would come fully into leadership roles after World War II.

Communal progress unions, similar to the ethnic associations of nineteenth-century Lagos but also clearly designed to serve the needs of people circulating within the colonial economy, provided another sort of input from the provinces to the center. These had first appeared early in the century but now blossomed into elaborate structures. From the late 1920s one was established in every large Yoruba town; Port Harcourt as well as Lagos had branches of many western and eastern associations by 1930. By 1940 extensive hierarchies of local, township, and regional unions reached across the south. Often started among "sons abroad"—village members working in the city—for their own mutual welfare, they soon began to promote the development of their respective home areas, establishing village branches, building schools, and providing scholarships. The sons abroad (usually better educated than those at home) ran the urban branches and guided the home branch from afar, returning home for the annual Christmas meeting. Initially the unions' search to secure a voice for themselves often conflicted with traditional rulers and the colonial administration. Eventually, however, they became established features of local and regional government, integrating and expediting the concerns of the local elite.[17]

These associations were important in the development of the Nigerian educated community in several ways. By providing scholarships and funding for schools at home, they accelerated the widening recruitment into the educated population. They also promoted ongoing and intimate contact within a widely dispersed community and between literates and illiterates in the cities and at home. They reveal that the educated were not "detribalized" and isolated, as some colonial-era observers feared or hoped, but rather interested in both Lagos and local affairs. Most importantly, they facilitated the rise of the educated community as the new elite beyond the urban centers. By assuming leadership roles in local politics, the interwar generations became more deeply rooted in the particulars of rural African societies than the educated elite of the nineteenth century had been. These locally focused organizations also, of course, advanced the development of local ethnic identities and the historical and cultural studies these required.

The intelligentsia of the interwar years had shifted their center of gravity from the Atlantic toward the Nigerian interior. Lagos was still clearly the center of literate culture, but the provinces now were also incorporated through both professional associations and progress unions. The east was rapidly overcoming its relative lag in education, and its voices were now heard both in Lagos and eastern centers. With far larger numbers than before World War I, the lines of division among the elite became increasingly complex, shaped by personality, political choices, and ethnicity. Relations were also troubled by the squeeze that the much-expanded younger cohort felt as they tried to reach the level of their seniors. But the expanding variety of journals and political parties did not yet have the regional, ethnic alignments that plagued Nigeria in the 1950s. As the provincial educated community grew local roots but did not sever its connections to Lagos and Calabar, the intelligentsia as a whole became better situated than ever before to define Nigeria's situation within the Atlantic horizons of their intellectual world.

## Split Affinities: Sojourners Abroad

Nigerians traveled to America and especially to Britain in ever greater numbers through the interwar period. These sojourners, especially the students, included some of the most influential interwar and postwar intellectuals. While abroad they confronted in person the contrary currents running through Atlantic attitudes to Africa in these years. Many went to Britain to acquire the training and culture that would mark them as heirs of Britain's "civilizing mission" in Africa, only to have their image of British civilization colored by exposure to its racial prejudice and paternalistic patronage. British critics of empire, long a source of inspiration for West African thinkers, now began to form with them an informal community of African experts. Close up, however, these critics often revealed their imperial attitudes. Travel to both Britain and America also placed Nigerians in seedbeds of Pan-Africanism, where more intense and continuous links were forged with continental and diasporan Africans. Intellectuals returned from or operating abroad were typically more supportive of these ideas than those who remained at home. But this exposure also divulged the differences and difficulties within the Pan-African world. Pejorative perceptions of Africa, opposed political philosophies, even personality conflicts, all emerged despite factors fostering solidarity. Nigerians' experiences abroad thus simultaneously reinforced and challenged their connections to the two Atlantic communities that had long exerted powerful influences on them.

The numbers of Nigerians abroad in these years remained small. Funding higher education required either wealthy sponsors or drive, innovation, and good fortune. Four Efik law students in the 1920s were funded by wealthy families or friends; the Ibibio Union sent six scholars abroad by 1938. The well-known struggles of Azikiwe reveal typical difficulties raising funds. Ayo Rosiji's family mortgaged and sold property to finance his departure in 1944. Davies pleaded to be let go from his government clerkship to acquire a year's severance pay to fund studies in London and helped pay his way by composing crossword puzzles for newspapers. These obstacles could frustrate dreams; they also tightened the links between the most highly trained intellectuals and the relatively wealthy. The effort had rewards. Students' departures overseas were much-celebrated events. Until at least the

1950s, when improved access to overseas education reduced its value, high social status derived from merely having been to school abroad.[18]

Nigerians destined for Britain joined a black population of West Indians and West Africans growing more numerous and visible after World War I.[19] Numerous associations of continental and diasporan African students existed in Britain before and between the wars, but the principal interwar organization for West Africans in Britain was the West African Students' Union, established in 1925. Nigerian Ladipo Solanke, the central figure, was like many WASU members a student of law. At the WASU hostel Nigerians not only could discuss African history and politics but also could create an enclave of African cultural life in London, partly for their own comfort and partly to fulfill the Union's mandate to expose and explain this culture to the world. Many Nigerian intellectuals, such as Davies, Louis Mbanefo, and Julius Ojo-Cole in the earlier years and Kola Balogun, F. A. Ogunsheye, and Okoi Arikpo in later ones, were closely associated with the Union. WASU eventually had branches in West Africa and Harlem; sales of its journal reached even farther. In 1931 the League of Coloured Peoples, headed by West Indian physician Harold Moody, emerged as another important forum, shared by West Africans and West Indians. West Africans developed and recorded their ideas in a number of publications, notably the Union's *Wasu* magazine and the LCP journal *The Keys*. They also wrote for the main journals concerned with West African politics and commerce, *West Africa* and the *West African Review*, to express their views and supplement their incomes.

African students' contacts with the Colonial Office were, as Hakim Adi has detailed, kept tense by contrary urges to avoid control by their patrons while securing financial and other support. Serious discussions about the situation of African students in Britain started before World War I among philanthropic, missionary, and Colonial Office "friends of Africa" and accelerated in the postwar context of race riots, Pan-African conferences, and Garveyism. The idea developed of sheltering African students from both British racism and the appeal of "dangerous" ideas by generously providing a social environment—in particular a student hostel—which could be kept free from radical influences. Both WASU and the LCP were attracted to this idea—not least because of their own financial difficulties—but resisted the prospect of Colonial Office supervision. Through the early 1930s WASU hotly disputed a Colonial Office project to found Aggrey

House as a rival to the WASU hostel, although in the end a compromise prevailed.

West Africans were, as always, attracted to Britons interested in African affairs, in part because of the latter's critical approach to some imperial policies but also simply because their interest contrasted sharply with the general British apathy toward Africa. Lord Olivier, once praised by Blyden, was similarly praised by Solanke as "one of the most famous champions in the cause and interest of the Africans," especially for his support for WASU. Macaulay praised the editor of *West Africa* as someone "who has the genuine interests of Africa and Africans always at the bottom of his large and generous heart." This common ground is illustrated by the way *The Keys* republished—and implicitly endorsed—a cartoon by David Low of the mainstream *Evening Standard* concerning the Italian invasion of Abyssinia in 1935 (fig. 1). The black community could quite aptly appropriate Low's depiction of the horror of Italian imperialism as their own. Politicians of the Labour and Fabian type were among the most prominent contacts,

BARBARISM                                    CIVILIZATION

1. David Low, "Barbarism/Civilization," *London Evening Standard*, 12 October 1935. © *London Evening Standard*/Solo, reprinted with permission; photograph courtesy of the Centre for the Study of Cartoons and Caricature, University of Kent, Canterbury)

along with African experts such as Margery Perham. Many events sponsored by WASU were, in effect, "British-African assemblies"; WASU hosted visits by leaders such as Labour Party leader Clement Atlee and Governor Bourdillon of Nigeria. West Africans also attended discussions of colonial questions organized by such groups as the Royal Society of Arts. Of 260 LCP members in 1936, about 100 were white.[20] The notion of belonging to an expert community which might better guide colonial policy attracted Nigerians, as the mission of the African Society had once attracted Blyden. Solanke appealed for the British colonial administrator to work with the educated African: "Let him embrace the educated as his brother, his co-partner in the duty of guardianship of Africa." He also hoped WASU Day would inspire West African cooperation "with every non-West African . . . especially with the White element of each community." Adeniyi Williams, a student of civil engineering, wrote to Perham after hearing her radio talk on the African future to thank her for her "courageous and unbiased views" in contrast to the general ignorance and patronizing attitude met among most Britons. He welcomed her assistance in developing Africa, insisting, however, that it be "on grounds of honour." Appeals to honor were necessary. The Africans' putative partners often exhibited attitudes of superiority or condescension that were resented as strongly as were attempts to control student hostels. West African reactions to racial prejudice became increasingly sharp in the 1930s. As one Nigerian pointed out, "Even the student agitator craves for nothing more than reciprocity of good feeling. . . . we prefer co-operation rather than patronage."[21] Davies recalls that he had to cut short one of Perham's talks at WASU to save her from a hostile audience.

The complex and unequal relationship between African experts and Africans is well illustrated by a little known chapter in Azikiwe's early career. Preparing to return from his studies in America in 1932, he applied to the International African Institute in London for a fellowship to do anthropological work on the Igbo. Azikiwe's case seemed quite promising: his American referees provided glowing letters; the Nigerian government provided a favorable evaluation. Bronislaw Malinowksi, the anthropologist to be in charge, met him in the United States and invited him to join the British Royal Anthropological Society; Perham interviewed him at Oxford. Both were impressed. Significantly, Azikiwe's character was as much an issue here as his intellect.

Further, both the Institute and the head of the Nigerian education department were keen to award an African a fellowship. In light of all this, the IAI executive committee approved one year's funding in 1933 for training in London, "subject to an entirely favourable report being received from the Nigerian Government." Provisional plans were made to fund two years of subsequent fieldwork. Soon afterwards, however, one of the executive committee members suffered second thoughts. Diedrich Westermann doubted that an African could in fact do the same kind of scientific work as a European and feared a failed African fellow would both "spoil" the African and harm the Institute's reputation. Others' doubts now surfaced: unease about letting an African do colonial fieldwork without direct European supervision, fear that Azikiwe was too "political" to be "objective." The director therefore invoked the requirement of unequivocal Nigerian government approval as a pretense. Azikiwe was told that the Institute was interested in him but had insufficient resources. Although the culture of colonial racism in the end defeated Azikiwe's ambition and perhaps accelerated his alienation from British rule, this episode also reveals the fleeting possibility of sympathetic cooperation between two communities keenly interested in understanding contemporary Africa. In much the same way, the general atmosphere in interwar Britain constantly offered—but could never really allow—sustained cooperation between colonial and metropolitan intellectuals.[22]

Such treatment no doubt enhanced the attraction of racial unity. Driven by international events such as the failure of the League of Nations to protect Abyssinia from Italian invasion and incidents of blatant racism in Britain, colonial sojourners and British blacks became increasingly active as spokespeople for black interests. Calls for imperial reform after World War I progressed into calls for self-government early in World War II. London was truly a center of Pan-African life, drawing in notable African Americans, South Africans, and even Africans from French-controlled territories. Indian nationalists, speaking in London, won rapt attention. African-American figures like entertainer and activist Paul Robeson became a patron of WASU, and philosopher Alain Locke came there to speak. Caribbean connections were legion. Garvey temporarily provided a WASU building; W. A. Lewis (later a Nobel Prize laureate in economics) contributed to *The Keys* and *Wasu* while studying at the London School of Economics.

C. L. R. James and George Padmore, with their Communist connections, also moved in these circles. Conferences and summer schools sponsored by the LCP on such topics as "The Negro in the World Today" (1934) or "African Peoples, Democracy, and World Peace" (1939) suggest how Nigerians were inspired to adopt Pan-African perspectives and to construct the world in terms of race. Solanke, for example, stressed that "we together with our brethren in America and West Indies must join and start to build our own steamships and man them." A. Ade Ademola, contributing with several Nigerians to Nancy Cunard's 1934 *Negro Anthology,* presented a historical argument "to render the solidarity of the whole African race almost as impregnable as the rock of eternity."[23]

But these repeated appeals for Pan-African unity were inspired in part by acute consciousness of the potential for disunity. West Indians were divided by territorial loyalties. The LCP and WASU sometimes competed for support from the same black constituency. The West Indian population in Britain outnumbered the West African and identified more closely with the League than with WASU. When WASU sought a boycott of Aggrey House in 1934, the League refused to comply, and the bulk of the Ghanaian students within WASU took the League's position against the Nigerians'. Cultural misunderstandings also troubled relations, as this comment on a debate at WASU about black cooperation reveals. "West Indians came in for the usual trouncing for their vanity, their ignorance of the culture of their forefathers, their desire to be imitation Europeans, and their blindness to the advantages of mutual understanding. The debate was lively, but itself showed signs that these charges are beginning to lose their original validity." Davies once disclosed his plans to generate a revolution for Nigerian self-government to Lewis. Revolutions, his friend replied dismissively, required oppressed masses, while "in Nigeria people sit under the banana trees and ripe bananas pop into their mouths."[24] Political perspectives also diverged. The left-wing views of activists such as James, Padmore, or I. T. A. Wallace-Johnson won significant acceptance (especially considering the elite ambitions of most West African students) but never held the field. Analyses decrying racial groupings as impediments to class action vied with the appeal of Pan-Africanism against racist denigration. This fertile cosmopolitan environment would generate the famous 1945 Pan-African Congress in Manchester, but in the process Pan-Africanism would emerge more clearly as a continental rather than a Black Atlantic concern, divided also by territory. Living through this process, Nigerians in Britain confronted the need to identify more clearly their specific place within the Black Atlantic.

Activities in the United States, although on a much smaller and less organized scale, had a similar effect. The Native African Union of America founded in New York during 1927 had two Nigerians from the southeast among its officers. The small exodus of students inspired by Azikiwe to retrace his path to Lincoln University in 1938 organized associations only in the 1940s. This and later waves found themselves treated as foreigners, even as novelties. This may have been expected within white society, but it was also widely true among African Americans. In spite of the common experience of racism and the advance of a positive black identity in the Harlem Renaissance, the African-American image of Africa long remained simply a mixture of "stereotype and sentiment." The students often were dismayed by American images of Africa as a uniformly dark, savage-filled jungle. At Lincoln, a black university, the early African students were drawn together by their shared exclusion. As Ojike remembered of the early 1940s, "In every activity, the thought that we were all Africans brought us together to encourage and help one another. Some of us from Nigeria had not met Gold-Coastians or Liberians before. All the same, we regarded one another as brothers." Through their organizations, speaking tours, and the press, the task of attacking misconceptions occupied much of the students' time, even in the 1960s. Thus, while exposure to the African-American world clearly advanced Nigerian students' awareness of the diaspora, the experience also highlighted the Atlantic divide. In Ojike's mind "black Americans were Americans whose slogan should be: 'Back *up* Africa,' rather than . . . 'Back *to* Africa.'"[25] Further, exposure to mainstream ideas about development and democracy drew Azikiwe and many later students toward generally American rather than specifically African-American ideas. But this appeal was limited. Brutal exposure to the last-hired, first-fired predicament of American blacks pushed them back toward both black solidarity and doubts about the virtues of American democracy.

The overseas experiences of Nigerian students were thus both formative and unsettling. Pan-African solidarity grew more intense but also more fractured and was crosscut by the development of a community of African, British, and American experts concerned with colonial development. But this community of Africanist specialists in turn was clearly divided by the hierarchies of colonial racism and thus subject to Pan-African critiques. This exposure to contrary influences augmented a process under way within Nigeria itself. The intelligentsia became more aware of Nigeria's unique condition within the Atlantic world and of their singular role as its emissaries.

### Atlantic Tides, Local Ties: The 1920s

The previous chapter argued that by locating themselves within a racial diaspora, the intelligentsia set askew their attempt to fully understand their own situation. This identity adopted an image of Africa from external observers in the Atlantic world, who tended to define Africa in counterpoint to Europe rather than through knowledge of Africa itself. In the 1920s, as local roots began to hold them in place despite the tides of Atlantic thought, the intelligentsia began to right themselves. Pan-African invitations were not ignored, and the idea of racial divisions lingered as a means of marking difference. But these same Pan-African appeals also revealed the divergent interests within the Black Atlantic. The intelligentsia also began to confront the problems inherent in asserting a distinct racial character while also seeking the rights once promised them within the British Empire.

Racewide activity reached its zenith in the years following World War I, which saw the Pan-African Congresses in Europe, Garvey's UNIA, WASU, and the NCBWA. Lagosians more directly connected to the African diaspora were more likely to be attracted to Pan-African ideas, as were many Liberian or Jamaican immigrants or Mojola Agbebi's son Akinbami who returned from New York to act as agent for Garvey's Black Star shipping line. Themes of racial unity also were prominent among Nigerians abroad. Thomas Jackson, son of an Americo-Liberian immigrant and now editor of his father's *Lagos Weekly Record*, entertained "no doubts whatever in the soundness" of Garvey's "doctrine of world-wide co-operation among negroes for their economic and industrial uplift." But the basic Pan-African message of redeeming the "African race" through combined action was widely welcomed even in the provinces, where Garvey's *Negro World* evaded government restrictions. Even at Marcus Garvey's death in

1940, the *Pilot* remembered how he had "inspired Africans to regard their black complexions with pride and to develop race consciousness." The Reverend Potts-Johnson, a Sierra Leonean, dedicated his *Nigerian Observer* in Port Harcourt to "Our God, Our Country and Our Race." As in the nineteenth century, the boundaries of West African identity remained unfixed. "Nationalism," the *Weekly Record* declared, "implies loyalty to the race or nation."[26] Progress was still understood as part of a racial, rather than a merely continental, saga.

But this pursuit of progress along with the entire "Negro race" stumbled over the issue of race leadership. African-American leaders such as Washington and Du Bois assumed—in keeping with many earlier African-American leaders—that they were the natural leaders of the Black Atlantic world. Garvey's Black Star Line—a transatlantic trading network intended as the foundation of a Pan-African empire under New World leadership—was an audacious adventure with an old theme. "If native Africans are unable to appreciate the value of their own country from the standard of Western civilization," Garvey asserted, "then it is for us, their brothers, to take to them the knowledge and information that they need to help develop the country for the common good." The majority of the West African intelligentsia, reluctant to subordinate themselves to this Pan-African imperialism, resisted on two grounds. Keeping to the language of racial peculiarity, some simply insisted that Africans on African soil had purer connections to the race. Already in 1904 John P. Jackson had blamed Liberia's woes on decultured African-American settlers. "The Africans" he asserted, "are those who had retained unimpaired their racial instincts" and therefore had a superior claim to leadership on the continent.[27] Kobina Sekyi, a Ghanaian intellectual, welcomed African-American assistance in 1925 but insisted that only Africans in Africa "are in possession and charge of the great and glorious traditions which our ancestors perfected long ago. . . . We . . . in Africa alone understand these forces and can direct them aright for the good of the whole Negro race." As the *Times of Nigeria* objected, "If at all that day should come and it must come in the process of evolution—when Africa shall be controlled by Africans, each distinct African nation while having the most cordial relations with every other sister nation, will infinitely prefer remaining as a separate political entity to being drawn into one huge melting pot of a universal Negro Empire."[28] Even the Lagos UNIA resisted Garvey's political program.

The second, less explicit response reflected the development of a distinctly West African and even Nigerian political perspective and program, embodied in such organizations as the NCBWA and NNDP. Numerous manifestos printed after World War I, along with NCBWA petitions and election material from the Legislative and Town Councils, reveal the assertion of a regional, "bourgeois" role. Their ongoing concerns included public sanitation, government "squandermania," and "autocratic obstinacy." Education reform—for both more and better schools—was a frequent topic, as were calls for the Nigerianization of the civil service. J. G. Campbell proposed "that two thirds of all positions of trust should be held by whites they being our Tutors and one third by us we being natives of the soil and that it is the duty of the Government to train natives to become fit for these posts."[29] The Lagos Women's League pressed for more women in the colonial service. The intelligentsia demanded elective representation in keeping with the intentions of the 1865 Parliamentary Select Committee and the political rhetoric of the British Empire; after it was granted they continued to request a larger role in government to criticize "obnoxious ordinances." In a 1928 survey of *Political and Administrative Problems,* Adeniyi-Jones pleaded for "official cognizance of the fact that the intelligent units of the population are not necessarily and diametrically opposed to Government, but are performing the duty of his Majesty's Opposition." The interwar political leaders spoke confidently for all communities on economic questions, especially on behalf of those involved in the burgeoning cocoa economy. They not infrequently presumed to tell farmers what was good for them, as when the *West African Nationhood,* lamenting overproduction, offered "our African producers" lessons in "the theory of Supply and Demand." British West African intellectuals were attracted to Pan-African appeals because they defended their race against imperial denigrations. They were especially attracted to Garvey's economic program because it offered economic security in the face of increasingly formidable foreign firms. But the West Africans' critique of Pan-Africanism both defended and defined their own position. As Stein argues, "Pan-African sentiments did not alter the Africans' appraisal of their interests."[30] Combined in a British West African "national" body, the Nigerians began to identify themselves as part of a West African middle class within the Black Atlantic, renegotiating but not rejecting racial affinities.

If West African class interests could be defended against Garvey on grounds of being truer Africans, this was less easily accomplished within the politics of colonial administration. British colonial policy developed in the early twentieth century on the premise of racial difference. Indeed, it turned to the ideas of African peculiarity developed by both Mary Kingsley and Edward Blyden in the African Society, the ideas West Africans had used to defend themselves against racist denigration. Not surprisingly, however, these ideas acquired a rather different import in imperial hands. Kingsley herself may have valued African culture, but she valued the British imperial mission more. Just treatment of African subjects required that they not be forced to abandon their culture; it also required maintaining—presumably forever— what she termed British *Oberhoheit*: "There is no English word for it—it means the power to rule at the top of things, the power to enforce peace among peoples, to secure commercial communication and provide an ultimate court of appeal in matters of Justice, to be king over kings, ruler over many peoples. This power we steal from no one and we have every right to have." Lugard advocated "equal opportunities" between the races but also supported "in matters social and racial a separate path, each pursuing his own inherited traditions, preserving his own race-purity and race-pride." The indirect rule model he developed used this principle to restrict the influence of the intelligentsia in colonial administration. Much as West Africans decried African-American claims to speak for the "native" African, Lugard laid down the "cardinal principle" that Nigeria's "large native population" would not be subordinated to "a small minority of educated and Europeanized natives who have nothing in common with them, and whose interests are very often opposed to theirs." Governor Clifford applied this principle to disqualify the leadership claims of the NCBWA. "It can only be described as farcical to suppose that . . . continental Nigeria can be represented by a handful of gentlemen . . . whose eyes are fixed, not upon African native history or tradition or policy, nor upon their own tribal obligations and the duties to their Natural Rulers . . . but upon political theories evolved by Europeans to fit a wholly different set of circumstances, arising out of peoples who have arrived at a wholly different stage of civilization." Judicial reforms in 1914 severely limited the scope for trained lawyers in various courts. Colonial officials argued that lawyers had lost their African qualities, while the British administrator "has made it his business to forget English politics . . . in order to study the customs and thought of the people for whose welfare he is responsible."[31]

Indirect rule in general was of course difficult for the intelligentsia to endorse. Few colonial measures aroused as much opposition as the court reforms; it did not relent until Governor Cameron's amendments in 1934. But composing a response posed a dilemma for the intelligentsia. They could, and did, insist on their racial and cultural connections to the African masses. In a letter to the secretary of state for the colonies, the Congress protested that many natural rulers had endorsed it. The educated community was practically indistinguishable from the natural rulers. Congress, it argued, "represents the bulk of the inhabitants of the various indigenous communities, and with them claims, as sons of the soil, the inherent right to make representations. . . . some of these very educated men are connected with aboriginal families, and are eligible to reign, and now and again do exercise rule over their people. Moreover, it is notorious that in the African system it is not likely that by reason of a man's education he can exploit the members of his own tribe or family, since according to that system he sinks or swims with them." William Moore stressed that educated and illiterate Itsekiri had identical interests.[32]

But if African leadership required fidelity to distinct African standards of legitimacy, as Blyden, Kingsley, and Lugard all maintained, there was no clear reason why the intelligentsia, and not the chiefs themselves, qualified to speak for the masses. The intelligentsia therefore also asserted that their education and skills, not their "African personality," qualified them for leadership. Attacking Lugard's denunciation of educated Africans, the *Weekly Record* declared that it was "the indispensable adjunct of a liberal education" and the "magic wand" of "command of the English language" which gave the intellectual, as "a son of the soil and a member of the subject race," the ability to "express himself most clearly and intelligently" and "criticize with logical precision the political measures of the Government." "The advanced or progressive units of the race will be those who through the process of natural selection can boast of elasticity or adaptation or who have the greatest power of making conscious adjustments to ever changing conditions."[33] Against the principles of indirect rule the intelligentsia stressed their worldly knowledge and legal training compared to chiefs. "Barristers," an association composed largely of lawyers argued, "are regarded no less by the Nigerian as the European communities as guides and protectors." "As lawyers increase," J. G. Campbell insisted, "so politicians increase and as politicians of the right sort increase the country will be able to take its place in the discussion of those subjects that build up a civilized nation."[34] But this argument, in turn, erased the defense developed in Blyden's era. Denying the significance of race and culture allowed British claims to imperial superiority full rein. There was nothing special Africans could contribute to the governance of empire that skilled British administrators could not.

The intelligentsia of the 1920s were caught between the demands of their civilizing mission—which required leadership based on metropolitan skills—and pride in their "African personality"—which required leadership based on birth and tradition. Race identity still seemed pertinent in the context of white domination and racism, but both the premise and promise of Pan-Africanism were proving problematic. The language of racial difference had once allowed a rejoinder to imperial racism. Now, incorporated in indirect rule policy, it seemed to bind them. The two broad identities developed in the nineteenth-century world were proving cumbersome tools for the work of defining and defending the interests of the West African medial classes. The "youth" of the 1930s would attempt to do more than merely cope with these contradictions.

### "Young Nigeria at the Crossroads": The 1930s

The Ghanaian educator J. E. K. Aggrey sensed in 1923 that "there is a Youth Movement coming in Africa that some day may startle the world." In 1926 a Nigerian university graduate explained to his fellow "thinking Africans" that "by a variety of well-known causes the present generation of West Africans may be said to have arrived at that stage of development which frequently leads a people placed in similar circumstances to grapple with, and adjust, many complex issues affecting their future progress and well-being."[35] A short-lived Union of Young Democrats had aroused little attention in Lagos in 1923, but youth organizations swept through West Africa after the appearance of the Lagos Youth Movement in 1934. By the end of this decade of "great intellectual ferment," there were youth organizations in Ghana and Sierra Leone, while Eyo Ita had founded a Nigerian Youth League Movement in Calabar and the Nigerian Young Democrats (in alliance with the NNDP) had emerged to compete with the NYM. "Young Nigeria," many thought, was "at the crossroads . . . half way between the old order and the new."[36] What explains this new spirit among the intelligentsia? The demographic changes outlined above offer only a partial explanation, not least because the "youth" included many elders. Crises of the 1930s also help explain this ferment. The economic depression raised questions about the viability of the colonial economy; the invasion of Ethiopia and the buildup to the Second World War pointed to a bleak future for African colonial subjects. There was also fatigue with what Carr labeled the "insanity" of Lagos politics, in which vitriolic fights among long-established factions effected little change.[37] A complete explanation, however, must also appreciate the new ideas circulating by the 1930s about colonial development and African society. The youth intelligentsia, seeking to displace the old guard, drew on these ideas to define a clearer role for themselves within Nigerian society, moving beyond some of the constraints of their seniors' positions.

One shift of fundamental significance for West Africans concerned the meaning of race in Atlantic discourse. The idea of innate race hierarchy of course did not die out in the interwar period; it is still with us. Notable and minor figures continued in these years to assert that Africans were incapable of understanding market relations or of absorbing a European education. Africans, many maintained in late Victorian fashion, could acquire at best a "shade of white veneer."[38] But the idea of innate racial differences had never been universally accepted, and by the 1930s it was under attack on a number of fronts. Scientists and anthropologists were finding it difficult to prove. Radical and humanitarian critics, wary of the uses to which it was being put in imperial and other contexts, used this confusion to discredit it as a "modern superstition." Franz Boas had been an early critic in anthropological and popular forums. Nazi eugenic programs in the 1930s enhanced suspicions of race science; the propaganda war against Germany in the 1940s effectively removed ideas about racial inferiority from respectable scientific discourse. Anthropologist Meyer Fortes concluded in 1945 that "the balance of scientific evidence and of practical experience" proved the cultural insignificance of race, a finding UNESCO promulgated after the war. These changes were traced in the British West African world. The Reverend A. G. Fraser, of Achimota College in Ghana, shared the views of colonial education expert Arthur Mayhew in the 1930s: Africans were not innately backward but only disadvantaged people who would respond best to universal, not race-specific, education. "Assuming, then, not only a universal capacity for cultural development, but also its universal necessity, and refusing to mistake difference in stages of development for difference in racial ability, we are bound as educationists to have in view an ultimate good, a common civilization, for the whole world, a framework, as it were, of universally accepted ideas and values." The secretary of state wrote in 1941 that "the Nazis with their false doctrine of the Herrenvolk have made it clear that there is no place in our conception of life for the doctrine that one race is superior to another." Margery Perham sketched a mock trial before "Judge Science" in which African laziness was accepted, but the charge of innate inferiority was dismissed for lack of evidence.[39] The idea of race as a biologically determined social group with a fixed place in a human hierarchy was being displaced by an idea of race as a historically determined social group at a certain level of development, superficially divided by environmental influences. European writers, of course, could still substitute African historical backwardness for racial inferiority, but Africans and Europeans were no longer placed on separate lines of development.

In this new atmosphere some African-American writers began to downplay the common racial identity within the diaspora and to recognize the cultural differences wrought by divergent histories. In a 1929 address to WASU, Alain Locke bluntly admitted that African Americans had seen Africa "through a glass darkly," following the "Euro-American outlook." The African-American historian Carter Woodson, touring Europe in 1932 to survey the state of African studies, stressed that Africans had to be their own spokesmen.[40] Some notable British colonial critics, for their part, now began to see the folly and danger of indirect rule policies that excluded an increasingly "disgruntled intelligentsia" on the grounds of preserving racial traditions that were changing anyway. C. R. Buxton, W. M. Macmillan, and others advised instead harnessing their special skills for colonial development. Governors Cameron and Bourdillon incorporated some of this new appreciation of the educated class in their administrative reforms during the 1930s. Native Administration Councils, Cameron told WASU in 1934, "should encourage the admission of the educated element, despite the latter's lack of title."[41] More generally, and elusively, the Colonial Office began a gradual shift away from the indirect rule commitment to preservation toward recognition that change had to be promoted. Only hints of this came before the very end of the decade; the full flood of reform came with the war.

These ideas may have been shifting only gradually in the Atlantic world generally, but the youth intelligentsia were disposed to appreciate their potential promptly. The nebulous spirit of the youth era is perhaps best first grasped as a matter of mood rather than policy, incorporating the new spirit of colonial reform. It was built on contrasts as much as substance: new against old, action against inaction. Davies, the most prominent Youth Movement writer in the 1930s, divided the West African political actors into the "Do-somethings" and the "Do-nothings." Despite past accomplishments, the old guard were too hobbled by "petty, personal squabbles" to offer effective criticism of the government. Azikiwe's 1937 *Renascent Africa*, which Orizu later called "the Bible of West African youth," appealed to the "young in mind" to apply their energy and ideas to "salvage the debris of old Africa through the supreme efforts of youth."[42] As Akinola Lasekan later represented Azikiwe in his cartoon "The Reformer" (fig. 2), the "new" Africans would erase all the evils of the "old." "It is the revolt of youth against injustice of the old which enables Old Age to realize that it needs a new set of values."[43] The youth ethic was defined in a more positive, if equally nebulous, way. NYM supporters presented the movement's "ideal" as "abnegation of self" or advocated "The Doctrine of Altruism." The Nigerian Young Democrats determined to challenge "immorality and unchastity, unfaithfulness and dishonesty, insobriety, reckless and riotous living" that threatened "the foundations of our race." S. L. Akintola hoped the new generation would create "a civilization which gives precedence to cosmopolitanism and not to patriotism[,] to humanity and not to nationalism[,] to reason and not to passion, to peace and not to war, to idealism and not to materialism[,] a civilization which recognizes the Fatherhood of God and the brotherhood of man."[44]

Beneath this high-minded rhetoric, however, were some more specific ideas. The Atlantic tradition of eliding the "Nigerian" and the "African" continued. Ita, the American-educated "spiritual father" and prominent pamphleteer of the youth era, saw youth as the source of "race energy" fit to disprove assertions that Africans were "a moron race, infant race, senile and dying race, and what not." But the notion of racial difference was explicitly attacked. Azikiwe cited Boas, Fraser, and other British and American authorities to make the point that "no reputable anthropologist of to-day entertains the notion of a racial inferiority for government or other institutions of society." Solanke argued that while there might have been distinct races millennia ago, the trend since that time had been "re-admixture" toward a "universal brotherhood." *Wasu* also accepted racial categories but denied that they meant much. "We shall be the last to deny or belittle the differences between the two races. But when all is said and done, the fact remains that the black man is the white man painted black, and the white man is the black man painted white."[45] A contributor to the *Lagos Daily News*, echoed by the editor, cited Kingsley, Dudley Kidd,

THE REFORMER

2. Akinola Lasekan, "The Reformer," (From *Zik of Africa* [Lagos: Zik's Press, 1947], p. 11)

111

Finot, and others—much the same group Blyden had once welcomed —to support an argument contrary to Blyden's. Negroes were only culturally different, not racially so, and they would become the equal of any other in the right circumstances. Another "Enquiring African," although citing Blyden as an inspiration (along with Aggrey, Hayford, and Agbebi), rejected Blyden's appeal for pure racial development. "The Africa of tomorrow . . . is going to be the first truly cosmopolitan continent in the history of mankind. . . . If . . . we are going to live together in this future land . . . is it not right that we should work in co-operation not marred by the whinings of race-apologists on the one side or any over-bearingly patronizing attitude on the other?" The ideal of a West African university, dear to Blyden and James Johnson, was not forgotten, but the idea of special education for the race was. The NYM, in its inaugural protest over Yaba Higher College, insisted that Nigerians have access to a European education either at home or abroad. Europe remained, Alakija insisted, "the home of knowledge." By 1948 Afolabi George assumed the evidence was clear "that the Negro's backwardness is only a geographical and historical accident."[46]

There was a corresponding movement narrowing further the trends apparent in the NCBWA: concern with racial—and even West African—uplift became specifically Nigerian. One Nigerian insisted that the broad category of Britain's "subject races" be refined to allow appreciation of the unique conditions in each colony. The NYM celebrated events with a "national anthem."[47] Azikiwe's writings reflect these narrowing horizons. *Liberia in World Politics*, written in America, was a defense of Liberia's vanguard role in the redemption of the African race. *Renascent Africa*, written in West Africa a few years later, was specifically continental in scope. His pamphlets in the 1940s dealt strictly with Nigerian issues. The range of Ita's writing was constricted on parallel lines.

New ideas for Nigerian development likewise eschewed the idea of racial peculiarity, proposing instead modern global standards. Indirect rule was rejected in favor of development along British Commonwealth lines, in articles that cited such sympathetic critics such as Charles Buxton and Perham. Their political demands leaped ahead of the NCBWA agenda, denying the need for gradual trusteeship on the road to self-government. Davies declared that the "British Empire deserves nothing but extinction as complete as that of the Dodo" but accepted that Nigeria could "live and flourish" in the Commonwealth. "The task of the present generation," another youth wrote, was "to lay a sound and solid foundation upon which may be raised in the fulness of time a nation worthy of an honourable place in the British Commonwealth and among the nations of the world." The NYM charter demanded "complete independence" both in the local management of affairs and within the empire.[48]

The youth intelligentsia were much clearer than the previous generation about the criteria that made them Nigerian leaders. They qualified not because of racial ties to their followers or because they were members of a privileged, Christian establishment but because they were prepared to serve as a modern intellectual elite, in ways chiefs and the older generation of leaders trained in the church could not. Davies welcomed the eclipse of "superstition" by the "scientific" and "rational world." The NYM strove to present a positive program, because "to be able to reduce a communal feeling to a written plan is to have won half the battle for the re-birth of our country." As Davies asked rhetorically, "Is there any other section of the community more capable of asking questions about his surroundings with a view to altering them, with open mindedness and with elegance, than the youths?"[49] The absence of explicitly Christian ethics is striking. Labeling the church a tool of imperialism, Azikiwe pointed out that "the term 'Christian' is not an honourable one, genetically speaking"; his program stressed the material and social requirements of African regeneration. Awolowo later went beyond this when he argued that ministers of the church were "the most unfitted persons" to sit on the Legislative Council, because they were trained to leave things to heavenly rather than human agency.[50] The youth could perform these tasks because of education, and education was now unequivocally proclaimed as the prerequisite for leadership. Oyinkan Abayomi of the NYM Ladies' Section pushed her companions to lead the "illiterate women of the community." Awolowo blamed "illiterate" traders, workers, and farmers for being inferior economic actors and implied literates in these occupations would be superior. Azikiwe carried this idea beyond its logical end, arguing in *Renascent Africa* that "illiterate" drivers, carpenters, and farmers should be displaced by some of the unemployed literates, who not only would do a better job by virtue of their education but also would unionize properly and thus advance African emancipation. In a more succinct 1934 speech, Azikiwe "postulated" that "it is the scholar who makes or unmakes society."[51]

The new intellectual mood of the 1930s may have been propelled by a new cohort of educated Nigerians seeking grounds upon which to define themselves against old guard competitors. It clearly was also shaped by the new pattern of recruitment. Education above all brought the new generation into the educated community, and this criterion was now privileged above all earlier ones: wealth, family background, or affiliation with the civilizing mission. Further, the increasingly Nigerian—as opposed to "native foreigner"—membership of the intelligentsia and the elaboration of the Nigerian state focused the youth intelligentsia on Nigerian rather than on racial or even British West African horizons. Azikiwe stressed that "only *from within the African* must the 'New Africa' become a reality and not through any other efforts, however noble and philanthropic, *from without*."[52] But the intelligentsia in the 1930s also absorbed new ideas about African development to move beyond some of the limitations apparent in the 1920s. Instead of trying awkwardly to balance the investigation of the "African personality" with adoption of British civilization, a new option was opened—of Nigerian experts solving Nigeria's social and economic problems within a modern state. The youth intelligentsia did not transcend the habit of constructing Africa against ideas of Europe. But they did engage ideas of development and leadership—and claim rights—that implied Africa and Europe could be understood in common terms. However implicit, this potent admixture, which took pride in both accepting difference and denying it, opened new possibilities for analyzing the Nigerian situation and devising prescriptions for it. These changes of the interwar years perhaps can be best brought into focus by looking at interwar economic ideas.

### "A Formidable Weapon"

The Nigerian intelligentsia devised an economic program between the wars, adapting African-American and British ideas into a platform supporting their own actions on behalf of the medial classes, especially entrepreneurs within the trade structure. Rising above but building on both Victorian ambitions to be a productive colony and Pan-African ambitions to redeem the race economically, their ideas moved closer to home. As fully expounded by the Youth Movement, this program encapsulates a unique Nigerian formulation of Atlantic ideas which illustrates one of the general arguments of this study: the intelligentsia sought empowerment by combining available ideas and rhetoric; they were not obliged simply to swallow whole imperial or Black Atlantic thought.

The interwar period was marked by economic crises. Fluctuating, low commodity prices promoted the rise of an oligopoly of large European trading firms, highlighted by the formation of the United Africa Company in 1929. These firms not only encroached upon the lower levels of the trade structure where African entrepreneurs had sought refuge but also arranged among themselves a series of agreements to regulate commodity and merchandise prices. African merchant princes had already been reduced to mere middlemen; now middlemen were being marginalized. As the Pan-African journalist Dusé Mohammed Ali warned from London in 1920, "Combines in African raw commodities, while crowding out the smaller European trader, threaten to undermine the very fabric of African agriculture and Native endeavour." In 1933 Robert Cole at WASU mourned that the "African middleman . . . has been swallowed up by octopuses of erstwhile wholesale houses whose tentacles peddle the lowliest commodities in little branch shops in the humblest side streets." The *Lagos Daily News* argued that from 1929 to 1934 the combines had caused the severe decline of palm oil and cocoa prices.[53] By the later 1930s the popular case against the evils of monopoly had been sealed shut, with the added weight of some British critics. The united forces of the "vested-interests," it was claimed, "suck all the good things of the egg leaving the shell for the native." The UAC was seen as "a steamroller under which they are being continually flattened out until perhaps the last breath is taken out of them, and only the human husk remains."[54]

Initially, the Nigerian response stressed the ideal of free trade as "the soul of business," a condition of civilization, and something required by Lugard's own principles of trusteeship.[55] This demand, dating from the nineteenth century, remained central to the NCBWA and NYM. But soon a more comprehensive and proactive agenda, expanding on ideas first sketched at the turn of the century, overshadowed this appeal. It was designed to reform and reorganize Africans to overcome their internal weaknesses, to fit the new realities of colonial commerce as the economic equals of the large European firms. This emphasis on empowering themselves gave increasing importance to getting beyond ties to the soil to stress the need for domestic industries.

As Dusé wrote in 1920, "This being an age of combinations of one kind or another, it behooves the coloured people of the world to show a solid front." In the 1920s this spirit of combination was undertaken in what Duffield calls the classic form of Pan-African business activity, formulated by both Garvey and the NCBWA, and attempted in Lagos between the wars by, among others, Winifred Tete-Ansa. Through a tripartite scheme of a cooperative society, an African bank, and an American-based buying firm, all held together by putative racial ties, Tete-Ansa tried in the 1920s to establish a commercial system that would break the hold of the European firms on the West African economy by connecting West African producers and middlemen directly with the American market. Cooperation was the way the many small owners of surplus capital could hope to form blocs appropriate to the scale of the colonial economy. His two attempts failed. Investment was never strong, the direct connection with the American market was never secured, official hostility and organizational problems proved intractable. But by the 1930s these general ideas became fashionable in the press. Unity, self-help, and cooperation were advocated variously as means to independence, economic strength, and national salvation. The National Bank of Nigeria, founded by Nigerians who had broken away from Tete-Ansa's failing bank in 1933, proclaimed that "the African's most ardent desire is to be economically independent. . . . He wishes to have his own capital to develop his agriculture, trade and industries. . . . The only solution is in Self-Help." Solanke wrote to Macaulay to stress that "neither the Government nor the (Commercial and) European Industrialists are strong enough to constitute our formidable or unconquerable foe if we really unite and cooperate." Azikiwe, with his characteristic flourish, admonished that "you may talk about monopoly, you may scream about fixing of prices, you may harangue about unfair competition until your epiglottis ceases to function, but unless African business organizations learn to *unite* their efforts in a *co-operative* (working together) *combine* (union), African business will continue to be a one-man's affair, and the economic emancipation of the African is a long way off." Awolowo, in a private memorandum to the Ibadan branch of the NYM in 1940, constructed an elaborate economic program imbued with this spirit.

> We have a formidable weapon which only awaits being properly utilized by us. We have the means of co-operation at our disposal. If we are united truly and indeed, we can change the economic aspect of this country almost overnight. By unity we could with one accord refuse to submit one minute longer to the economic exploitation we have bitterly suffered. We would refuse to buy imported goods if we knew that their purchase would amount to a serious disadvantage to us. We would refuse to sell, should the sale appear tantamount to an exploitation of the African producers. . . . That is why I say that the economic salvation of this country lies in Co-operation.[56]

This program quite clearly drew on ideas offered by both African-American and British colonial ideas about African development, but it also was clearly drawing away from them, taking its own distinct form. Economic programs developed by African-American leaders were, like Nigerian thinking, pervaded by "the doctrines of self help and racial solidarity."[57] Facing a similar need to advance in an economy weighted against them, they urged African Americans to invest in and patronize the businesses of their peers as a means of building up industrial, retail, and service enterprises to equal the scope and prosperity of the mainstream economy. This economic prescription involved both cooperative and private enterprise, but successful individuals were lauded as the economic vanguard of their race. The Nigerian version also advanced individual interests in the name and for the sake of the larger group. Awolowo's "Economic Programme" saw that pooling resources could strengthen the joint position of produce traders and transporters but did not suggest the merger of their individual companies. Their success might redound to the benefit of the nation or race, but that success was to start with their individual fortunes. The Nigerian version was also tailored to Nigerian circumstances. It aimed to earn Nigerian entrepreneurs substantial control of the colonial economy, not just carve out a share, while it was less diverse in scope, focused on produce marketing and processing rather than a full range of goods and services. It also, of course, rejected African-American claims to race leadership, while retaining the idea of using transatlantic links to their own advantage.

British plans for Nigerian cooperatives, which surfaced in the early 1930s and took legislative form in 1935, were pushed by the need to reinvigorate the export sector. Cooperation was an attractive organizing principle because it would gently rework the natural African order without violating racial characteristics. It was deemed an ideal mixture of African communalism and modern economics. Lugard suggested that indirect rule could well be renamed "Co-operative Rule." The government's adviser on cooperatives urged just such a grand amalgamation. The "African race, swept off its balance by world currents and confused by a thousand new opportunities and temptations, has to find a new footing, to re-adjust itself to a revolution, to acquire painfully those virtues and self-constraints for which in the simpler surroundings of thirty years ago there was little demand. . . . there is no beneficial activity to which the co-operative method, if it is truly co-operative, may not legitimately be applied." Cooperation had the further attraction of promising to integrate the "detribalized and Westernized lawyer" into the colonial order. As Lugard pointed out, "The *intelligentsia* have the opportunity in this era of transition and adaptation to be of inestimable service to their country, or to clog the wheels of progress by causing racial animosities and preaching doctrines as yet impossible of realization. Work in connexion with co-operative societies . . . will . . . create new openings for the educated African."[58]

Some of this cooperative ideology converged with lingering Nigerian concepts of race-specific development and the need to foster in their economy "that spirit of co-operation which is the genius of the African."[59] Moreover, many Nigerian traders wanted to restructure the export sector. However, the conservative and paternalist aims of these ideas aroused Nigerian resentment. The NYM vehemently rejected government proposals for cooperative marketing societies as a threat to their entrepreneurial ambitions. Further, Nigerians wanted to reshape rather than merely reinvigorate the colonial economy. In 1926 Tete-Ansa had declared that West Africans wanted only to exchange their tropical produce for British manufactures. By the 1930s it was more typical for the intelligentsia to advocate limited-scale industrialization. Journalists pleaded for West Africans to have faith in their ability to succeed as manufacturers. Many programs for industrial development were proposed through the 1930s, often highlighting the successful efforts of African industrial pioneers. Heavy industries such as iron or steel were avoided in favor of light industries concentrating on import substitution or agricultural processing, such as textiles, oil pressing, papermaking, and leatherworking. The Nigerian economic prescription thus appropriated British rhetoric without accepting much of its content. Lugard proposed cooperatives as restraints to both change and the intelligentsia; the intelligentsia invented a tool to unchain themselves.

### Seeking "The Soul of Nigeria"

If these economic programs represent one aspect of the promise of interwar intellectual life—a pragmatic response to the felt needs of specific Nigerian groups—a much more diffuse body of writing on history and culture reveals another: a deepening involvement in local knowledge and problems. This more local focus was most powerful among the provincial intelligentsia, but not unknown among Nigerians abroad. Late nineteenth-century writers like Obadiah Johnson and J. O. George had explored Yoruba history to establish virtues of the whole African race first and of the Yoruba second. Interwar writers tended to reverse these priorities, in keeping with the growing abandonment of racial themes. Ojo-Cole neatly illustrated the change of orientation: a proclamation about the glories of "the West African civilisation" became simply a description of "Yoruba civilisation." He also apparently prepared but failed to publish a "Comprehensive History of Nigeria" and founded the Nigerian Institute in 1933 to promote a school curriculum of African languages and history. The WASU mission included exploring and explaining the "African mentality," but Solanke understood the need to work from detailed knowledge of diverse cultures rather than in generalized terms. "It is the duty of Africans to investigate and give to the world in suitable literary form, an account of their history, laws, customs, institutions and languages. Without such materials it would be impossible for us to know what lines our development should take."[60] He published extensively on Yoruba and especially Egba culture and apparently made some audio recordings of Yoruba folklore. Isaac Delano launched his search for *The Soul of Nigeria* with an extended tour to immerse himself among the people. Less grandly, S. O. Temietan addressed the question of cultural variety within Nigeria by comparing marriage ceremonies among his own "Jekri" and "the Hausa tribes," pointing out how "tribal hatred and prejudice" would result from barring intertribal marriage.[61]

This shift derived more from factors inside Nigeria than outside. It was in part simply the result of the now established provincial intelligentsia investigating questions that mattered to them. Folarin noted that his "idea of writing a *Historical Review of the Life of the Egbas* rose from natural causes." Like a merchant taking stock or a government taking a census, "ought not therefore a nation find out how far she has been fairing in this world's field of battle, after an existence and toil of one hundred years." These works often expressed the concerns of broad segments of provincial communities who had awaited a local author to put them in the most powerful colonial medium: print. William Moore wrote his *History of Itsekiri* in 1936 "in response to the felt need of the Itsekiri people, both literate and illiterate, for a written History of our Nation. . . . amendments by any Itsekiri, be he or she educated or uneducated, and all others who have the interest of the Itsekiri Country at heart, will be welcomed." Many works appeared in a Nigerian language as well as English, indicating concern for a local audience. But this work also was clearly structured by the institutions of indirect rule, which incorporated preexisting African polities—or at least their simulacra—as units of identification, requiring both subjects and administrators to have knowledge of their history, laws, and customs. Colonial intelligence reports provided some of this, but so did local intelligentsia. Indeed, the two bodies of writing often crossfertilized. C. O. Omoneukanrin wrote his *Itsekiri Law and Custom* in part for "the British Government to whom the value of a thorough knowledge of African institutions, laws and customs cannot be overstated." The Warri resident, in whose office Omoneukanrin worked, assisted with the book. Egharevba gathered data for his *Short History of Benin* at a 1932 conference called by the Benin resident to gather historical testimony. Folarin's *Native Laws and Customs of Egbaland* was intended precisely as a handbook for the Abeokuta native court. Disputes within and between Native Administrations generated much writing designed to establish certain claims, such as the debates over Abeokuta's constitution or the Eleko's claims to the Lagos throne. Iweka-Nuno, for example, intended to set right "misapprehensions" arising from "misleading representations by the people of the neighbouring Towns, as well as by some inhabitants of the Town themselves, who, in order to benefit themselves and their affairs, are altering the customs and good systems of Obosi."[62]

Such local writing received a fillip from a community of expatriates in Nigeria concerned both to preserve the beauty of Nigerian cultures and to oversee their progressive development. Their support was based on the common ground shared by Blyden and Kingsley but now typically lacked notions of innate racial difference. The central figure here was E. H. Duckworth, editor from 1933 to 1953 of *Nigeria,* a magazine initially associated with the Nigerian education department. Duckworth pushed educated Nigerians to value their own culture and potential, sounding very much like a native cultural nationalist. Nigerian writers, Duckworth told them, "by researching into and describing the antiquities, the craftwork, the customs of the country, can help to create in the mass of the people an appreciation of Nigerian art and culture. Help build up an appreciation of the old things; do not be afraid of them. Respect the past, record its history, treasure its signposts, help build museums in Nigeria."[63] Numerous Nigerian authors, many of them provincial schoolteachers, responded to Duckworth's appeal, no doubt from diverse motives of their own.

But this work also rose above the horizons of Native Administrations to pursue wider aims. Yoruba writers, building on a body of literature well established by the time Samuel Johnson's *History of the Yorubas* appeared in 1921, continued a multifaceted project of developing a pan-Yoruba identity from the many constituent Yoruba polities. The *Nigerian Daily Times* publicized a contest to write a Yoruba national anthem; plans and pleas were made to develop the Yoruba language and maintain its integrity. J. D. Y. Peel has analyzed this "Yoruba ethnogenesis" as the work of especially the Yoruba Christian intelligentsia, who sought to create an identity matched to both their pan-Yoruba roots and the framework of the colonial state. Similar projects were being launched elsewhere in these years, in studies of Onitsha by Azikiwe and Ibeziako and on Benin by Egharevba.[64] The motives for these interwar cultural studies were diverse, ranging from the pursuit of race redemption to local rivalry, from language preservation to ethnogenesis. Whatever the original motivations, they flowed into the regional identities of postwar politics.

If the intelligentsia appropriated local historical and cultural knowledge to meet their needs or to substantiate arguments in colonial politics, they were also shaped by it in complex ways. Andrew Apter has outlined how Yoruba politics since at least the eighteenth century have been shaped by two competing "ritual fields": one, centered on Ife, is used within the competitive structures of Yoruba polities to resist another set, centered on Oyo. Fuller delineation of these patterns in interwar historical writing must await future work, but even a cursory reading of passages on group origins suggests how the interwar Yoruba intelligentsia were replaying and redeploying these elaborate arguments. Similarly, Peel has revealed how the histories written in early twentieth-century Ilesha were shaped by the forms and idioms of the oral historiography upon which they drew. The colonial intelligentsia thus drew more than just data from local bodies of historical and cultural knowledge. There was inspiration here from long-standing and living critical traditions, connected by efforts to create knowledge fitted to the colonial context—an inspiration which requires more careful study.[65]

The interwar intelligentsia knew they stood in a long line of African figures who had grappled with their essential problem: how to secure the interests of the medial classes in British West Africa. The numerous editions of Deniga's *African Leaders* and *Nigerian Who's Who*s captured this procession. Essien placed Prince Archibong "amongst the Aggreys, the Blydens, the Sawyerrs, the Gibsons, the Macaulays, the Saparas, the Ani-Okokons—the glorious company of the dutiful sons of our dear Mother Africa." Ikoli, editor of the *African Messenger*, saw Aggrey as the intellectual successor to Blyden. Solanke, Azikiwe, and Ojo-Cole continued to praise African-American leaders like Garvey and Washington.[66] The fruit of these efforts had reached a state of ferment by the 1930s, more remarkable perhaps for its potency than its body. Echeruo has argued that Azikiwe's work up to 1937 was an eclectic adaptation of nineteenth-century Black Atlantic ideas rather than a leap into postwar themes. Ayandele talks of a "total ideological barrenness" in the interwar intelligentsia, who were "borrowers of the forms but not the spirit, the shadows but not the substance" of European culture.[67] I would argue, in contrast, that the spirit of this period reveals the intelligentsia at their most adept—borrowing widely and critically and adapting these ideas to fit their situation. They had stressed their Victorian attributes in the mid-nineteenth century to better secure their required colonial setting and then emphasized their Black Atlantic ties to counter denigrations of all Africans. But the "Africa" of earlier Black Atlantic discourse was now being disaggregated by an intelligentsia less dependent on and less comfortable with Black Atlantic thought and more rooted in southern Nigeria. British colonial critics were studied critically; Nigerians still attached some significance to the assertion of historically rooted African difference even if ideas of racial difference were dissolving. Their most notable achievement was a pragmatic economic prescription of "Unity, Self-Help and Cooperation." Written to fit the needs of colonial entrepreneurs and matched to their capacity for organization and capital formation, it would have reduced dependence on raw produce exports and added value to the Nigerian economy. It spoke the language of Pan-Africanism but calculated things closer to home, even subordinating peasant producers to the traders' cause. Another achievement was the expanding corpus of cultural and historical writing, diversely motivated and informed, which began to provide specific content to various identities required in the colonial context: "African" and "Nigerian," but also "Yoruba" and "Itsekiri." Rising above the mid-Victorian habit of praising things foreign and above the Blydenesque agenda of defining Africa merely against Europe, this was the work of a modern intelligentsia, shaped by contemporary Atlantic thought, colonial politics, and indigenous intellectual traditions.

My argument here is not that these diversely motivated—and in all still rather scant—studies of Nigeria finally revealed the true "soul of Nigeria." But in the Atlantic context of the time—inspired by anticolonial sentiment to assert universal rights while also embedded in an imperial order which bolstered the enduring imagery of African otherness—interwar colonial subjects at least began to find some kind of imperfect balance within these unsettling forces. They began to reach toward a perspective which recognized that ambitions to modernize Nigeria had to be checked by a sense of African difference, that diasporan affinities and connections between African cultures might figure along with imperial linkages in this project. The interwar ferment, in short, allowed the Nigerian intelligentsia to develop a sense of their own situation and problems, held by local ties against Atlantic tides. Condemning imitation of any source, they now talked of African "fusion with the civilised nations of the West," recognizing the need to constantly assess "how far the fusion should extend and when the African should commence to evolve distinctive traditions."[68] Their new, inchoate sense of being Nigerian was no less contingent than earlier identities and no more stable or reassuring. The familiar lament about their lack of foresight, sincerity, courage, and enthusiasm as leaders continued. But the malaise of the 1930s had a different quality from that of a generation earlier. The intelligentsia were less disturbed by the gap between their image of Africa and their reality or by the tension between Pan-African solidarity and claims to British imperial citizenship. Rather, they were disturbed by their inability to fill the role of modern national leaders that they now wanted to assume. The multiple changes from the 1940s forward disrupted this search and profoundly altered their quest both to define and to lead Nigeria.

# 5.

## "Who Are the Nigerians?"

### Nationalism and the Future, 1940–1960

**M**ANY CONTEMPORARY OBSERVERS, entering the 1960s hopefully, looked back on the period since World War II as an uplifting story of Nigerian economic growth and nationalist victory. In fact, however, those postwar decades were weighted with sensations of disorientation and pessimistic foreboding. Until World War II, Nigerians had been able to pursue, though not solve, the nineteenth-century agenda of discovering their place in the Atlantic world in an atmosphere of comparatively gradual change. During the 1940s pressure for self-government and economic reform gave a direction and focus to much intellectual activity. But as the certainty of British withdrawal became clear, the intellectual quest for the route to African modernity was all but lost in the urgent search for constitutional and national development, both pursued on the premise that Nigeria's future would follow a universal model. Moreover, the intelligentsia had to change agendas while undergoing complex and rapid alterations in their own social makeup. More widespread recruitment, competing loyalties, diversifying educational careers, a renewed attachment to the state, and divisive stratification all served to disrupt established patterns. As these changes unfolded, we can sense a deepening atmosphere of confusion from many sources. Thus, while postwar Nigerian political history progressed along an apparently linear path toward the realization of self-government, Nigerian intellectual history did not follow a parallel trajectory. All but overwhelmed by their exposure to new ideas and conditions, the intelligentsia on the eve of independence lost sight, at least temporarily, of much of their earlier tradition.

## A "Reading Public"

The Nigerian economy remained unsettled through the 1940s. The attempt by major European firms to arrange a cocoa price agreement in 1937, coming at the end of the depression, had threatened both Nigerian middlemen and government revenues. The war obliged the state to assume broad control of exports, imports, and production before a commission of inquiry could fully address the crisis. However, the "Cocoa Pool" firms used their influence under wartime constraints to enhance their power at the expense of African and other smaller traders. Falling export prices, rising import prices, and food shortages combined to make the war years very difficult for Nigerian producers, middlemen, and urban dwellers. While export demand improved after 1945, continuing British control over Nigerian export earnings extended wartime hardship and unrest. By 1950, however, British controls had relaxed, demand had improved, and imports had become more available. Nigeria entered a boom unknown since before 1914. Although government policies favored urban dwellers over rural producers, both improved their real incomes. This trend slowed slightly after 1955, but a spirit of economic optimism still obtained in 1960. This change of economic fortunes accompanied a profound shift in colonial policy, from defending indirect rule to defining the devolution of power. Prewar ideas of reform generated political concessions under wartime pressure, starting with the appointment of two Nigerians to the Executive Council in 1942. A new constitution promised by Governor Richards in 1944 was enacted in 1946. Popular discontent with these measures and parallel trends in Ghana that climaxed in widespread riots in February 1948 propelled the British to further action. Governor Macpherson launched an early constitutional review in 1948 involving widespread consultation with the educated community and espousal of democratic principles. This set events rolling toward self-government, although this had not been the immediate intention of the Colonial Office. The 1951 constitution introduced a federal structure; further constitutional reviews in 1953 and 1956 paved the bumpy but fast-traveled road to independence in 1960. There is, then, a stark contrast between the two postwar decades. From early in the war until about 1948, economic conditions and political grievances generated an atmosphere of heated protest which general prosperity and political reform in the 1950s largely dissipated.[1]

126

The rate of social and economic change accelerated. The percentage of Nigerians in urban settlements increased by one-third between 1931 and 1953. Expanded agricultural output was complemented by a manifold increase in industrial production, albeit from a small beginning, especially in agricultural processing and consumer goods manufacturing. Foreign firms dominated these new sectors, but they also now left more room in retail trade for Africans and others. At the same time, the government sector expanded rapidly in size and power. Regional and federal levels of government used marketing boards and other public corporations to direct the economy. By the late 1950s Nigeria was certainly neither developed nor industrialized, but it could display many attributes of such economies, including an expanding government bureaucracy, a large urban population, a university, and technical colleges.

Carried by these developments, the population of Western-educated Nigerians now expanded more rapidly than ever before, quickly filling many of the gaps left from previous uneven expansion and dwarfing earlier totals.[2] Primary-school enrollments more than doubled through the war, to about 540,000 by 1947. Universal Primary Education, launched in the mid-1950s, multiplied this figure some five times to about 2.6 million by 1960. Secondary-school enrollments grew as remarkably. The approximately one hundred secondary schools and teacher-training institutes in 1947 had increased perhaps eightfold by 1960; the number of students grew over tenfold. In the early 1950s around 30 percent of school-age children were attending school; by 1960 the figure was 75 percent. Women steadily narrowed the gender gap after the war but did not close it. At the primary level the male-to-female ratio was close to two to one by 1957. At the secondary level the 1957 ratio was five to one (and only about three to one among teachers in training). The gap with the northern region narrowed as well, but with less dramatic results. Excluding Koranic schools, primary students in 1960 amounted to about one-tenth of the southern total; secondary students in 1957 equaled about one-eighth. Data from 1953 surveys reveal the fruits of all this schooling in some detail. An estimated 10 percent of the southern Nigerian population over seven years of age, excluding Lagos, had at least basic competence in English; about 16 percent were literate in English or a Nigerian language rendered in Roman script. The new expansion did not completely erase earlier differences. Literacy rates of up to 25 percent obtained where colonial trade, evangelization, or administration had been more intense, such as in provinces close to the coast in the east and in the core of the west. Port Harcourt township had 43 percent, Lagos perhaps 50 percent. Morrill thinks it likely that no Efik adult in Calabar in the late 1950s was illiterate. More remote provinces fell far below the average. The educated remained more concentrated in urban than in rural populations and in larger than in smaller towns. In 1953 the towns of Onitsha and Enugu, with only one-fifth of the Onitsha Province population, had one-third of the "educated"; Ibadan Town, with only three-tenths of the provincial population, contained six-tenths of its "educated." But they were still found mostly outside urban settings, as they had been in 1921. In 1953 some 1.6 million southern Nigerians were literate in Roman script, while the combined population of the eighteen largest southern urban centers amounted to less than 2 million. If 40 percent of this urban population was literate—a generous approximation—fully half the literates lived outside these major centers. Thus a literate population now reached across southern Nigeria in a thin but well-distributed layer, reaching beyond the larger cities and by no means disconnected from village life.

Tertiary education expanded similarly.[3] Teachers emerged as a significant occupational category in their own right. There were over 3,000 teachers in training in 1947 and over 23,000 by 1958. In 1946 nearly 200 Nigerians were in the United Kingdom in university or other institutes of higher learning; another 100 were in America. Numbers jumped sharply thereafter under the prospect of extensive Nigerianization. Government overseas scholarships began slowly from 1937 to replace private and communal association funding. Only 137 awards had been made by 1948, but there were 171 government scholars in the United States alone by 1949. The federal government's 500 scholarships in 1961 were supplemented by awards from all the regional governments. These sources of support still did not meet the demand (many Nigerians hopeful of higher education sailed to Britain as stowaways), but they did allow students without personal wealth to challenge the access of the privileged to higher education and higher status. By 1950, 938 Nigerian students were in the United Kingdom while a further 300 or so were in American universities. By 1959 an estimated 800 Nigerians were graduating from universities overseas each year, implying an enrollment of well over 2,000 on the assumption that programs lasted three years. To this rapid postwar increase in overseas education we must add higher education within Nigeria. The University College Ibadan opened in 1948 in affiliation with the University of London and boasted 615 graduates by 1960. The Nigerian College of Arts, Science, and Technology produced an additional 200 graduates annually by Independence. The variety of university careers increased as the numbers rose. The majority of Nigerians in British schools were in medicine, law, or engineering. But as UCI offered no degrees in law or engineering until after 1958, about two-thirds of its early students were in science and medicine and about one-third were in arts and social sciences. Students in America could not read British law; in 1958 over half were studying in science and professional faculties. By 1959 Nigeria had its first atomic physicist and psychiatrist, but no psychologist. The university population also became more balanced in terms of gender and ethnic origin. When UCI opened there were twenty-five males to every female. By 1958 the ratio had closed slightly to seventeen to one; similar ratios applied among Nigerian university students in America. The advantage once enjoyed by the Yoruba in higher education was now all but gone. By the early 1950s around a third of Nigerian doctors were Igbo, and Igbo more than twice outnumbered Yoruba in American universities and probably at least equaled them in British universities. In 1955 eastern and western students in residence at UCI were almost balanced. Only about fifteen northerners were at UCI in 1957–58. By the late colonial period, then, there was a highly educated intelligentsia spread above the thicker layer of mere literates representing most parts of the south, in a broad variety of occupations.

The intelligentsia now not only reached but also communicated across the Nigerian south, through various institutions. The circulation of the *Daily Times* almost quadrupled through the 1950s, to 96,000. By 1959 national dailies alone had a circulation of 193,000 (about ten times the 1937 figure) while southern provincial weeklies had a total circulation of almost 43,000 (about twice the 1937 figure). Libraries created as propaganda reading rooms by the government during the war were taken over by local governments and became the bases of public libraries in many villages and towns beyond the three active libraries in Lagos, despite the fact that Nigeria had only eleven trained librarians in 1955. Small and large printing presses and publishing companies proliferated as never before, in and beyond Lagos. CMS Bookshops, the largest single bookdealer across southern Nigeria, imported half a million printed books of various types in 1945. Books of secondary or local importance had substantial sales, often sustained through informal contacts. Christopher Chukwura stocked 1,000 copies of his *History of Eastern Motor Transport Union* in 1954. Timothy Uzo's political tract, *The Pathfinder,* sold over 5,000 copies in five months during 1953. Thus, having started from Lagos and extended first to provincial centers, by the 1950s the communications network of the intelligentsia left few areas unconnected. If still open to improvement, it was adequate for sustaining dialogue across the country. Writers could publish their arguments and advise readers to use "the medium of the Newspapers for the discussion of the reading public." The intelligentsia were recognizably analogous to the intelligentsia of Europe, if still also recognized as inchoate and small relative to the population. As a British observer noted at Independence, "Nigeria has a gratifyingly experienced and mature leadership class; a core of intellectuals who are beginning to run institutions like schools, newspapers, and radio."[4]

## Opportunity and Disunity

But being more numerous and more connected did not mean the intelligentsia were now more powerful, united, or agreed among themselves than before. Indeed, the fractures in the community were probably now deeper, and certainly more significant, than in previous eras. First, even though many of the graduates produced by the sharp upturn in late 1950s enrollments won their degrees too late to figure much in events before 1960, the explosive growth in these short years and the new diversity of education were in themselves enough to inject a certain confusion. An observation made in 1960, that "the number of students abroad in any given year now exceeds the total number in any decade before 1940," probably understates the case but indicates the imbalance between the established and new cohorts.[5] Second, if no single provincial center displaced Lagos as the anchor of intellectual life, the collective bulk of provincial centers surely threatened to outweigh it. Leading provincial figures were, as before the war, more likely to be clerks, clergymen, and teachers than doctors and lawyers, but this did not prevent them from entering national forums in their own right. The dominance of Yoruba intellectuals and themes that had given interwar writing a certain coherence was now submerged in a much broader community of writers with more diverse concerns. By 1959 the sixty-odd functioning newspapers in southern Nigeria were split evenly between Lagos and provincial centers. These provincial papers now included dailies and national weeklies from such diverse places as Warri and Ilesha. Ibadan and Enugu, as regional capitals, were acquiring new importance. Port Harcourt professionals were numerous enough to form a Welfare Society in 1960, to offer "intellectual guidance" to the government. Provincial observers demanded that political parties extend themselves "beyond the borders of rabid and irresponsible Lagos . . . outside of the turbulent island of discord."[6]

The political history of the period also reveals fragmentation, as Lagos became less a center of elite culture and more a political prize to be won by regionally based parties. Nigerians entered the war expecting hastened political change. Disenchantment with British policy inspired a variety of political and other organizations to form the National Council of Nigeria and the Cameroons in 1944 as a common front under the leadership of Azikiwe and Macaulay. The NCNC dominated the nationalist movement through the 1940s, as other groups, including the radical Zikists, joined it in several united efforts against British intransigence and violence. But when British policy shifted in the late 1940s, diverse organizations entered the prelude to competitive self-governing politics. The Action Group in the west, the NCNC in the east, and the Northern Peoples' Congress established the basic tripartite structure of Nigerian political life, each representing regional ambitions within the federation and becoming associated with each region's dominant ethnic group. They were complemented by a dizzying array of smaller parties, often focused on local issues and not always aligned with national blocs. The Warri Peoples' Party, for example, was established to "take keen interest in all political matters affecting Warri Division in particular and Nigeria in general." Other movements, like the United Middle Belt Congress, were intent on redrawing the federation's units. Ethnic considerations figured in all these politics, even entering student union life at UCI in the 1950s. Political parties acquired newspaper chains through the 1950s, and most newspapers assumed a party loyalty. Azikiwe's *West African Pilot* became the flagship of a press empire supporting the NCNC; the Action Group started one from Awolowo's *Nigerian Tribune*. The government entered the competition for public opinion with ardor during World War II and established a swelling output of newspapers, books, and pamphlets explaining its policies and celebrating its achievements. As regional governments came under Nigerian control, the government press fell in line with party positions. The intense, vitriolic nature of party politics renders much of the partisan press without interest as a source of independent criticism or original thought. The independent papers, such as the *African Echo* or the *Eastern States Express*, although often short-lived and poorly produced, are more valuable.[7]

Political and ethnic divisions were powerfully felt, but perhaps a more important source of the postwar sense of confusion was the way fluid social trends were imperfectly contained by increasingly defined social strata. As Africa approached self-government, international scholars devoted considerable effort to discovering the nature of its emergent leaders, a group broadly characterized by high social status, wealth, and education.[8] The empirical details these studies provide illuminate these contrary qualities well. These scholars resisted casting this group simply as a ruling class or African "bourgeoisie," adopting instead less restrictive notions of "elite" or "political class." A variety of reasons were offered, especially in the Nigerian case. Until Independence this group did not have the political control of a ruling class. Nor did it have any special hold on economic power, land, or resources, except for some privileged access to the state. Illiterate traders and contractors could still control more wealth than many school graduates. Marriage and residence patterns, typically shared within classes, were crosscut and sometimes severed among the elite by ties to extended families and home villages. Wealth and education opportunities were thereby distributed widely rather than inherited narrowly among the elite alone. The ease with which Nigerians could rise to elite status through education also kept class identity diffuse. Further, seething ethnic and political divisions among the educated obscured lines of class. Although many contemporary scholars correctly predicted that hardening lines of division would make class analyses more relevant to postcolonial Nigeria, attempts to apply it retroactively have not rendered late colonial Nigerian society with more clarity than did elite theory.[9] We may take from this, then, that class identities in late colonial Nigerian society were at most inchoate and be warned away from seeking a class ideology in elite ideas. Diverse educational, ethnic, regional, and occupational origins were not erased by accession to the educated community. This assertion does not undermine one of the premises of this study—that the educated constituted a significantly distinct colonial group. Education, as in earlier times, opened economic possibilities otherwise closed and placed graduates in a medial position which they still sought to secure. The core elite did in fact devise an economic program well suited to their group interests. The point remains, however, that the educated community, despite certain shared interests, was too fluid a group—pulled by too many ties—to move in concert. These same characteristics apply to the intelligentsia, who were drawn from the same diverse sources as the educated community at large.

Another pertinent lesson to be drawn from contemporary scholarship is the way divisions were forming among Nigeria's educated community. That individual careers still could cross these lines does not mean that lines were not forming. In 1946 Ojike listed the groups within the intelligentsia "in a descending order of their personal security and social vision combined." They were "journalists, doctors, teachers, lawyers, clerks, ministers, managers, police, soldiers, students and artists." While his order might be revised, it suggests both a hierarchy within the intelligentsia and contemporary awareness of it. By 1960 it was commonplace to assert that a wide gap separated the rich leaders and the impoverished masses. Pursuing exact divisions would be fruitless, but it is necessary to recognize emergent strata to appreciate the growing complexity of Nigerian intellectual life. We can divide them loosely into three sets with imprecise and permeable boundaries between them: a small elite core; a larger group with less secure claims on elite status; and a less well educated, rapidly growing periphery. Such differences were not new—there were both lawyers and mere school graduates among the intelligentsia in the 1890s. In late colonial society, however, several factors made such differences more significant. Each level of school graduates on its own now rivaled or surpassed the size of the entire educated community from a few decades earlier. Further, income standards were markedly disparate. Perhaps some 2.5 percent of the population of Lagos fell in the upper elite in the early 1960s. They earned perhaps twenty times what wage laborers earned, and five times what middle-level managers earned. Senior government servants could outearn middle managers by a factor of eight or ten.[10] Finally, the intelligentsia of each ring tended to belong to different organizations with discernibly different perspectives. Describing each group will reveal the significance of these circles of influence more clearly.

## Circles of Influence

The core intelligentsia were the most commonly recognized by contemporary studies and figure centrally here. Obvious members include government ministers and senior civil servants, professionals, editors of important newspapers, university faculty, and some university graduates. T. O. Elias, who taught law at Manchester University in the 1950s and was later a justice at The Hague, described his peers as the "hard core" of the intelligentsia, derived "from among those who have been educated abroad. . . . they are often able to afford a reasonable standard of comfort and modern amenities for themselves and their families largely because their education has fitted them for higher incomes." This was a fairly exclusive club. Various statistics suggest a group of a few thousand growing to at most five thousand by 1960.[11]

Many of this group came from elite families literate for several generations who took pains to educate their children. Mann could trace many nineteenth-century elite families back from the 1970s; many of the legal "giants" of early 1950s Lagos boast old elite surnames.[12] The continuity with at least the previous elite generation is reflected in Lloyd's data that about 80 percent of the Ibadan elite in the early 1960s had fathers with at least primary education, when until 1950 less than 30 percent of school-age children attended school. One-quarter of this elite had fathers with postprimary education, again far above the average. The percentage of UCI students in 1964 with fathers in professional, managerial, teaching, and similar careers was four times the percentage of such jobs in the Lagos workforce. But the provincial educated community established in the interwar period, now in accelerated growth, was producing a new flood of first-generation school graduates. Increasingly, the old elite found themselves competing for status rather than merely assuming it.[13]

This group fared well in the process of decolonization as the state, parastatal corporations, and foreign firms expanded under policies of Nigerianization. In 1948 only 172 Africans held senior posts in the civil service, but there were 685 in 1952, and 2,308 in 1960. Professional career opportunities also multiplied. Through the 1940s, 32 lawyers were called to the Nigerian bar. During the 1950s more than 360 enrolled. Over 100 more enrolled in 1960 alone. Many professional careers, once sought as an escape from government employment, were now funded directly or indirectly by the state. Of the 156 elite examined by Smythe and Smythe, for example, over 70 percent were in "government-connected jobs."[14] Thus the close attachment of this group to the state, more obvious in later periods, was already emerging in the 1950s. Ever since the late nineteenth century, the Nigerian intelligentsia had faced the dilemma of depending upon a colonial state from which they were alienated. For this core group, at least, this dilemma was now resolved. Released from this long-standing tension, their agenda took on a new shape.

It seems the social habits of the educated elite and of the intelligentsia among them were made over to mark off their location as a rising privileged minority. As Plotnicov observes of the Jos elite, they wanted to be "admired and respected by all" for their "wealth, power, knowledge, and modern social sophistication." Students at UCI, receiving their "Training for Snobbery," dressed in white flannels and played cricket and tennis. One of the first Nigerians to become an assistant district officer, in 1955, felt the acute need to acquire the demeanor and equipment of his British peers.[15] Politicians, civil servants, and professionals moved into exclusive—and formerly exclusively European—residential districts, from which they organized cocktail parties and ballroom dances. Observers often remarked at their similarity with the departing British, not least in terms of their distance from the unlettered. Pronouncements by more elite Nigerians also reveal a growing sense of superiority over the less educated and less privileged masses. Ojike, describing the social hierarchy, pointed out that "the trousered or white-collar class are the most informed on social problems as a whole. . . . And no class pretends that it is wrong or unfair for it mainly to rule the society which no other class knows as well as it does." Trying to convince the British of this same point, Awolowo asserted that "it must be realized now and for all time that this articulate minority are destined to rule the country. It is their heritage. It is they who must be trained in the art of government so as to enable them to take over complete control of the affairs of their country." Although Awolowo objected to British representations of the African as "backward, superstitious, primitive and . . . ignorant," he himself used precisely such words to describe the "masses." They "will not be bothered by politics. Their preoccupation is the search for food, clothing, and shelter of a wretched type."[16] At a 1950 constitutional conference, one delegate was sure that at least 90 percent of the people had no idea what their leaders were doing for them; he judged that "universal suffrage at this stage is a mere farce." Ita's leadership duties did not shy away from coercion: "For the sake of democracy a free compulsory and universal education must be imposed if necessary by force upon an unready illiterate people. Even if it may mean pain and suffering it should be done because it is for their own ultimate good. If it may be regarded as an error or brutality it is blundering in the right direction." As observers of the First Republic noted, "The mass of the population were regarded by the elite as objects of manipulation rather than real participants" in public life.[17]

However, as in the mid-nineteenth century, the postwar elite did not, and did not want to, merely imitate Europeans. As an elite, conscious of their leadership role, they had to maintain social distinctions from the noneducated and less educated masses. At the same time, as nationalist leaders, local notables, and people of business, they could not cut themselves off from Nigerian cultures. As the more astute observers noted, and fiction set in the period depicts, the educated elite still operated within their extended families, took traditional titles, and played leading roles in communal associations, dressing equally impressively in European or African costume as the occasion required.[18] As they moved between the various possibilities inherent in their position, they may have been Westernized but were not becoming Western. Rather, they were living as the products and creators of a new but distinctly Nigerian social order. Echoing their mid-nineteenth-century predecessors' display of British attributes was merely an effective means of reinforcing their assumption of new privileges within the late colonial order.

Well served by the colonial dispensation of the 1950s, this core intelligentsia tended to follow a moderate nationalist line. The Nigeria Society, formed largely by university students and graduates in London in 1948, epitomizes their activities. Its aims included "the fostering of a spirit of Nigerian citizenship and the general dissemination of a Nigeria-wide outlook among its members and other Nigerians, the encouragement of social, cultural and other useful contacts and understanding among the various ethnic groups of Nigeria, and . . . studies of various aspects of Nigerian problems." The society's interests centered around practical policy issues germane to the transfer of power and organization of the Nigerian state, well evidenced in its collections of *Occasional Papers* in 1954 and 1955 and its *New Nigerian* journal launched in 1961. It also worked behind the scenes as a valuable "brains trust" to Awolowo as Western Region premier. In 1965 it claimed members "from all walks of life—Civil Servants, Judges, Lawyers, Ministers, Legislators, University Lecturers, Schoolmasters, Businessmen, Journalists and others"; contributors included such notable Nigerian intellectuals as economist S. A. Aluko, historian S. O. Biobaku, and civil servant and diplomat Chief S. O. Adebo. A Citizens' Committee for Independence composed submissions to the government in a similar spirit but embodied one of the splits among Nigerian intellectuals with its marked majority of American university graduates.[19] The still nascent Nigerian academic community at UCI made contributions through journals such as *Ibadan* and *Black Orpheus* and in public lectures.

Outside this core intelligentsia was a broad range of less clearly elite Nigerians who participated actively in intellectual life. At the inner border they are not easily distinguished from the core. This ring recruited inner elite as patrons, as when R. Kano Umo's *History of Aro Settlements* was edited and published by Ojike. Graduates of UCI or American universities, commanding less prestige than those trained in Britain, might be placed on this border. Many moved across the line as their careers advanced. The populist Ibadan leader Adegoke Adelabu, for example, gained some prominence with the publication of his *Africa in Ebullition*. But barriers were forming. This middle group launched stinging attacks on the leadership claims of the core intelligentsia. Those more firmly outside the border ranged from editors of smaller papers and university students to grammar-school and teaching college graduates, ministers of religion, traders, junior civil servants, and clerks. Compared to the core, they were thus less likely to live in exclusive areas, mix with Europeans socially, or have substantial incomes and more likely to be in the provinces. Their numbers are difficult to determine, but an estimate that in 1960 only about 20,000 Nigerians had two or more years of postsecondary education suggests an order of magnitude about five or six times the size of the core elite.[20]

In a reprise of the education expansion of the·1930s, the youthful members of this group could not quickly find the employment they expected. With their promotions and aspirations obstructed by a relatively young cohort placed above them on career ladders in the first wave of Nigerianization, they became frustrated. Contemporary observers frequently remarked on this division between the "haves" and the "have-nots" as contributing to a growing atmosphere of popular dissatisfaction with the emergent order.[21] As observers rather than leaders of political life, outsiders tended to be more critical of the status quo than the core intelligentsia. However, because they shared the interests common to the educated community in colonial society and retained hopes of mobility, their radicalism was often transient. They did not necessarily want structural change or new departures but rather reforms and employment to match their expectations. Nevertheless, this was the most vibrant group of the intelligentsia and produced some of the most trenchant critiques of Nigerian affairs. Their newspaper, pamphlet, and book publications far exceed those mentioned in this study.

Some organizations within this group in the 1940s illuminate their characteristics. The Nigerian Economic Society, established in Lagos in 1943, sought to investigate and publish studies of Nigerian conditions in a nonpartisan manner. It solicited the patronage of Macaulay, but its members were former commerce students at Yaba Higher College, now mostly government and commercial clerks, concentrated in Lagos but also dispersed throughout Nigeria, many of whom were reading for a University of London external degree in commerce. The Nigerian Fabian Society, formed from an earlier study group in 1943, characterized its membership as educated chiefs, journalists, teachers, clerks, farmers, traders, religious leaders, and laborers. The Olympian Society, formed in the late 1940s by "a group of intelligent youngmen" largely from the east, established the Olympian Publishing Bureau as "an effective instrument for disseminating political education and guiding the emotions and aspirations of the people of Nigeria into right channels." The Pan African Bureau of Information in Lagos (later the New Era Bureau) and the African Literature Bureau in Onitsha proclaimed similar missions. Students at UCI quickly established their own journals, such as the *University Herald* and the *Beacon,* while students in the United States and Britain offered opinions on constitutional and other issues through the 1950s.[22]

A third ring—again hard to delineate with precision—comprised largely of recent male graduates of primary schools, stood at the periphery of intellectual life. In major urban areas at the end of the colonial period such school leavers, and even secondary-school graduates, sometimes described their occupation as "applicants" during their long search for a suitable placement. This was because, as Abernethy observes, the expansion of primary education had "destroyed the efficacy of the First School-leaving certificate as a sufficient condition for employment," at least in urban centers. According to one Nigerian biographer, a university matriculation might now open doors a mere primary-school certificate would have unlocked in 1920. The more fortunate could still hope to be junior clerks or minimally qualified teachers in the expanded school system; many, it seems, also became writers both to be heard and to secure income. The producers of Onitsha market literature exemplify this widespread group. A mass of inexpensive pamphlets and chapbooks flooded out of Onitsha as aspirant writers found a supply of secondhand presses made available by a printing industry under refurbishment. By the mid-1960s there were some twenty-five publishing houses and nineteen printing presses at work. Obiechina describes the authors as "school-teachers, local printing press owners and booksellers . . . journalists, railwaymen, clerks, traders, artisans, farmers and even grammar school boys." Romantic fiction and how-to literature were their stock in trade; they also produced local histories, accounts of "laws and custom," and other books of parochial concern.[23] We might also include here critics in other media, such as Herbert Ogunde's theater troupe that flourished in the later 1940s, addressing its work to political as well as social questions, or the political cartoonist Akinole Lasekan. These various authors offered many insightful critiques of British rule and Nigerian society and formed an important part of the audience of and contributors to the national press. Despite the often poor technical quality of their publications, ignoring their contribution would obscure an important element in the vitality and complexity of Nigerian intellectual life.

## Activists and "Unofficial Ambassadors" Abroad

Relations with Europeans went through some unsettling shifts in these same years, in the spirit of much else in the last colonial decades. The wartime flow of troops and others through Nigeria expanded both the scope and variety of contact between Africans and Europeans but did not improve relations. The propaganda war against Nazism made racism increasingly indefensible, rendering unchanged colonial habits and attitudes all the more intolerable to the intelligentsia. Arthur Richards, arriving as governor in 1943, was much less sympathetic to nationalist ambitions than Bourdillon and no doubt contributed to the escalating wartime and postwar tensions. By 1945 Richards reported that sporting events between Europeans and Africans too frequently ended in racial incidents; by early 1947 some officials feared rebellion. Perham had argued energetically in the late 1930s for a scheme involving the British Council and Colonial Office which would try to bridge the social chasm between West Africans and Britons, hoping mutual understanding might preempt unwanted radicalism. Wartime attempts to make a few restricted European clubs nonracial had little impact; the continued resentment of European-only hotels and even hospitals rose to a public furor in February 1947, when a black Colonial Office official was refused a room in a Lagos hotel. Thenceforth, as part of the general policy of consultation and conciliation, official policy forbade all discriminatory practices and promoted social contacts between Africans and Europeans. Nigerians did not flock to the newly nonracial clubs, still regarded as symbols of expatriate superiority, but tensions eased. A British friend of Perham's reported in 1957 that Africans comprised about a fifth of the "club" members in Abeokuta, and "all fit in well."[24] Indeed, social relations soon became rather confused. The "second colonial occupation" and overseas education expanded the scope of social contact on two fronts just as the reordering of power raised awkward points of etiquette. The new generation of Europeans and Nigerians blithely transgressed old rules. Increasing numbers of Nigerians returned from education abroad with European or American wives. British women administrators invited male Nigerian colleagues to dinner (although in one case this obliged her older British male colleague to patrol protectively—unasked—outside). Kola Balogun, as the new (and young) federal minister of information in 1955, had to fire his resentful British civil servants of considerable seniority. Race relations between Europeans and educated Nigerians, then, moved quickly from hopeful expectation under the Bourdillons, to radical discontent in the middle 1940s, to less tense but also less ordered relations in the 1950s.

The confused nature of postwar intellectual life was also strengthened by Nigerians' experiences abroad. If affinities had been split between imperial and Pan-African networks between the wars, after the war patterns frayed. Pan-African ardor peaked at the war's end. Thereafter, Nigerian students in Britain emerged as widely connected spokespeople for specifically Nigerian interests. At the same time, they were pulled apart into factions replicating the Nigerian domestic scene, despite exposure to the racism and other conditions that had once inspired sojourners overseas toward Pan-African solidarity.

Britain remained the single most important overseas destination. Waves of official delegations, traveling for constitutional conferences and fact-finding missions, now added pomp and prestige to the life of Nigerian students in London. Contacts with British officials intensified, partly because from the early 1940s officials redoubled their efforts to protect Africans from racism and radicalism. In 1950 the British Council, acting on behalf of the Colonial Office, augmented piecemeal charitable initiatives with extensive programs to assist newly arrived students. But West African contacts with British colonial officials, experts, and critics also expanded, as ever, because of African initiatives to connect with what Davies called a small but "growing and influential section of the British public" who "organized Colonial Conferences, and wrote books and pamphlets" concerning colonial policies.[25] Very significant links made with the Fabian Colonial Bureau and certain Labour Party members ranged from political alliance through organizational linkage to personal friendship. In 1942, for example, Labour Members of Parliament Reginald Sorensen and Arthur Creech Jones joined with Solanke of WASU to form a committee which raised West African issues in the House of Commons. Awolowo, like many of his peers, belonged to the Fabians and campaigned for the Labour Party in the 1945 British election. Funmilayo Ransome-Kuti maintained correspondence with Sorensen, Creech Jones, and others after her 1947 tour of Britain. Davies invited Sorensen and Rita Hinden of the FCB to tour Nigeria in 1948 and became a friend of Hinden. Requests for organizational advice, Fabian literature, and political support continued into the 1950s, from, for example, the Nigerian Union of Teachers. These contacts suggest at least the partial realization of Solanke's earlier dream that metropolitan and African experts join forces to oversee Africa. There were many reasons why M. C. K. Ajuluchuku could proclaim in 1954 that the Fabians were the "conglomeration of the best brains in Britain" and "really tops with most Africans."[26] S. A. Aluko recalls that even studying under more conservative scholars like Lucy Mair and Perham in the 1950s was fruitful, disagreements over colonial policies notwithstanding. Both sides shared enough ideas to make dialogue not only possible but also rewarding.

However, it is clear that the Nigerians viewed these contacts critically and did not confuse shared interests with agreement, especially in the 1940s. West African students increasingly engaged experts on Africa in debates on African development. Academics, Colonial Office officials, and governors were invited by WASU to defend British policy, not merely to explain it. In 1947 a newly appointed Governor Macpherson was told he was "inheriting more ill-will, distrust and suspicion" than any present colonial governor, but he was still welcomed to WASU for a "frank exchange of views."[27]

Conditions in 1947 provoked heated disputes despite basic consensus on the need for colonial development. But more enduring divisions also separated British and colonial critics, notably a certain paternalism and self-righteousness not only among die-hard imperialists but also among the advocates of colonial reform. Perham's response to Awolowo's request for a foreword to his *Path to Nigerian Freedom* is revealing. She wrote Awolowo that he seemed "unhistorical and unjust" in many passages, especially regarding the efforts of many colonial servants, and reminded him that the future health of Nigeria required "men of your station being not 70% or 85% but 100% reasonable and clear-sighted." Her foreword, directed at a British audience, hoped British sincerity and service could overcome the nationalists' "highly sensitive and emotional state of mind," which obstructed their cooperation with British efforts. Walter Miller, a missionary with many years' experience in northern Nigeria and vocal critic of British actions, still insisted that Africa will be "renewed only through us." Hinden could see why African nationalists seemed ungrateful about colonial development plans. At the same time, she also betrayed the assumption of superiority that nationalists reviled. The vehement protest against postwar colonial policy was, in the end, "all for one simple reason." The African, she observed, "can no longer tolerate our imperialist attitude, even though it is no longer the imperialism of exploitation, but the imperialism of a benevolent, paternal trustee. . . . While we bring him beer and skittles, and prove by statistics that our generosity is unprecedented, he is thinking only of his independence."[28]

Not without cause, Nigerians asserted their proper place with aggressive pride. Ojike insisted that "Nigerians write about their own towns and country, not leaving this basic task to aliens who always see us as inferior." Adelabu declared that since Nigerians had "donned the Toga of Maturity," only they could write their new constitution. "Any hints from anywhere, beyond the confines of our country, that anyone dares to imagine that he is concerned with our own internal problems and domestic affairs, we shall regard as an unwarranted attack on our national dignity, which precludes our subjugation or owing any allegiance to any other Power on the surface of the globe."[29] Further, with the approach of self-government, West Africans were better placed to assert their intellectual independence. While the British had once been experts in colonial administration, now Nigerians could emerge as fellow experts in the pages of *African Affairs* or as private critics of even Fabian writers. Where once Nigerians had sought Fabians' insights into imperial politics, now Fabians sought out insiders to explain Nigerian current affairs. Nigerians also drew on other sources to reduce the importance of metropolitan contacts, such as the Nigeria Society, the growing government bureaucracy, and official tours of wider Europe and the Commonwealth. The Nigerian intelligentsia were claiming the status of experts in their own home.

In America, Nigerians moved away from the interwar pursuit of diasporan Pan-Africanism to act as generic African or specifically Nigerian spokespeople to both black and white America. New York was the center of much activity, notably by three members of the 1938 student exodus: Ojike, K. O. Mbadiwe, and A. A. Nwafor Orizu. The African Students Association established in 1941 and Mbadiwe's African Academy of Arts and Research established in 1943 were based there, producing various sporadic publications on African culture and affairs, such as the academy's short-lived *Africa: Today and Tomorrow*. But Nigerian students were more widely dispersed than in Britain. The 123 listed in a 1949 study were on fifty different campuses, from California to Florida. Thus while a network did link at least some African students, they were frequently on their own in American society. Nigerian students had extensive contacts within African-American communities, held by a shared (if different) interest in African affairs. Ojike became acquainted with some middle-class African Americans in the northern United States. Many students, from Azikiwe on, wrote for African-American and other newspapers. They kept current on wider debates within the black world, debates that sometimes involved British contributors. As in Britain, African students in America also established dialogue with the small group of whites interested in African and colonial affairs. This circle provided important and often prominent contacts. Ojike followed both Ita and Azikiwe in seeking help from the Phelps-Stokes Foundation. More academic and political contacts also developed. As part of an International Student Assembly in 1942, Ojike met President and Mrs. Roosevelt. Eleanor Roosevelt, along with such other notable Americans as Pearl S. Buck and Wendell Willkie, supported African endeavors in speaking tours, publications, and festivals. African students felt a pressing need to explain Africa to an American audience which remained woefully misinformed. Ojike, who claims to have made over 1,000 public lectures on Nigerian and African affairs, distinguished himself in a role many assumed as "unofficial ambassadors" to all America. Four Nigerian students—Ojike, Mbadiwe, Orizu, and Nwanko Chukwuemeka—published six books in America between them from 1942 to 1951.[30] In short, the Nigerian students in America had within ready reach a wide range of contacts and ideas, with whites and blacks, in which specific Pan-African ties played an increasingly minor role.

Both in America and Britain postwar students assumed their roles as ambassadors and experts while interwar hopes of black unity faded. The Britain-based West African Society rekindled Pan–West African themes from the 1930s, but its *Africana* magazine survived only three issues, in 1948 and 1949. The stronger trend was for West African organizations to divide into territorial organizations and for these to fracture as domestic forces invaded the former centers of Pan-Africanism. The LCP disappeared in 1947. WASU began to lose its dominant place and became associated with an important minority of more radical students. Garigue reported over 1,000 West African students in Britain in 1951, but only 300 WASU members. In 1948 the Nigerian Union of Great Britain and Ireland was revived from the precursors of WASU. An Ibo Student Union was formed in 1944 at Cambridge, followed by the original branch of the Yoruba Egbe Omu Oduduwa in London in 1945 and a countergroup, the Yoruba Federal Union, in 1948. In America the specifically Nigerian Union of Students formed in 1949 gradually succumbed to ethnic politics.

The interwar period had been dominated by an intelligentsia connected to the Lagos elite and the alliance between the "youth" intelligentsia and cocoa entrepreneurs. In the postwar era voices left in the background earlier and groups just defining their interests in the context of decolonization complicated this simplicity. Distributed in fluid but distinguishable strata and crosscut by a multiplicity of other loyalties and linkages, they no longer fit any easily summarized pattern. Pan-African ambitions, not untroubled before the war, moved from the diaspora to the continent but no longer framed the vision of Nigerians abroad as they once had. Instead, segments grouped by various criteria—as insiders, ethnic minorities, or radicals—now vied for a place on the national stage. This may well have been an advance on the more focused agendas of NCBWA or NYM campaigns, as it generated debates more representative of Nigeria's complexity. It also, however, introduced competition and disorientation at a time when momentous decisions about the future had to be made. Whatever the long-term results, the short term had all the confusion one might expect when established patterns are frayed by the forces of social and ideational change.

## "New Ideas Are Stirring," 1940-1943

Just as this social fragmentation emerged over time, so too did intellectual life move gradually toward its late colonial confusions. During the war and in its immediate aftermath, the stratification within the educated community remained largely hidden behind a wave of protest which moved all levels of the intelligentsia in a common direction. Indeed, through a series of rapid and sharp changes in the 1940s, the colonial intelligentsia brilliantly exhibited their enduring ability to adapt Atlantic discourse. As the consensus in British thinking shifted leftward—on both the domestic and imperial fronts—toward a new vision of the future, Nigerians borrowed both energy and suggestions from it to push their own agenda of political reform and economic development. Pan-African forums remained important for restating the Black Atlantic case for recognition as equals, but the innovations derived from new possibilities opened by the metropole. This happened in two stages. Until about 1943, the Nigerian intelligentsia marched hopefully in step, expanding and elaborating upon promised changes. From the later war years to the late 1940s, frustrated by promises left unfulfilled, they adopted a more radical, often socialist rhetoric. For most this was a phase; for a minority it inaugurated a more consistently radical strand of criticism. After the demands of this era were addressed, the unfolding social and intellectual confusion surfaced dramatically in the 1950s, all the more unsettling for having spawned truly radical critics.

Wartime policy changes had been foreshadowed during the 1930s and had received avid notice among the youth intelligentsia. By the late 1930s the British colonial vision was in flux as changing ideas about race combined with growing skepticism that colonial societies were, in fact, becoming more ordered, healthy, or productive. Observers began to see that indirect rule could contain neither rapid social change nor, more disturbingly, unrest. New departures suggested by Fabian colonial critics as well as academics like Perham, W. M. Macmillan, and Reginald Coupland gained adherents within official circles on the eve of the war. Lord Hailey's 1938 survey of the African situation, commissioned by the Colonial Office, soon displaced Lugard's *Dual Mandate* as the fount of colonial policy. Under the pressures of war, the new policies acquired a wide following and took firm form in the 1940 and 1945 Colonial Development and Welfare Acts and the Nigerian Ten-Year Development Plan adopted in 1946. Opinions ranged within a spectrum. The cautious Hailey still suspected colonial peoples needed guidance; Leonard Barnes called from the left for them to rise up on their own behalf. Both, however, now advocated change instead of preservation, and British "partnership" instead of trusteeship. The major emphasis was now on economic and social de-

146

velopment, to be initiated through injections of foreign capital and expertise. Education was to be revamped for developmental needs and extended to the university level. Government planning was to ensure efficiency and speed. The political future was less clearly described, but wartime propaganda designed to inspire loyalty and sacrifice armed Nigerians with a case against colonial rule which the British were hard put to answer. From America such notable figures as Wendell Willkie voiced criticisms of empire for all to hear; the 1941 Atlantic Charter seemed to certify colonial rights to self-determination. By 1943 the British secretary of state for the colonies declared that the British intended "as soon as practicable to develop self-government" in the colonies. Hailey succinctly summed up the new standards of colonial government by pointing out that henceforth the British "shall ask ourselves if in our dealings with the Dependencies we are performing the normal functions of a modern state."[31]

The *West African Review* warned policymakers in 1942 that "the British West Africa of 1939 is dead and a new one is being born. . . . Sleep will not again come to those eyes—no matter how skilfull the nursing." The Nigerian intelligentsia were fully awake to the new possibilities at hand. Davies welcomed Macmillan's *Warning from the West Indies* in 1940 as part of a "new order." Henry Carr recognized from the 1940 Colonial Development Act "that new ideas are stirring in England, that day by day these new ideas gain power and that almost everyone of them is the friend of His Majesty's black subjects and not their enemy." From the start of the war, Nigerian writers also did their best to keep the British restless. Even before the Atlantic Charter, Allied calls to join the fight for democracy provided ample ammunition. One writer dubbed the war at its outbreak a fight for "Liberty, Freedom [and] Enfranchisement."[32] In 1943 the West African Press Delegation to England, WASU in London, and the NYM in Lagos all demanded that the crown colony system be replaced by more democratic government and a clear timetable be established for the realization of self-government. In more extended works of the period by Udoma, Awolowo, Orizu, Ojike, Mbadiwe, and Azikiwe, Nigerian writers made a more sustained and systematic case for their right to self-government. Udoma and Awolowo in Britain tended toward a more conciliatory and conservative position than did Mbadiwe, Ojike, and Orizu in America, but their arguments shared common elements.

Well-established Black Atlantic claims about Africa's glorious culture and history were cited as proof of African ability. Self-government was asserted as a precondition of further progress and as the only way to prevent Africa from becoming an insoluble problem of postwar international relations. The arguments were not always consistent. Restoration of precolonial sovereignty was demanded as a right, overlooking that sovereignty would now return to Africans situated in quite different polities. The Atlantic slave trade and colonial rule were censured as the causes of African weakness, while recent accomplishments were noted as proof that colonial rule had sufficiently prepared African for independence. But definite action was demanded and even mapped out. Azikiwe sketched a two-stage, fifteen-year plan in 1943; Ojike followed a few years later with a ten-year plan. J. G. Campbell dated himself by labeling impatient demands for self-government "childish"; the deaths of Campbell, Macaulay, and Carr during the mid-1940s marked the passing from a generation which had accepted imperial rule as a necessary evil to one which demanded imminent sovereignty.[33] After the 1950 constitutional conference, if not before, events rendered arguments for self-government superfluous.

The new road to colonial development and welfare provided equally effective material for a new Nigerian economic prescription. In the first war years the prewar preoccupation with foreign monopolies was augmented by suggestions for limited state action. But Nigerian commentary soon incorporated the new ideas. In 1942, for example, some Western Region chiefs requested imperial development funds to promote industries within their Native Administrations. By 1943 such tentative suggestions were surpassed by much more comprehensive appeals for state initiatives, economic planning, industrialization, and nationalization. The NYM, in a memorandum to the visiting secretary of state, assigned the government the following onerous tasks: "guarantee for the African workers a reasonable standard of living"; fund "free education"; "enable the peasant population to derive maximum benefit from the land"; and plan to ensure free medical service to all Nigerians within five years.[34] A. B. Olumayiwa's suggestions "towards post war economic reconstruction" described more specific mechanisms the state might apply to similar ends. Drawing especially on Fabian and Labour critics, Azikiwe insisted that Nigeria needed a Beveridge Plan far more than

England did; his *Economic Reconstruction of Nigeria* recommended increased spending of tax revenues and imperial grants on education and other social services. A solely agricultural Nigeria, Awolowo insisted, was as vulnerable to tumbling as a one-legged man. Suggestions remained centered on the minor manufacturing industries familiar from the 1930s, but these were now clearly seen as the first step toward a fully diversified modern economy. As Ojike asked, "If the people do not industrialize, if they do not produce modern goods within their country, if all money earned from the soil is spent outside Africa, just how can people's standard of living rise?" Many authors cited the arguments for nationalization of important industries and public services being made for Britain or, more often, referred to Rita Hinden's *Plan for Africa* (which K. A. Abayomi broadcast on the Lagos Rediffusion Service in 1942). Soyemi Coker, toward the left end of the spectrum as vice president of the Trades Union Congress, wanted this nationalization "to save the workers of this country from the yoke of capitalists and exploiters." Most, however, like the NYM, proposed more limited lists, for the "benefit and enjoyment" of all citizens. Azikiwe looked forward to "a better planned society which should be devoid of the profit motive" and asserted that the "philosophy of rugged individualism must give way to that of a planned economy based on mutual aid."[35]

### "Atlantic Chatter" and Radical Rhetoric, 1943-1948

Imperial promises and programs had expanded the realm of the possible by 1943 beyond familiar horizons. Programs only hinted at by both British critics and the NYM in the 1930s were now policy. Returning from England with the West African Press Delegation in 1943, Azikiwe counseled consultation and cooperation between government and governed, confident "that our problems are receiving meticulous study and observation in England." "The age of economic imperialism," he thought, "appears to be on the wane." But these rosy vistas soon dissolved in the face of British caution about headlong political change, imperial prerogatives, and wartime realities. Economic hardships felt acutely late in the war—such as inflation, price controls, and shipping restrictions—and postwar problems of low wages and returning soldiers' treatment were seen by some as deliberate European tactics to weaken Africans, not develop them. The limited concessions in Governor Richards's constitution came as an "imperialist bombshell." Ordinances introduced to establish powers deemed necessary for colonial development plans were received with protest, largely it seems because they empowered a government still beyond Nigerian control. The Labour Party, so sympathetic to colonial demands during the war, disappointed many with its conduct in government after 1945. The dollar crisis of 1947 created deeper doubts, as the British government blatantly used colonial resources for metropolitan needs. It seemed, as Ejimofor recalled a few years later, that the British had "disclaimed their pledge and converted the Atlantic Charter to the Atlantic Chatter."[36] Azikiwe's sense of having an imperial audience became a sense of colonial alienation, a moment captured in Lasekan's "The Critical Observer" (fig. 3).

3. Akinola Lasekan, "The Critical Observer." (From *Zik of Africa* [Lagos: Zik's Press, 1947], p. 8)

This disillusion generated an atmosphere of radicalism in Nigeria and abroad. The Pan-African Congress in Manchester in 1945 pressed the case for colonial freedom. The West African National Secretariat formed with more adamant demands for self-government, as WASU itself became more radical. In America, Nigerian students led by Ojike and Mbadiwe allied with more radical groups, notably the Council on African Affairs, and presented their case to the fledgling United Nations. In Nigeria the radical phase was marked by many protests of economic conditions, notably the 1945 General Strike. The NCNC launched a colonywide protest campaign against the new constitution and the "Obnoxious Ordinances." Azikiwe toyed with radical alliances and insinuated ominously in 1948 that "in truth, my faith in Great Britain has waned and I am compelled to admit openly my belief that freedom for Nigeria and the Cameroons can no longer be expected to descend to us easily without tremendous sacrifice." British action from 1948 eased tensions, but they lingered under the surface. Fronts of nationalist unity were formed against instances of imperial brutality, notably the shooting of workers at Enugu in 1949.[37]

In this context demands from within Nigeria for self-government became blunt. At the same time, attacks on colonial development policies became more cynical and damning. Wartime policies were seen as favoring the established firms at the expense of African traders. A Lagos merchant, for example, wrote from personal experience about "the transparent determination of the Government of Nigeria to prevent all classes of African from carrying on overseas trade of any kind in fair competition with European firms." Ransome-Kuti, tapping an old vein of resentment, likened the plan for colonial development and welfare to the cocoa pool, draining away Nigeria's wealth. "Obiahwu" noted caustically that the colonial welfare scheme simply revealed that the British finally had found some value in their colonies. "Now that she is a debtor-nation casting about for means of economic recovery, she suddenly 'discovers' Africa as the long-lost Aladdin's lamp, and rubs her eyes in wonder for all to see. But it is consummately poor acting, most unexpected for the land of Shakespeare." Ayo Rosiji feared that the Colonial Development Corporation would only tighten the grip of "British capitalists" and doom the colonies to the "stranglehold" of "foreign control."[38]

The consensus over new visions of development was broken by more than nationalist anger at apparent policy reversals or a passionate collision between paternalism and pride. The British approached the problem of African development from a perspective rooted in the civilizing mission tradition which the Nigerians did not share. Colonial reformers like Macmillan admitted that imperial rule had not cured scarcity in Africa but insisted that "the outstanding fact about the colonies—their poverty—is absolute, not Marxist (induced) poverty; it is natural—and the dominant fact is that there is and has been all too little to 'exploit.'" In the similar vision of Hancock, "with rare exceptions, the ideas and techniques of economic progress were never a living force in African life until the restless and innovating European brought them in." Africa required, thus, outside help. In many cases, Hinden made clear, "the act of [imperial] withdrawal would not, of itself, open the gateways to prosperity. On the other hand . . . if the imperial powers remained, at least for a time, and instead of exploiting these lands, acted as trustees to develop and enrich them for the sake of their own people, then the crushing problems of poverty and backwardness might indeed be overcome." The reformers' primary mission, then, was to alleviate poverty, not advance political participation. As Creech Jones explained the Labour Party's colonial policy, "It is marked . . . by the emphasis on social and economic progress as a condition of political advance. Political progress must be supported by the establishment of sound social services, such as health and education; and in turn these social services require a sound economic basis to maintain them. It is only through such planned and balanced development that political democracy in the colonial territories can take root in a sound economy and adequate social standards, and be worked by people with knowledge and responsibility."[39]

The Nigerian intelligentsia held an opposite view, starting from the Black Atlantic premise that Africa was not initially and fundamentally backward. They might have been quite prepared to admit that Africa lagged behind the world in many respects, and that it was plagued by many social evils, but it was imperialism that above all had inhibited Africa's ability to prosper. As Orizu pointed out, "One must try to distinguish between the simple life of the African as a cultural type, and the poverty imported into Africa by European imperialism as a new

152

development." The "European powers," Mbadiwe maintained, "have set back our progress thousands of years. They have thrown us in the most terrible confusion ever to be recorded in history." The assertion of African vitality was rooted, in part, in the intelligentsia's direct knowledge of African life, which British observers could not easily obtain from the outside. It followed that the Nigerians' primary task was not advancing social welfare within a colonial framework but obtaining control over their own affairs. As Ojike made clear, "The claim of the British is that they want to help us to modernise our countries; but the trouble is that the very presence of the British or any other white men in Nigeria or Africa as political advisors retards the pace of progress which the people have the ability to pursue according to their own standards, under their own leaders, if free from imperialistic controls." The *Labour Champion* simply rejected the "red herring" that economic development must precede political advance.[40] This divergence lay behind the disagreement between the NCNC and the Fabians over the "Obnoxious Ordinances" associated with the 1946 Nigerian Development Plan. The Fabians supported the idea of creating state ownership of Nigerian mineral resources; what was good socialist policy in Britain was good socialist policy in Nigeria. To the Fabians, theirs was "a struggle for the securing of social justice—of which freedom is an essential part—in the Colonies." But as Hinden also perceived, Nigerians could not be convinced that the British Empire, "even when run by socialists, is anything but the same old wolf flaunting a new lambskin."[41] It is not clear that political reform advanced because the Nigerians convinced the British of their case; it is clear that their insistence on political change first was deeply rooted in a divergent view of Africa's needs. In other circumstances the inauguration of planned development might have occasioned impassioned and intricate discussions over the best mixture of state and individual control. In this context all that resulted was confrontation, as nationalist pride stood firm against imperial conceit. The tide of nationalism pushed back the forces of imperialism, but without fully addressing the complexities of the political and social transformations that Nigerians faced. The Nigerian intelligentsia had a long history of contemplating social questions, but the context of decolonization submerged much of this legacy and led them into independence with an agenda for action marked more by hubris than the humility their daunting tasks called for. This set the stage for simplified solutions in the 1950s, once this point of conflict was dissolved by British concessions.

In this mood, Azikiwe proposed a Socialist Party of Nigeria; some young Nigerians founded a National Socialist Party in 1945. Nigerian writers began to identify themselves as socialists, introducing the slogans common to virtually all nationalist economic programs in the 1950s. The curious logic of this adoption can be traced through the battle of "Nationalism *vs* Capitalism" that the NCNC conducted on its 1946 national tour. Foreign firms remained the principal threat to the economic ambitions of the Nigerian medial classes.[42] But the nationalism of "Unity, Self-Help and Co-operation" had never borne much fruit, and the scale of Nigerian entrepreneurs was now more than ever dwarfed by the combined power of foreign firms and an interventionist state. Socialist rhetoric—made accessible and acceptable by the rise of the Labour Party and Britain's alliance with the Soviet Union—came to the rescue. If capitalism was understood as foreign, then national interests would naturally be served by socialist ideals.

It is clear that the socialist rhetoric of the late 1940s did not involve abandoning the medial classes' long-standing search for economic security. The interests of workers were defended, but usually in the context of the nation's welfare, not as a distinct group. On the other hand, the *Pilot* attacked the administration especially for stifling African initiative and demanded that development funds provide more help for small African businesses. NCNC leaders criticized the Nigerian railway partly for not being a model employer but also because no Nigerians held directorships in it, and they rejected the "Obnoxious Ordinances" because there was no "African bourgeoisie" in place to benefit from the development schemes they facilitated.[43] For many, then, the radical moment was more rhetorical than real. However, it did begin the transition from the "Unity, Self-Help and Co-operation" ideals of the 1930s to the "Nigerian socialism" slogans of the 1950s. Both programs shared the ambition to remedy the economic weaknesses of the middle classes in the colonial economy. But the experience of the 1940s served to reveal and entrench the new idea of using the state in this pursuit. Identifying nationalism with socialism may have flowed from circumstance more than analysis, but it did begin to define a program aptly suited to the medial classes' longtime pursuit of economic security in the decade of decolonization.

But this same moment also marks the beginning of a more genuine radical tendency in Nigeria, more consistently critical of mainstream thinking, often expressing more durable solidarity with workers and the underclasses. The labor movement, with the 1945 General Strike, raised leaders like Michael Imoudu to national prominence. In the press the short-lived *Nigerian Worker* of 1943 was followed in 1950 by the *Labour Champion,* a socialist paper owned by the Amalgamated Union of United Africa Company African employees. The most dramatic indicator was the Zikist movement, formed in 1946. The Zikists took their label from Azikiwe's popular nickname and their inspiration from his 1937 *Renascent Africa,* reworked in Orizu's 1944 *Without Bitterness.* The *African Echo* proclaimed their message from 1948 to 1950, followed briefly by the Port Harcourt *People* in 1950. Leaders included Kola Balogun, M. C. K. Ajuluchukwu, Abiodun Aloba, Mokwugo Okoye, Osita Agwuna, and Nduka Eze. The Zikists were not incisive analysts as much as they were impatient for change and committed to the ideal of self-government. They revived and extended the youth ethic of the 1930s, calling not only for independence but also for social rebirth and revolution, sometimes with more urgency than clarity of thought. Indeed, their radicalism was more apparent than any consistent left-wing position. They proclaimed their goal to be a "Socialist Republic" and wanted Nigeria to "be ruled according to the wishes of the majority." But Zikism was also presented not as "a creed but an attitude of mind, a synthetic cause aiming at the harmonization of the diverse ways of life in the world," open to those of any class or philosophical disposition. Nonetheless, the tension between their ideals and the realities of the late 1940s inspired extreme action. Judging that they could "no longer hope to have reason where, it is evident, respect for reason does not exist," the Zikists laid plans in 1948 to "wage war" through civil disobedience and attacks on foreign and government property.[44] This led to government banning in 1950 and the dissipation of the movement within a few years. Its legacy, however, was carried on.

The social and intellectual roots of this radical strand deserve brief comment. Radical ideas did not belong exclusively to any of the groups of intelligentsia I have sketched. American-educated Nigerians have been seen as a more radical group than their British-educated peers, because of the more blatant racism and anti-imperial attitudes encountered in America.[45] But the militancy of some American alumni such as Azikiwe, Ojike, and Orizu is balanced by the moderation of others, such as Okechukwu Ikejiani, a medical doctor, and I. U. Akpabio, an educator. Racism and anti-imperialism were not absent from Britain, which also produced radicals such as Chike Obi. In any case, most Zikists were not (or not yet) educated in America. Radicals of the 1940s included people from the labor movement, the periphery of the educated community, and those qualified for the core group, such as the lawyer Amanke Okafor. However, it seems the bulk of the radical movement derived from the middle and outer groups. Iweriebor's study shows that the Zikist leaders were emergent journalists, typically with at least a grammar-school education. The membership included the peers of these men, as well as thousands with less education, wealth, and status: labor leaders, teachers, commercial and government agents, primary- and grammar-school students, ex-servicemen, and petty traders. Early radical critics thus had their broadest base among groups of outsiders beginning to recognize the privileged insiders in the new order. This set the pattern for the 1950s, when writers in the second and third circles of the intelligentsia made many of the most trenchant critiques.

### "On a Platter of Gold," 1948–1955

Fearful by 1947 that Azikiwe and others might choose the radical path, the British proposed an early constitutional review and other measures to win over potential moderates, while suppressing extremists. These changes successfully evoked a new mood of cooperation among the intelligentsia, even if they did not eliminate all points of conflict. The *Nigerian Eastern Mail* welcomed Governor Macpherson in 1948 as the "harbinger of a new political era . . . from a new Colonial Office—the Colonial Office of rebirth, the Colonial Office that has revolted against the old ways of leopards and wolves, of the strong devouring the weak." *The People*, disowning its Zikist past three years later, argued that the new constitution was a sure step toward freedom, and that the time for radical nationalism had passed. "In a nut shell, through evolution even the most vocal nationalist would agree with me that we are nearing freedom which violence had made more difficult." By the 1953 Constitutional Conference, Ogunsheye admitted that "the issue of whether self-government will come or not is a dead one. It will come, but the pertinent questions are: what kind of self-government? And self-government for whom?" Azikiwe now declared that Britain had awarded freedom on a "platter of gold."[46] This late colonial contentment, especially among the core intelligentsia, marked a striking break with the preceding years of vehement anti-imperialism. The promise of imminent economic and political power now drew the intelligentsia more closely and uncritically toward a seductive new discourse on democracy, development, and nation building provided not only by Fabians but in British policy and the United Nations.

This shift involved on one side a move away from notions of racial identity and solidarity that had long influenced Nigerian thought. Traditions rooted in the Black Atlantic had little to offer when decolonization offered so much. The very idea of racial community was often dismissed. The intelligentsia now saw themselves primarily as Nigerians rather than as Africans, or even West Africans. Occasional references to race leadership implied that Nigeria would lead other black nations, not that race would supersede nation. Even WASU relaxed its Pan-African posture. In 1927 Solanke had lectured, typically enough, on "Africa, Yesterday and Today, from the Negro's Point of View." By 1948 WASU discussions were dominated by talks on the administration, economies, and constitutions of individual West African territories.[47] The early insistence that Africa was not inherently benighted was not withdrawn, but the issue was now largely forgotten as the British accepted that political change had to accompany social development. Instead of thinking about African difference, the intelligentsia now sought to show how the new principles of development applied to them.

Universal models of the past and future replaced ones based on racial peculiarities. K. O. Dike, an early professional historian, appealed for new approaches that would integrate Africa in global history and dismantle racist models. An amateur historian expressed a similar sentiment: "Basically, man is man under any age, under any climatic conditions, under any colour or race. He has the same basic characteristics." Orizu insisted that "the trend of social change in modern Nigeria is the same as in other societies which developed from agricultural, rural, and localized life into industrial, urbanized, and cosmopolitan nations." Elias's study of Nigerian law argued similarly that all legal systems were essentially the same, therefore African law was likely to evolve in much the same way as had English common law. Marxist ideas of universal stages of history—more explicit among the core intelligentsia, less so among more marginal figures—were sometimes employed to locate Nigerian events within universal processes. Optimism abounded that Nigeria would become a modern industrial power. Akinsuroju was adamant on this: "It is evolution, and evolution is a law of nature. It has to occur to a people at one time or the other." African customs were not to be wholly discarded, but the sights of the intelligentsia were firmly set on attaining modern institutions rather than on preserving African traditions. According to Epelle, *The Promise of Nigeria* was that chiefly rule would quickly give way to parliamentary government, universities, and airlines. The absorption with novelty was at times overwhelming. Ita, for example, insisted that the African "needs the world's new inspiration, new energies, new tools of production. He needs a new vision of himself in the context of the new world situation. . . . He must have the new knowledge and he must use it and the new energies and his own resources to build the new world community."[48]

The other dynamic in this shift was a broadening agreement with the plans elaborated under the decolonization scheme. Although during the radical phase Governors Richards and Macpherson had described some of their extreme opponents as mentally unbalanced, others had detected an underlying consensus which now became more evident. A Colonial Office official dealing with Solanke during the war recognized "that in his own way he is fighting for exactly what we want him to have, if only we spoke the same way of reasoning." Despite fears of Azikiwe's radical potential after the war, FCB secretary Hinden told the Nigerian colonial secretary in 1949 that she doubted if there were really "any basic differences between him and the rest of us." As the mood eased, the common ground of colonial subjects and reformers resurfaced. Marjorie Nicholson of the FCB told Ita in 1950 that his ideas were clearly "running along the same lines as ours." The proposals in J. O. Ajibola's 1949 *Economic Development of*

*West Africa* relied heavily on works by Fabians as well as Perham. Even Nigerian and expatriate criticism of colonial policy often harmonized, as when Ita warmly proclaimed that the spirit of Walter Miller's observations made him "as much 'Native' as any Nigerian can be 'Native.'"[49] The development plan adopted by the Nigerian Federal Government in 1955 was little changed from proposals offered by World Bank experts. Chief Adebo, head of the Western Region civil service at Independence, recalls a workplace atmosphere consonant with the findings of Falola's detailed study of Nigerian development planning: the emergent government elite accepted the experts' essential elements of development, despite disagreements on particulars. Having assumed the role of speaking for Nigeria, they now described for it a future defined by universal models of economic modernization.

This transition from the radical phase to the broad acceptance of imperial development plans did more than simply confuse long-standing Nigerian patterns of inquiry by overlaying imported designs. It also forced a reorientation in Nigerian approaches to enduring questions, notably the task of defining, as Arikpo put it, "who are the Nigerians?" The nineteenth-century intelligentsia had answered by contrasting themselves as blacks against whites. In the early twentieth century, the intelligentsia gradually had narrowed their horizons, from the African diaspora to Africa to West Africa, arriving finally at the boundaries of Nigeria. But they still had defined themselves against the wider world. Specific Nigerian virtues had been used to defend Africans in general against the claims of European imperialism. Now, as the idea of empire retreated, so too did the need to define Nigeria against it. Ita captured the new context: "Hitherto, we have been held together like sand in a box in an artificial bond by the force of an alien imperialism. It is now imperative that we should find effective cementing forces to bind us together into one organic entity called a nation."[50] The problem now was not only to defend the nation against external threats, nor only to define it against external standards, but also to find in its internal dynamics and cultures the substance of the Nigerian national identity.

This need to understand Nigeria from the opposite direction had roots in factors more diffuse than the need to frame a constitution. Since the youth era the intelligentsia had been dominated by indigenes rather than recruits from the diaspora and therefore were more deeply rooted in local identities than earlier generations had been. More important, the agenda of domestic politics forced local identities to the fore. The intelligentsia had always exhibited loyalties to particular polities and groups within Nigeria, evident in their nineteenth-century sectional associations and later in their progress unions. But as the intelligentsia sought to protect and advance local and regional interests in the evolving federal constitutional structure, these interests came to be viewed as the material that not only would build the nation but also needed protection in the new edifice. Mbanefo already had sensed in the 1930s that "men from opposite ends of the country must be made to realize that there is a bond of national interest holding them together." By the late 1950s it was even clearer to Oluwasanmi at UCI that Nigeria was a nation to be forged from "a conglomeration of small and insignificant tribal societies," by building contacts and national institutions across cultural boundaries within the country. The Dynamic Party's memorandum on the 1956 constitutional review carefully defined local identities as component units in the Nigerian administrative structure. Attempts were made to study the major cultural groups in the context of their shared nationhood. To bolster this quest, efforts were made to identify the natural and historical forces that were forging Nigerians into a nation. Arikpo implied that a nation-state was the inevitable and perhaps ultimate stage of Nigeria's development. Pulled together by the Niger and Benue Rivers, sealed off by the coastal forest and northern desert, the nation had been formed by successive waves of migrants who had since mixed. "From all these accounts there is one inevitable conclusion, namely that Nigeria is not an accident. It is not an artificial creation nor an arbitrary block of land chipped off the surface of tropical Africa. On the contrary in Nigeria we are dealing with a cultural melting-pot where cultural influences from all directions have met to produce a most virile cultural complex." Oluwasanmi was more inclined to stress the significance of human agency—especially British intervention—in creating the conditions in which a "common nationality could develop." Awolowo, rather exceptionally, asserted in 1945 that "there is no such thing as a Nigerian nation," reducing the term *Nigerian* to "merely a distinctive appellation to distinguish those who live within the boundaries of Nigeria from those who do not."[51] But even he implicitly accepted the need to make something of this yet inchoate collection of cultures. Professional historians after 1960 would inherit from these amateurs the search for the inner qualities of the Nigerian nation.

In 1953 Ogunsheye judged that of all the problems facing Nigerians, "perhaps none is more urgent than that of finding an appropriate elastic political and constitutional frame-work in which the various nationalities and tribes can live and work with the minimum of friction."[52] Writing tracts on these questions became a minor industry for all levels of the intelligentsia, driven by the almost continuous series of constitutional reviews. But this shift in their established perspective made this urgent task more confusing and challenging than it already was and left the intelligentsia scrambling for means to make sense of their urgent two-directional task: defining Nigeria against the world while finding its inner connections. These publications amply reveal an intelligentsia obliged to pick up the tools of constitution mongering provided by their departing British rulers and wield these hastily imported implements as if they fit all circumstances, in the contemporary determination to follow universal patterns. Black Atlantic thought, concerned less with nation building than with locating Africa within European discourse, seemed largely irrelevant. Certainly the nation-building project required deeper knowledge of Nigeria's many cultures; it might also have benefited from a more critical perspective on solutions offered by British policies. What was lost here was the legacy of exploring how Nigeria might diverge from putative universal patterns, of asking how British constitutional models might not fit. Blyden's notion of racial difference was perhaps well forgotten, but attention to historical difference and the search for elements of particularly Nigerian or African politics were not.

However, if Black Atlantic perspectives clouded over, another long-standing tradition perdured: the ability of the colonial intelligentsia to adapt the general discourse about Africa to serve their own search for security in the colonial order. This is again most evident in the economic prescription of the core intelligentsia. At one level it reveals a departure from the pragmatic attempts of the 1930s to match Nigerian entrepreneurs' potential with a program. But seen more fundamentally and in historical context, it signifies the long-desired achievement (at least for some) of economic security, paralleling the attainment of self-government. Monopolies retained their scapegoat status into the

1950s. Chukwuemeka described the UAC in 1950 as a threat "whose octopus claws stretch far out into every remote corner in Africa," as Azikiwe had feared monopolies' "octopus grip" in 1943, and Robert Cole had dreaded their spreading tentacles in 1933. The potential of state support had been sensed with the birth of the colonial development and welfare scheme and advanced under the socialist rhetoric of the mid-1940s. The problem, however, was that the colonial state under British control could not be trusted. Ogunsheye made a popular observation in 1951: "No colonial government can call forth the necessary enthusiasm to sacrifice for development and that for two reasons. Not only does it not enjoy the necessary confidence but the colonial ruling group is so laden with economic and social privileges that it cannot set that example of self-sacrifice and self-denial." Closer to the heart of the medial classes' concerns, Chukwuemeka feared that "it is not the intention of the British Colonial government to pursue an economic policy that will accelerate the development of an independent African middle class, and perhaps bring about the early cessation of political domination." Indeed, under colonial control rapid development might even be harmful. Capital investment from foreign sources, for example, would only tighten the hold of foreign firms at the expense of Nigerian entrepreneurs. Awolowo succinctly summed up the middle classes' fear: "The moment you allow these foreign investors to invest in the various industries, you are shutting the door to Nigerians, and you are going to reduce the people of this country perpetually to Clerks, Sub-Managers, Semi-Directors and what-nots to serve under foreign investors."[53]

As long as the state remained beyond their control, Nigerians hesitated to forsake the ethic of self-help promulgated before the war. It seemed wiser to advance slowly with capital squeezed from the limited Nigerian economy than to strengthen foreign economic hegemony. Ojike's "Economic Philosophy," reminiscent of the Youth Movement's Million Shilling Fund, advocated "investing our own capitals together to run big business that can rival the alien combines." Industrialization schemes focused cautiously on small-scale African enterprise; proposals were made to break the UAC's grip through direct trade with America. These suggestions echoed Tete-Ansa's calls from the 1930s, with the significant and fitting change that these were no longer Pan-African ventures but were directed at tapping the economic potential of America in general. However, when the British finally retreated from their position that economic and social development was a prerequisite for political progress, Nigerian views advanced. Economic ideas were reformulated around the application of state power, now wielded by Nigerians through such agencies as regional development corporations. The Action Group made plans to use its new authority "to arrest the tendency of our industrial activities being concentrated in the hand of foreigners, and, in the long run, to ensure that all major industrial activities are either vested in the state or in our fellow countrymen, as is now the case in Europe and America."[54] In lieu of an established native entrepreneurial class, the government was to act as "the motor-force of economic development."[55] Education and training for businessmen, financial support, partnerships of Nigerian private and public capital, model farms, tariff barriers, controls over foreign investment, and enforced partnerships of foreign capital with Nigerian private capital were some of the means the state could now use to have Nigerians benefit from foreign investment.

With this power the Nigerian leadership assumed a more cordial attitude toward foreign capital and expatriate experts. Awolowo quite correctly observed in 1955 that "today, we hear and read less of attacks on 'British Imperialism,' than we do of intelligent discussion on the various aspects of our economic problem." Mbadiwe welcomed the new "economic partnership" with Britain in 1956, remarking that he could not have done so five years earlier. The scale of suggested projects now also increased. By 1959 the NCNC was promising to reduce restrictions on foreign investment. The need "to abide by the rules of the game" in the world of business—a theme familiar to later years—now displaced fear of foreign firms. The *Pilot* even made the plea in cartoon form, representing "The Race towards Economic Stability" as a man labeled "Nigerian Business Prestige" struggling on the road to the "World Market," shackled to a huge stone marked "Dishonest Businessmen."[56]

The mainstream economic prescription thus had assumed a new form by 1960. All the main political parties in the 1950s and First Republic invoked the magical power of welfare socialism to win votes. But as observers recognized at the time, this socialism promoted rather than protested the ambitions of Nigerian capitalists. It was not necessarily opposed to foreign capital, as long as Nigerian interests were not threatened. The socialist quality of these programs came largely from the idea of using the state to control foreign and state capital in the interests of developing an indigenous middle class. This prescription worked in the interests of merchants and business entrepreneurs but was also effective for the educated community in general. By virtue of its members' skills, they too stood to benefit from the expanding opportunities—licit and illicit—to be found administering state, parastatal, and publicly supported agencies of development. Armed with this prescription, fortunate segments of the Nigerian medial classes now found the economic security within the colonial trade structure that their predecessors had long sought. This climax, however, should not blind us to the break here from their long tradition of self-help schemes that had attended to enduring limitations of scale and organization among Nigerian entrepreneurs. Old ambitions were being realized through state power but also were being skewed as promises outstripped realities. The NCNC, for example, proclaimed on the eve of independence that "we will, during our tenure of office, guarantee to our people and enforce political freedom, social equality, economic security and religious freedom."[57] Instead, the gap between the haves and have-nots grew wider. The disruptive effects of differential economic success did not go unnoticed; popular criticisms of mainstream thought flourished as independence approached.

## "Not in Peace, but in Pieces," 1955-1960

As the core intelligentsia forged ahead on the road to self-government and self-development through the 1950s, the sense of nationalist victory was increasingly tainted by a sense of unease. As early as 1948 some feared Nigeria was en route to "a Dark Ages in a Modern Time"; by 1957 dread of a looming "political Sodom and Gomorrah" had only grown. Oji foretold "civil and intertribal warfare"; Akak predicted, with more flourish, that Nigeria would reach independence "not in peace, but in pieces."[58] The passionate, sometimes violent rivalries among the principal parties and the anxiety of approaching the empire's end no doubt explain part of this, but these qualms also have profound roots in the social fragmentation and intellectual discontinuity of the postwar years.

Members of the core intelligentsia shared this unease. Even by the later 1940s, many thought Nigerian society had fallen into an "abysmal state of moral bankruptcy." Awolowo in 1945 thought Nigerian political organizations "weak, flabby, colourless, and utterly lacking in honesty and intelligent leadership." Tai Solarin, beginning his long public career as a critic as colonial rule ended, did not see much improvement.[59] As Robert Tignor has argued, accusations of corruption probably outnumbered actual cases, as both British officials and losers of elections used them to challenge officeholders. He overlooks, however, the deep-seated unease from which these postwar commentaries flowed. There was a growing fear that the new leadership lacked the ethical integrity to wield power wisely or unselfishly. Enahoro feared that the educated had become "mere carriers-of-degree" who believed "that while the people swallow the bitter pill, their own aristocratic work should merely consist of scraping off the sugar for private consumption." Ita chastised his peers in similar terms: "Are we not revelling in our own cultural aristocracy? In spite of our early vows that if only God would grant us to receive our university education we would turn over heaven and earth to save our people, have we not come back to exploit and destroy the very people as lawyers, doctors, even ministers and teachers?" A few perceived problems deeper than mere moral weakness. Bishop S. C. Phillips feared poor judgment from a national leadership marked by youth and inexperience. "You would not because of intense hunger pour down your throat a boiling hot soup," he warned, advising that those with the "grey hairs of experience" be consulted to prevent this. Legislator Alvan Ikoku, with insight, judged that the intelligentsia were too closely identified with the civil service to be sufficiently critical. Some more provocative analyses were at least intimated but not far developed. Ita argued that the intelligentsia had to recover from the "poison of the psychology of dependence . . . of dependence on imported ideas . . . and the vain hope that one day after long benevolent tutelage, freedom and salvation will descend from heaven like manna upon lazy parasitic worms." F. O. Onipede, a doctoral student at Columbia University, was especially concerned by how resentment of British rule, coupled with the desire to emulate British achievements, had tended "to impose a painful schizophrenia on the emergent 'moral being' of the new African," while no coherent ideology had formed.[60]

But despite finding these faults with their peers, the core intelligentsia by and large did not question that the most educated were the most qualified to lead, or the basic nationalist premise that sovereignty had to be achieved before social and economic problems could be properly solved. Among the more numerous, less elite intelligentsia, these premises were often challenged. There was a general sense that politics had gone awry. As one observer noted in 1953, the political stage was crowded by many actors. "Some were conservative, some reactionary, some liberal while others were radical. . . . it was difficult to understand who was the real enemy which the parties were fighting against. Personal abuse, fault finding, libelous accusations, resulting in bitterness and rancour went a long way to damage the citadel of Nigeria Political Theatre."[61] Long gone was the "serene atmosphere" of the 1940s, "when the country fought imperialism with one voice under a united leadership." More important, there was a clear sense that the elite leaders were to blame for this. In 1950 *New Africa* deplored the growing number of men who had failed in previous careers, then entered politics "with songs of nationalist romanticism on their lips" in search of personal gain. A columnist in the *Nigerian Statesman* made note of this tendency. "What puzzles me now-a-days is the new turn Nigerian nationalism is taking. When so-called 'nationalists' are out of office, they emit sparks of fiery speeches—even r-r-revolutionary ones. But let them put on the toga virilis of office, they change their attitude, and as long as they have their own three decent meals a day, the world is moving perfectly on its axis." A Protest Committee of Nigerian Youths established itself in the late 1940s as "a clearing house of public opinion" to protect the public welfare and political freedom.[62] Many among the middle and outer circles of the intelligentsia thought "it was high time we killed the impression and the idea that a trip to England and return is a qualification for leadership." A doctoral student abroad wanted Nigeria to be led "by a multitude of men and women—farmers, traders, lawyers, doctors, contractors, teachers," who would not fall into the errors of the current educated minority.[63] Lasekan captured popular doubt about the values of literates in his cartoon "Nigeria: A Country of Pen-Pushers?" (fig. 4). Oji condemned the educated class generally as "bribery takers" and exploiters of the poor. From the outer edges of the intelligentsia, Juwe claimed flatly that "if you look carefully into the life of our people to-day you will see that troublemakers are the people whom we call men of good education." Educated political leaders, he claimed, "like to go to the high seats in the Assembly House and ride in Saloon Cars, earn fat salaries with the expence of the poor tax payers and yet they claim themselves to be the leaders and saviours of men." It was not unreasonable, given these fears, for the Nigerian Anti-Self Government Party and the Nigerian Radical Party to question the wisdom of a headlong rush to independence. As early as 1951 the *Nigerian Daily Record* suggested "benevolent foreign domination" might indeed be better than tyrannical self-government.[64]

No sooner had the nationalists' demands had been granted, it seems, than Nigerians became unsure of the way forward. As Onipede observed in 1956, "Today, as never before in the history of West African nationalism, there is a marked feeling of doubt about the objectives of nationalism." Attacks on those *Pan-Africa* had dubbed mere

4. Akinola Lasekan, "Nigeria: A Country of Pen-Pushers?" (From *Nigeria in Cartoons* [Lagos: African Art and Craft Studio, 1944], p. 19)

"paytriots," however, often merely reiterated vague platitudes. To argue, as Ita did, that Nigerians "must make our victory over an evil social order sure by entrenching and organizing goodness" did little to establish a practical forward program.[65] Effective social criticism and visions of the future required traction on more substantial ground. In the confusion wrought by the rapid, many-layered changes of the 1950s, diverse attempts were made to define such ideologies. Colonial rule ended, however, with the intelligentsia—especially those outside the core—still struggling to situate themselves in an unsettled and largely unfamiliar environment.

Diverse sectional interests articulated positions, often presenting these as synonymous with the national interest. Adunni Oluwole's Nigerian Commoners' Party and D. G. L. Olateju's Nigerian Taxpayers' Association merged on an antitax platform as the Nigerian Commoners Liberal Party in the mid-1950s. Chike Obi's Dynamic Party, critical of the prospects for self-government, survived the 1950s with limited electoral success. Graduates of King's College in Lagos established the League of Bribe Scorners in the early 1950s to censure corrupt practices. Women were prominent in many of these parties, but some also identified and defended their collective interests as women. Charlotte Obasa's prewar Lagos Women's League was succeeded by the Lagos Women's Party in 1944, concerned with a range of women's education, health, and labor questions. Funmilayo Ransome-Kuti, seeking to assist market women and illiterates, published the *Nigerian Woman* in 1951 and 1952. In 1949 she and others with NCNC affiliations formed the Nigerian Women's Union; it in turn helped form the Federation of Nigerian Women's Societies in 1953. The Nigerian Council of Women emerged with Action Group affiliation in 1954. The issues raised by these groups, however, struggled for general recognition.[66]

At least some continued to rely on Christian principles, which had played in the genesis of the colonial intelligentsia's tradition of thought. Religious movements—especially millenarian ones—gained new energy and adherents through the war years, especially among semiliterate and self-educated urban dwellers. In the 1950s the National Church of Nigeria rendered nationalist politics into religious form, to lend the nationalist struggle clarity and purpose. Both highly placed intellectuals like Ilogu and popular authors like Ejimofor argued that faith could regenerate social order. Bishop Odutola feared the country was headed toward profound troubles unless God-fearing Christians acquired political office. But such appeals could not get far against the general sense, growing since the youth era, that government was a matter of rational rather than religious concern.[67]

Many sought the way forward along the cultural nationalist paths well established in Nigeria and the Black Atlantic. Various organizations were formed, devoted to researching, publishing, and promoting Nigerian cultural traditions against the tide of change and imported institutions. A vast popular body of writing appeared under and outside their auspices. The Egbe Omo Oduduwa, a cultural and political organization of elite Yoruba, was joined, for example, by the Society for Promoting Igbo Language and Culture, while Jacob Egharevba's continuing work on Benin history and culture was echoed by dozens of local historical and cultural studies. Beyond historical investigations, efforts were made to revive traditional dress, reveal scientific insights in traditional medicine, provide schoolchildren with books on their traditions, and vitalize indigenous languages. These efforts echoed Blyden's call to define the African way, although this path was now clearly shaped by history and environment rather than race. As Orizu put it, "Modern Nigeria must be reconstructed on the basis of what fits Nigeria as Nigeria and not as British-Nigeria or Europeanized-Nigeria," and only Nigerians could properly guide this process. But the weaknesses of this cultural nationalist tradition also reverberated through this literature. Prewar cultural nationalist ideals were being widely distributed among the rapidly growing postwar intelligentsia, but not being developed far beyond broad, long-established principles. Although these efforts detailed at length what, for example, Igbo customs were, the task of assessing them was addressed in vague terms. The Afikpo Youth Welfare League, like many similar associations, set out "to seek and to preserve all that is good and noble in our native customs and usages, and at the same time refine and modify such customs as are bad and unprogressive." Arguing that "African aboriginal innocence has been polluted by European Materialism," Adelabu willed Nigerians "Back to your Virtues." The *Eastern States Express* invoked Aggrey's maxim in 1951. "Let us introduce civilization capable of breaking evil institutions among us, but the good in our way of life must be preserved, guarded and handed down to posterity. Only the Best is Good enough for Africa."[68] It did not, however, go on to explain what exactly defined "good" African elements, let alone "the Best."

Further, for many, notions of the "Nigerian" or "African" way were still defined by contrast with European ways, driven by the need to disprove imperialist myths rather than discover historical truths. The historian J. F. Ade Ajayi, while still a university student, stressed that African historical research was needed to counter racist denials of Africa's meaningful past. Many of the efforts by the lesser intelligentsia to "preserve a permanent record of our people and race" betray a greater concern for reform than preservation. Idigo, typical of many, sought the "abolition of archaic and undesirable customs" such as witchcraft trials and twin killing, so that Aguleri might more readily "progress in the assimilation of Western civilisation."[69] Two of Lasekan's works, "Back to the Land" and "Illiteracy" (figs. 5 and 6), convey the way postwar writers continued their habit of defining African values against "Western Civilization" while also seeking to unchain Africa from its cultural impediments. The specific content of "Nigerian" culture, or of cultures within Nigeria, remained plagued by Blyden's habit of defining the African against external norms; com-

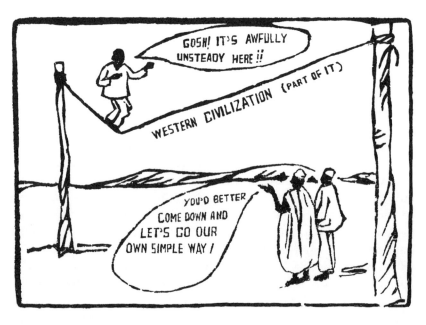

5. Akinola Lasekan, "Back to the Land." (From *Nigeria in Cartoons* [Lagos: African Art and Craft Studio, 1944], p. 49)

prehending Nigerian society required less constrained study of the situation in its own terms.

The anti-imperial sentiment is muted in the numerous local histories of the 1950s and 1960s, but this did not necessarily clear the ground for more intimate local knowledge. Cultural nationalist efforts, embedded in the politics of ethnic competition and institutionally supported by ethnic progress unions, now often aimed at providing political ammunition rather than producing knowledge. Authors typically highlighted accomplishments important to local pride, such as the achievements of educated sons of the soil. They also stressed the historical and social significance of the area in question, hoping to augment its weight in the balance of Nigerian politics. Idigo's efforts at cultural reform were, significantly, intended to "make Aguleri take her rightful place in Nigeria in the race for economic, social, religious and political development." Local minority writers, fearful of domination by the major groups, saw their struggle within Nigeria as analogous to the earlier anti-imperial struggle. J. U.

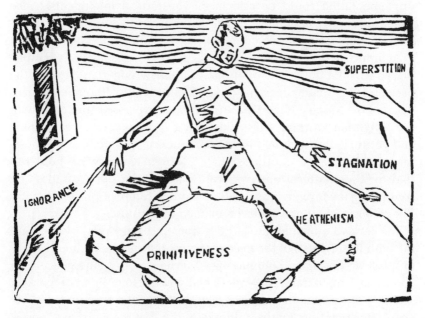

6. Akinola Lasekan, "Illiteracy." (From *Nigeria in Cartoons* [Lagos: African Art and Craft Studio, 1944], p. 14)

171

Isuman's appeal for a new state in the Benin and Delta Provinces, for example, was a battle for "the freedom of my people" who might otherwise be "doomed to political slavery and economic servitude."[70] Knowledge produced under such conditions did little to explore the common threads that might weave a national culture.

Of all the efforts to find critical perspectives, the Left perhaps pursued the most coherent critique of the emergent order. Despite suppression of the Zikists in 1950 and Cold War anti-Communism, a series of radical, often socialist, organizations appeared, including the Freedom Movement in 1950 and followed by the United Working People's Party, a Workers' Solidarity Conference, and a Convention Peoples' Party of Nigeria. New recruits from a younger generation joined former Zikists such as S. G. Ikoku, Eze, Ajuluchuku, and Okoye in these parties. Conditions before decolonization were not conducive to the formation of a vibrant left-wing critique. The mainstream parties' socialist programs, vaguely and variously defined, all implied equality, scientific planning, and a strong state. They also campaigned against foreign capitalists. These ideals were hard to attack; only their implementation could be criticized. The radical intelligentsia also were profoundly nationalist and little disposed to question the mainstream premise that foreign domination was a more pressing problem than internal divisions. A *Labour Champion* cartoon, for example, placed a white imperialist, not one of the new Nigerian elite, on the back of a struggling Nigerian worker. Even in 1961, although the manifesto of the Marxist Nigerian Peoples Party expressed solidarity with the "Nigerian Working Class" including farmers, peasants, women, and youth, it also included in its constituency "progressive businessmen, intellectuals and professionals." Moreover, the party hoped to find for these latter groups "salvation and better opportunities" by controlling the foreign interests that had heretofore oppressed them.[71] The problem of foreign control remained uppermost.

Insofar as a more definite left position emerged, it was by identifying with the interests of the masses against the emergent elite. Numerous *Labour Champion* columns had warned of the emergence of a "bourgeois aristocracy" in leaders ready to exploit Nigerian workers like any other capitalist class. Agwuna sharpened this advice a few years later, pointing out that, ultimately, the "bourgeois" was a "spineless, cunning conservative whose only complaint against imperialism is that he is not himself the imperialist. He is deadly opposed to the dictatorship of the proletariat." After Independence had reduced the threat of foreign interests, the left intelligentsia focused more clearly on class tensions within Nigeria. In 1964 the Socialist Workers and Farmers Party, identifying as its enemies not only foreign capitalists but also the new national elite, vowed to "fight for power not for chiefs, businessmen and professionals but for our cheated and neg-lected people."[72] Although this critique of Nigerian society was slowly moving more clearly away from mainstream parties, it was still sus-ceptible to appropriation by mainstream politicians looking to capital-ize on popular discontent. This dynamic led Awolowo and his Action Group to return to radical rhetoric as the opposition party after 1960. Further, the left-wing attack remained a rather stock Marxist position, still weak on understanding the actual nature of postcolonial social categories.

There was, then, a climate of diverse, vibrant criticism in the last colonial decade, emanating from all levels of the intelligentsia but most powerfully from the groups outside the elite. In one sense, this showed promise as old models with just African and European op-tions dissolved. In another, however, it revealed more confusion than reconceptualization. Its spirited nature could not make up for its weak grounding. Attacks focused on the abuse of power but still assumed that more ethical leaders could secure the future. Political leaders were rebuked for misapplying World Bank development plans but not for adopting them in the first place. This confusion was evident in the eclectic variety of ideologies proffered alongside the socialism ubiqui-tous in the final colonial decade. Adelabu, consciously taking up the work of *Renascent Africa,* explicitly cautioned against ideological pu-rity. "An overdose of doctrinaire socialism without a judicious mix-ture of progressive conservatism, or orthodox liberalism, and of that centre-stabilising process, leads inevitably to communism, to totalitar-ianism. . . . I commend to my countrymen the Stabilised Democracies of the English-speaking world, with perhaps a deeper hue of Chinese Agrarianism and a little touch of Indian Mysticism and Reliance on Spiritual Values." He hoped someday "to propound and amplify in all its ramifications" his "coherent philosophy" of life based on the num-ber seven, which would "do for intellectualism what Einstein's Gen-eral Theory of Relativity has done for the Physical Sciences." Some of the new "isms" had recognizable roots in West African thought; others appear to have been sui generis. Orizu looked to "aggreyism" as a foundation for his "zikism." Juwe advocated "Macaulism." E. O. Akak promoted his anticorruption "Akakism" in conjunction with other contemporary "philosophies": Zikism, Orizu's "Horizontal Education," Ojike's "Boycott the Boycottables," and Eyo Ita's education theories. T. K. Utchay promoted a unifying philosophy of the world —"Knodubi"—constructed from the trinity Know, Do, and Be. Indeed, as G. I. Mbadiwe once noted, "a good number of books have been written about patterns and modes of life we adopt in order to derive the fullness out of living. Many systems are set out, some weird, some earthly."[73]

The intelligentsia, especially those outside the core, left the British Empire in a state of doubt and fragmentation rather than of certainty and resolution. This was not necessarily a permanent condition—the beginnings of more orderly analyses were already apparent—but it was an amply evident quality of intellectual life at this moment of political empowerment. The climax of the anticolonial struggle thus was not fully paralleled in intellectual life. Established themes continued, but they mixed freely with many new coined "isms" in a free-for-all competition of incompletely formed critical perspectives. The unique perspective on African and Nigerian problems that had fitfully emerged between the wars was, at this critical juncture of decision making, lost in the scramble. Ideas were now judged more by their modernity than by their applicability to Nigerian conditions. The separate perspective marked out by Black Atlantic discourse—however limited it may have been—at least had raised the question of difference and established a Nigerian distance from Atlantic thought. In this hectic decade difference was too often understood merely as the gap between Nigeria's undeveloped present and its desired "modern" future. The enduring spirit of Nigerian intellectual life—adapting available ideas about Africa toward particular ends—was more evident in elite economic thought than in other spheres. It would resurface in the sobering crises of the First Republic and civil war.

# 6

# Colonial Subjects in Context

To APPRECIATE the qualities of Nigeria's modern intellectual history, we must recognize and deal with the intricately interwoven patterns of change evident over more than a century of Nigerian engagement with the colonial situation. This book was not intended as a comprehensive survey of the intelligentsia and their ideas but as an attempt to outline these broad patterns over four broadly defined periods. This narrative framework has served some themes better than others. Rather than simply recapitulate that same structure, a summary along thematic lines might better serve to highlight the complexity of these colonial subjects' lives.

The social composition of the southern Nigerian intelligentsia changed profoundly over time. In the mid-nineteenth century, the educated were largely coterminous with the elite of traders, missionaries, and civil servants spawned by the civilizing mission. Trade remained the heart of their economic life, but through the twentieth century their interests diversified into service industries and a widening variety of professional, commercial, and government careers, directed toward but not monopolized by law, medicine, religious ministry, and teaching. By the 1950s occupations spanned—if sparsely—a spectrum representative of other modern societies. Before World War I the intelligentsia were recruited mainly in other parts of West Africa and the diaspora and were led by an upper echelon educated in Britain. While still looking outward to the Atlantic world from centers in Lagos and Calabar, the intellectual community came to be dominated by Yoruba between the world wars. In these same decades, however, the Black Atlantic culture of the coast spread through the southern Nigerian hinterland, recruiting from a much wider cross section of Nigerian societies. The results of this penetration became rapidly apparent after the Second World War; by the 1950s the intelligentsia were overwhelmingly indigenous, rooted in the hinterland, and far larger than in previous generations. Graduates of British schools were now rivaled by graduates in a diverse range of subjects from schools in the United States and elsewhere. From the late nineteenth century, increasingly rapid expansion in the numbers recruited created an educated population with a pyramidal profile. School enrollments also tended to expand more rapidly than prestigious jobs. In the early colonial years, schooling led easily to high social status; by the late colonial period, schools had generated rings of educated Nigerians reaching far out from the elite core to frustrated perennial "applicants." This set the stage for at least two moments of intergenerational conflict. The rise of the Youth Movement in the 1930s marked both the career competition of a new cohort with an entrenched older one and the displacement of the diasporan elite by local recruits. Trenchant criticisms of the emergent order in the later 1950s were powered by the tensions between younger have-nots and established haves. The Western-educated community was not a simple or homogenous group upon arrival in Nigeria; over time, it is clear, new and old political, status, and ethnic divisions made it an ever more complex social group.

The attitude of the educated toward the colonial order varied, despite their enduring medial position within it. Through the mid-nineteenth century the intelligentsia promoted the expansion of the colonial state; as a marginal group on the coast, they needed its endorsement and support. The colonial order in return offered status through careers in commerce, church, and state. At the turn of the century imperial partition and deteriorating economic conditions, combined with less concrete but equally pressing changes in British thinking about the improvability of the "African race"—and indeed about the significance of racial difference itself—forced a reevaluation of initial positions. Although their medial functions in it broadened, and their dependence on it remained, their attitude toward the colonial order shifted from admiration to aversion. The colonial state was something from which the medial classes now wanted to escape, through independent careers, economic self-help, and Pan-African attachments. This antipathy endured through the Great Depression of the 1930s, spawning a period of innovative attempts to put solutions to Nigerian problems proudly in Nigerian hands. From the late 1930s, however, this relationship became more ambivalent and less stable. Promises of reform, signaled by the 1940 Colonial Development and Welfare Act, engendered hopes of a new dispensation. The failure and betrayal of this promise through the middle 1940s inspired instances of the most hostile and militant anticolonial thought yet, most power-fully from the Zikists. But from the late 1940s imperial political conces-sions, economic growth, and the expansion of the state under Nigerian control quickly appeased mainstream opinion. A nationalist commitment to independence was now all but unquestionable among political leaders, but so too was the mainstream commitment to the new economic and social order being planned with foreign expertise. This appeasement was nonetheless incomplete; elements within the increasingly diverse intelligentsia—especially those outside the core— continued to develop a radical critique after the 1940s, combining de-mands for self-government with qualms about how social justice would be served in the postcolonial future.

At no time in the colonial century is the self-image of the intelli-gentsia easily described. They formed a diverse and expanding com-munity, often riven by factional disputes. Portraits of the community varied with each individual's vantage point, and even according to the issue or context at hand. But periods can be determined during which certain images dominated—all of them pierced by unease and self-doubt. Through the middle of the nineteenth century, the small coastal enclaves of Christian converts wanted to see themselves and be seen as African representatives of British civilization. The novelty and ambition of their agenda—to alter the direction of African history with themselves at the vanguard—juxtaposed with their feeble foothold on the coast, not surprisingly induced insecurity. Stressing their British affinities and proudly assuming the role of "black Eng-lishmen" to lend themselves substance, the midcentury intelligentsia were not much inclined to contemplate the problems inherent in being African agents of a foreign culture. After 1860—and especially from the 1880s—the intelligentsia faced the combined challenge of scientific racism and imperial control. Forced to reexamine their self-image, they joined with African-American and other writers to present themselves as members of a racewide elite, in search of their own "African personality." This response, well developed by 1900 by men such as Edward Blyden and Mojola Agbebi, survived in the interwar period—especially among Nigerians abroad and those who had returned. But it did not free them from their discomfort. The idea of asserting African difference was at odds with their attachment to European culture. Pan-African connections sustained and inspired, but they also revealed that the "African personality" was not single but multiple. African Americans' own sense of what their racial identity involved incorporated little appreciation of the cultural variety and recent achievements of West Africans, let alone West African ambitions to develop under their own leadership. Further, the assertion of African difference proved a two-edged sword in colonial politics. It defended the right of Africans to resist imperial encroachment on the grounds that Africans had to define and defend their unique cultural sphere, but it also effectively undermined attempts by the intelligentsia to resist indirect rule policies that favored "natural rulers" over modern elites. Agbebi's sphinx was left with an insoluble riddle. The later interwar years saw the intelligentsia adopt a more narrow West African and even Nigerian identity, as colonial boundaries acquired meaning and electoral politics inspired active participation. They also saw the rise of a new generation more explicitly concerned with issues pertinent to its role as an elite within colonial society, retreating from the search for a racial identity in favor of advancing the clearly Western-style development presaged in the early ruminations of British colonial reformers. Sharp grievances with the colonial order, in particular by Yoruba involved in the burgeoning cocoa economy against the power of foreign firms and lack of government protection, also inspired ambitions for a more effective economic leadership. This shift of focus avoided the earlier dilemma by largely abandoning the need for unique racial development, but the aspiration to oversee Nigeria's modernization gave rise to new frustrations, as the knowledge, skills, and political power of the intelligentsia confronted both British resistance and the inherent immensity of their task. In the radical phase that followed, rising from the disruptions of war and its aftermath, elite dreams of self-government became popular demands. The unity of this moment, sustained by shared hostility to postwar colonial policies, supported a sense of confidence that nationalist faith would lead to genuine change and new unity. Lingering doubts were temporarily pushed into the background. But as Nigeria entered the often bewildering process of constitutional remodeling and decolonization after 1948, doubts quickly returned. Nationalist heroes came to be seen as self-serving politicians; the ideas of nationalism were found wanting both as a guide for policy and as a foundation for nation building. If much of the core elite remained hopeful and secure in their basic direction, many others worried acutely about the future. As they rushed toward a putative nation-state, the intelligentsia, increasingly divided by political and ethnic loyalties as well as by social and economic strata, struggled to construct a sense of Nigerian nationhood despite this fragmentation. As David Williams, editor of *West Africa,* later recalled, there was a notable lack of festivity in Lagos streets on Independence Day. The unease certainly did not subside through the civil war and has not ebbed since, although the reasons no doubt have continued to change. Problems of constitutional reform, military government, and environmental degradation, among others, have played their part in postcolonial times.[1]

The intelligentsia's views of societies within Nigeria changed in ways often similar to their views of themselves, because these too were shaped by alterations in Atlantic discourse about Africa and in Nigerian colonial society. Their interest in Nigerian societies began with the first generation and continued thereafter, but with varying stresses and intentions. The mid-nineteenth-century generation, notably Samuel Crowther, sought local knowledge that would make their missionary work more effective and informed. Others, lacking Crowther's direct connections to Nigeria, approached as more complete outsiders, treating indigenes as others. The Yoruba renaissance of the 1880s witnessed the first of several intense efforts to better understand the inner qualities of cultures within Nigeria. Typically, however, this local knowledge was sought as proof of generic "African" achievement relevant to the debate about racial difference. Historical and other writing continued to develop thereafter; but in the Pan-African fervor after the First World War, local knowledge was put to an additional purpose: to mark off the differences within the Black Atlantic and particularly to deflect African-American claims to leadership over Africa. Yoruba writers entered another period of high activity in the 1930s, joined by increasing numbers from elsewhere within Nigeria. Like much else in this decade, these explorations of local cultures held much promise. Intellectuals were still interested in defining African societies both to counter European racist denigration and to insist on West African claims within Pan-African schemes. But their notion of what constituted their identity and difference was more open than it had been in the heyday of scientific racism. Some, such as N. A. Fadipe and Isaac Delano, attempted to combine history, race, and the colonial situation to explain the shape of modern Nigeria. This promising ferment narrowed again during and after the Second World War, even as the frequency, scope, and volume of local studies increased markedly. In the radical anti-imperial mood of the later 1940s, Nigerians joined in Pan-African solidarity as victims of imperialism. During the frantic confusion of the 1950s, local knowledge was still sought for its own sake, by a new cohort of writers intimately tied to diverse communities within Nigeria. But it was often sought—and more often used—to promote and defend these communities in the preindependence battles over rights to representation. Nevertheless, all these phases generated considerable historical and cultural writing. British and diasporan Africans contributed to this body of knowledge in various modes, but they did not share in it, or care about it, in the same ways.

The complex qualities of the Nigerian intelligentsia are made powerfully evident by contrasting this enduring unease with their innovative and (for some) eventually effective search for an economic program which could secure their interests. Demands for imperial protection of free trade and limited diversification in the mid-nineteenth century were narrowed at the turn of the century by notions that Africans' racial destiny tied them to the soil. At the same time, however, the need to contain the power of larger foreign firms in the interest of smaller traders led them to insist more heavily on the sanctity of free trade and the evils of monopoly. These ideas developed between the world wars into a program of "Unity, Self-Help and Co-operation" which held much promise as a means of making the most of Nigerian entrepreneurs' strengths. Class, national, and racial solidarity were marshaled to join Nigerians' efforts and capital on a scale which at least could hope to compete with ever-expanding foreign rivals. Although widely elaborated during the 1930s, this initiative remained largely frustrated. Atmospheric changes beginning on the eve of

World War II introduced and made legitimate notions of an interventionist state. By a process of accident and ambition and the rhetorical opposition of the foreign and capitalist against the nationalist and socialist, Nigerian writers moved toward their version of African socialism, in fact another program for middle-class enrichment in the name of the nation. The basic urge behind this tradition of economic thought —a search for security in the dominating presence of foreign firms— finally found an effective tool after 1950, when state aid became a popular and available option, at least for those aptly situated to take advantage of it. The end of empire coincided with the rapid growth of an elite, associated with the state, espousing an economic program well suited to their position. But as this economic prescription took shape, critics inaugurated a more truly socialist tradition within Nigerian economic thought. All of these economic ideas developed within the rather strict confines of what was allowable but remained critical within these constraints: not accepting prevailing ideas unless they were useful and pushing the potential of new ideas until they proved more useful. This is most clearly revealed during the 1940s, as Nigerians quickly comprehended and deftly manipulated emergent imperial ideas of reform and wartime propaganda to move from a program of self-help to one of state intervention. Economic thought, then, marked by astute innovation in the pursuit of middle-class self-interest within the constraints of the colonial situation, contrasts sharply with enduring self-doubts concerning identity and leadership.

Certain of these patterns of change have a linear quality about them: from small to large, from simple to complex, from the Black Atlantic to the more specifically Nigerian. Recognition of such progressions have long sustained characterizations of the colonial intellectual history as a predictable movement from colonial to independent, from "African" to "modern." But this study has recognized that such linear patterns combined with both constant factors and repetitive themes. The intelligentsia were always part of a medial community seeking security in the colonial order. But they initially welcomed, then resented, then again welcomed the colonial state. Similarly, both the mid-Victorian and late colonial intelligentsia played down notions of African uniqueness that had strongly attracted Blyden and his contemporaries at the turn of the century. Moments of intergenerational conflict injected another dynamic. Clearly no single or simple pattern, certainly not one of gradual modernization, can capture the results of such movements.

Similarly, many scholars of colonial literature have remarked at the dualisms around which colonial thought has been constructed. Abdul JanMohamed, for example, has observed the insistent operation of a "manichean allegory" in colonial texts.[2] Atlantic discourse about Africa, it is clear, often dealt in posed opposites. It frequently posed the choice of either conserving African difference or converting Africa into something quite different. Black Atlantic and British writers invented images of Africa suited to their own agendas, which became the raw material for Nigerians facing the task of locating themselves in the modern world. Mid-Victorians accepted Africa as a benighted wilderness in need of European enlightenment. Blyden's West African peers countered racist denigration with their imagined genius of Africa, comprised of all the virtues Europeans seemed to lack—spirituality, communalism, attachment to the soil. Pan-African activists perceived the world in black and white and sought to unite the former in resistance against the latter. In the decade of decolonization, a new dualist imagery operated. "Africa" was marching inexorably toward the "modern," leaving its old ways for the new, erasing its markers of difference. As colonial subjects, then, Nigerian intellectuals were indeed often caught up in a discourse which employed crudely opposed categories in attempting to analyze the complex processes through which they were living. The point this study establishes is that they were not bound in predictable ways by these choices. They could dissemble these ideas and rebuild them from more fundamental parts. The intelligentsia of the Youth Movement years, notably, loosened these bonds by combining images of Africa based on racial difference with others premised on notions of universal human attributes. They took ideas of cooperation offered within the context of indirect rule and Pan-African solidarity and reissued them as a program to empower Nigerian cocoa-marketing entrepreneurs. But other generations of the intelligentsia also played with received dualist notions in attempts to define and understand the problems of their times. The mid-Victorian intelligentsia welcomed the chance to identify with their British peers but maintained a sense of their special relation to Africa, creating their singular role as "black Englishmen." The late colonial intelligentsia, for example, Adegoke Adelabu, pieced together vibrant visions of the future from widely divergent sources including Yoruba, American, and imperial ideas. If later dispassionate analysis reveals inner incoherence, this does not detract from the popularity of these programs in their time. If the Nigerians worked with found objects delivered by Atlantic tides, they also broke these down and rearranged the fragments in their own unique, complex mosaic. The result may have been less refined than something composed with original materials, but it was not less their own for this. Through over one hundred years they created patterns of thought that matched those of no other community participating in the Atlantic discourse on Africa, patterns that reflected their unique location in this intellectual world.

Postcolonial critics such as Homi Bhabha have tried to make sense of colonial intellectuals with insights about mimicry and hybridity. Such attempts, I hope it is clear, are not necessarily incompatible with the observations offered here. What I am arguing for is the application of such general characterizations in carefully drawn historical contexts, alive to the way the colonial context changes in content and intent over time and aware of the changing locations of various colonial intellectuals within that context. I have attempted here to understand the southern Nigerian case, rather than offer abstract insights about colonial subjects and their texts. I want to point up problems with the assumption that colonial intellectuals are predictable simply by virtue of being colonial. This holds, at least, for southern Nigeria; arguably these insights are worth testing in other contexts. There are constants in colonial intellectual history, but this observation can only serve as a more or less useful insight for entering its study; it cannot serve as a summary characterization. If we define the southern Nigerian intelligentsia simply as colonial, we reinforce the sense that their lives revolved around the single, fixed axis of the colonial presence. Clearly they were colonial subjects, and the subjects that occupied their interest revolved around the colonial situation. Further, the colonial situation imposed limits on their powers and imposed material and ideational conditions that were not of their choosing. But the colonial presence alone cannot explain the development of their thought over time. Over the course of southern Nigeria's colonial century, the nature of the colonial situation, the location of the colonial subjects, their ideational resources, and their problems all changed. Many of these changes were neither prefigured by the fact of empire nor necessary to it. Different factors changed at different times; the lives and ideas of Nigerian colonial subjects must be understood in the unpredictable contexts these alterations created. If the colonial situation provided some kind of axis for the intelligentsia, they were in constant irregular orbit around it. As they moved through the colonial period, their perspective on this axis was always shifting. As the formal British presence faded into neocolonial interest, some of the patterns that had been generated around this central axis continued, relevant still both to the broader question of Nigeria's place in the world and the multiple questions about the inner workings of Nigerian society.[3]

It is necessary to recognize the limitations of colonial intellectual life and to see that it was shaped by inventions imposed by both European and diasporan African thought. But to dismiss colonial intellectual life as merely dependent and derivative discourse misses the point. The southern Nigerian colonial intelligentsia were also active, self-interested participants in the construction of Africanist knowledge. They were complex colonial subjects who created within certain constraints. And it is their creations and their creativity—their inventiveness—that need to be stressed and explored, instead of continuing to stress their dependence. Understanding how modern Nigerian thought was constructed in the colonial period helps establish its dynamics and allows better assessment of its potential. The task that African intellectuals and Africanists now face, of thinking through our past imaginings about Africa toward a more effective grasp of the problems and prospects facing Nigeria and Africa, requires that we appreciate both the construction and the virtues of this tradition.

This study has tried to displace simple treatments of southern Nigerian intellectual history with a more careful, contextual one. I have not, however, attempted even to mention all the elements at play. I have not, notably, examined how issues of gender figure, either to the actors or to my analysis. What does it mean that women remained a minority among the colonial intelligentsia? How did Nigerian writers deal with the notoriously gendered language of imperial conquest and rule? Similarly, I have merely illustrated rather than adequately investigated the ways in which the content of colonial intellectual life was shaped by ideas, idioms, and insights from intellectual traditions more deeply rooted in Nigerian societies, or not rooted in the group I have defined here for study. How, for example, did Yoruba ideas of progress or good government play into similar notions within colonial discourse? Incorporating intellectuals not within the medial community defined in this study would bring into view other social strata as well as other cultural traditions within the broader treatment of Nigerian intellectual life. Any study that wants to go beyond the 1960s usefully will also have to go back and trace the development and integration of northern Nigerian intellectuals into southern Nigerian trends. Already by the 1950s northern figures played important roles that have not been treated here. Any or all of these themes could have been used here to help make my case about colonial complexity; I stopped short because of the risk of providing an excessively dense survey. Such themes, and many others, deserve careful and extended treatment as the study of the lives and ideas of colonial subjects develops. But they would, it seems, still amplify the basic argument of the present work—the need to recognize colonial subjects as complex. One study that seems especially promising is the examination of Nigerian historical writing during the colonial period. The African past was central to the many images of Africa at play in this era, not least among diverse groups of Nigerians. All participants in the Atlantic discourse on Africa projected images of Africa's past that sustained divergent visions of its future; historical knowledge was also a crucial element of intellectual and political life at the more local level. A careful study of how historical knowledge was constructed in various spheres by women as well as men, and how these bodies of knowledge were combined or competed, promises to be a fruitful way of applying, extending, and revising the basic insights and admonitions offered here.[4]

It has not been my purpose to confirm or deny inevitable or ultimate ends in the development of the colonial Nigerian intelligentsia, but only to establish a framework for the more fruitful investigation of this community and its members' ideas. Simply put, this involved not only understanding who the intelligentsia were in colonial society but also appreciating the changing contexts in which they operated. They were not obliged to deal with imperial ideology as a monolith they could only resist or accept. Rather, they were aware of the minority opinions and contrary elements within British and Black Atlantic thinking about Africa and were able to exploit new premises that promised somehow to serve their interests. If this was not done with great skill or insight, if Nigerian intellectual history disappoints many for its lack of luminaries of global import, this observation about their critical ability is nevertheless the most useful way to approach the study of them, for it opens rather than preempts questions about how Nigerians dealt with the impact of colonial rule. The intelligentsia were dependent in the sense that they were in a medial position within colonial society, and they could not affect the broad changes of ideas concerning race, Africa, or empire. But they were not wholly enslaved by their location. Rather, their position also enabled them to find perspectives and combine ideas that marked out their own intellectual tradition of adaptation, invention, and reinvention. It is a tradition at the same time colonial and modern, creative and dependent, prefigured and unpredictable.

# Appendix A

Approximate primary school populations in Lagos Colony and southern provinces, 1912–60

| Year | Government, assisted voluntary agency, and native administration | Unassisted voluntary agency | Totals |
|------|------|------|------|
| 1906 | — | — | 12,000 |
| 1912 | 16,000[a] | 20,000 | 36,000 |
| 1926 | 42,000 | 96,000 | 138,000 |
| 1937 | 81,000 | 137,000 | 218,000 |
| 1947 | 80,000 | 359,000 | 539,000 |
| 1952 | — | — | 917,000 |
| 1957 | — | — | 2,200,000 |
| 1960 | — | — | 2,630,000 |

*Sources:* Coleman, *Nigeria,* 134; Nduka, *Western Education,* 73; and Fafunwa, *History of Education,* 245.

[a]The sources differ slightly. For example, Mann gives only 14,000 students in 1912 (*Marrying Well,* 18).

# Appendix B

Approximate secondary school populations in southern Nigeria, 1912–60

| Year | Number of students | |
|------|------|------|
| 1912 | 67[a] | |
| 1926 | 520 | |
| 1937 | 4,000 | |
| 1947 | 10,000 | |
| 1957 | 60,000 | (30,000)[b] |
| 1960 | 130,000 | (49,000)[b] |

*Sources:* Coleman, *Nigeria,* 134; Fafunwa, *History of Education,* 190–91, 246; Nigeria, *Annual Abstract* (1963), 193; Abernethy, *Dilemma,* 195–96.

[a]Mann lists 800 students in 1912 (*Marrying Well,* 18).

[b]In the mid-1950s secondary modern schools with three-year programs appeared as an alternate to the traditional six-year secondary grammar schools (changed to five-year programs in 1956). The numbers in parentheses are for grammar schools only.

# Notes

## 1. The Invented and the Inventive

1. Gilroy, *Black Atlantic*, 29–40, 197.

2. Page, *Crowther*, v.

3. Notable examples of the first wave of interest include Emerson, *Empire to Nation*; Emerson and Kilson, *Political Awakening*; Hodgkin, *African Nationalism*; July, *Origins*; Kimble, *Ghana*.

4. Kohn and Sokolsky, *African Nationalism*, 15; Shepherd, *African Nationalism*, 3; July, *African Voice*, 228, 231.

5. Emerson and Kilson, *Political Awakening*, 16. Notable studies along themes treated by Said include Inden, *Imagining India*; Mudimbe, *Invention*. For a sense of how widely the idea of invention has been applied, see the references in Bassin, "Inventing Siberia," 764–65n. Several scholars developed this insight for the African case before Said, e.g., Curtin, *Image of Africa*; Hammond and Jablow, *Myth of Africa*.

6. Prah, *Society and History*, 7. An early but still useful study of nationalism is Coleman, *Nigeria*; more recently, see R. Okonkwo, *Heroes*. For the radical critique, see Fanon, *Wretched*; also Onimode, *Imperialism*, 127 and passim; Daniel, "Culture of Dependency." Regarding Nigeria in particular, Nwala, "Ideological Dependency"; G. Williams, "Nigeria." On colonized minds, see, e.g., Chinweizu, Jemie, and Madubuike, *Decolonization of African Literature*; also Ngugi, *Moving the Centre*; Okoth, "Dependent Culture."

7. Davidson, *Burden*, 49–50, 39; Ayandele, *Educated Elite*.

8. Ranger, "Invention of Tradition"; Ranger, "Invention of Tradition Revisited." For detailed thematic studies of invention by colonial Nigerians, see Zachernuk, "Lagos Elite"; Zachernuk, "Origins and Colonial Order"; Zachernuk, "Johnson."

9. The point that imperial thought is diverse and contradictory has been variously made, for example, Thornton, *Imperial Idea*; Trotter, "Colonial Subjects"; Comaroff, *Revelation*.

10. Davidson, *Burden*, 42. On imperial romantic appreciations of Nigerian cultures, see Zachernuk, "Imperial Culture."

189

11. See, for example, July, "Nineteenth Century Negritude."

12. Ashcroft et al., *Empire Writes Back,* 196; Asad, "Afterword"; Hountondji, *African Philosophy,* 164–65. A striking recent example of an approach to transcend is the monochromatic clash of Europe with "the mind of Black Africa" presented by Mungazi, *Mind.* I draw broad inspiration for the spirit of this book from works such as Appiah, *Father's House;* Barber, "African-Language Literature"; Chakrabarty, "Postcoloniality"; Clifford, *Predicament of Culture,* esp. "On Ethnographic Authority"; Dirks, *Colonialism and Culture;* Gilroy, *Black Atlantic;* Said, *Culture and Imperialism;* N. Thomas, *Colonialism's Culture.*

13. Prakash, "Post-Orientalist Histories." On the failure of nationalism, see Davidson, *Burden,* especially chap. 1; Osaghae, "Colonialism." The broad current interest is reflected in Mudimbe, *Idea of Africa;* Hountondji, *African Philosophy;* Lindfors, *Nigerian Literature.*

14. Recent trends are represented by, e.g., Barber and Moraes Farias, *Self-Assertion;* Falola, *Pioneer.* Some of the earlier valuable studies include Echeruo, *Victorian Lagos;* Kopytoff, *Preface;* Mann, *Marrying Well;* Olusanya, *Second World War;* Olusanya, *Students' Union;* Omu, *Press.* There are many more; a more complete sense of this literature and my debts to it can be found in the notes and bibliography. Recent additions to the supply of biographies and autobiographies include Biobaku, *When We Were Young;* Mba, *Rosiji.*

15. July, *African Voice,* ix. July treats the interwar period in an epilogue in *Origins.* Neither volume examines some prominent interwar and even postwar figures, for example, H. O. Davies, I. O. Delano, Eyo Ita, or T. M. Uzo.

16. In connection with the former, see, e.g., Paden, *Bello.* In connection with the latter, see, e.g., A. Apter, *Black Critics;* Barber, "Discursive Strategies"; Bastian, "Bloodhounds"; Peel, "Pastor and the *Babalawo.*" The primary sources mentioned here by no means equal those available for examination. A rather more extensive bibliography as well as biographical sketches of some 115 Nigerian intellectuals can be found in Zachernuk, "Intellectual Life."

## 2. The Race to Civilize:
## The Roots of Colonial Intellectual Life, 1840–1880s

1. This chapter and the next draw on a large body of published literature on the Western-educuated community in West Africa. On West Africa generally, see Wyse, *Krio;* Priestley, *West African Trade;* Kimble, *Ghana;* Spitzer, *Creoles;* July, *Origins;* Lynch, *Blyden.* On Nigeria in particular, the major works are Kopytoff, *Preface;* Ajayi, *Missions;* Ayandele, *Educated Elite;* Ayandele, *Missionary Impact;* Ayandele, *Holy Johnson;* Mann, *Marrying Well;* Echeruo, *Victorian Lagos;* P. Cole, *Elites.* See also Ajayi, "Nineteenth Century Origins"; Mann, "New African Elite"; Brown, "People of Lagos."

2. Nair, *Politics and Society,* 66–69; Forde, *Efik Traders,* viii; Hair, "Africanism." On the diversity of Krio culture, see Wyse, "Misunderstandings." On the

migrations from Brazil, see Boadi-Siaw, "Brazilian Returnees"; Mba, "Literature"; Turner, "Brazilian Ex-Slaves"; Ralston, "Brazilian Freedmen."

3. On nineteenth-century economic history, see most recently Law, *Slave Trade;* Lynn, *Commerce;* see also Dike, *Trade and Politics;* Hopkins, "Economic History of Lagos"; Hopkins, *West Africa,* 124–66; Flint, "Economic Changes"; Falola, *Ibadan;* Ohadike, *Ekumeku,* 21–43. Studies of nineteenth-century slavery are useful for appreciating the upheavals entailed. See, for example, Uchendu, "Slavery in Igboland"; Oriji, "Re-assessment"; Agiri, "Slavery in Yoruba Society."

4. Ayandele, *Ijebu,* 5–6, 23. On the Yoruba, see also Falola, "Hospitality to Hostility." On the southeast, see Northrup, "Patterns of Slavery," 9; Nair, *Politics and Society,* 43–51; Dike, *Trade and Politics,* 153–65.

5. Lynn, *Commerce,* 159–60; Fyfe, "Nichols."

6. Mann, *Marrying Well,* 11; Hopkins, "Blaize"; Omu, *Press,* 117–19. For the relationship between Christianity, trade, and elite economic life, see Webster, "Bible."

7. The intriguing colonial term *Native Foreigner* referred to "any person (not being a native of Nigeria) whose parents were members of a tribe or tribes indigenous to some part of Africa and the descendants of such a person, and shall include any person one of whose parents was a member of such tribe" (Talbot, *Southern Nigeria,* 4:19). Informed guesses about the early Lagos population vary. Compare Osuntokun, "Christianity and Islam," 131; Echeruo, *Victorian Lagos,* 16; Talbot, *Southern Nigeria,* 4:176, 180, 183–85. On literacy patterns, see Akere, "Linguistic Assimilation," 167–68. On the hinterland, see Pallinder-Law, "Abeokuta," 21–22; Latham, *Old Calabar,* 106–8; Lynn, "Technology," 428.

8. On early colonial education, see Fafunwa, *Education,* 81–91; Afigbo, "Education Code"; Nair, *Politics and Society,* 68; Mann, *Marrying Well,* 18. On women's education, see Denzer, "Women in Government," 3–4; Nwabara, *Iboland,* 49.

9. Euba, "Dress and Status," 152; Brown, "People of Lagos," 133–38.

10. Adewoye, "Antecedents," 15; Adewoye, "Sapara Williams"; Adeloye, "Pioneer Doctors." Hair notes thirteen certain Nigerian graduates of Fourah Bay before 1900 ("Fourah Bay," 155–57).

11. On blacks in Britain generally, including this period, available surveys are: Fryer, *Staying Power;* Lorimer, *Colour, Class;* Scobie, *Black Britannia;* Walvin, *Black and White;* see also Duffield, "Skilled Workers." On early organizational links, see Geiss, *Pan-African Movement,* 166–69; Brown, "People of Lagos," 210–30. On Delany and Campbell, see Blackett, "Return to the Motherland."

12. Adewoye, *Judicial System,* 48–52, 73–76; *Anglo-African,* 7 Jan. 1865. On Lagos conditions, see Ayandele, *Holy Johnson,* 85–87, 114–15; Nwanunobi, "Incendiarism"; Brown, "Public Health." On Abeokuta, see Pallinder-Law, "Abeokuta," 21–22; Harunah, "Lagos-Abeokuta Relations"; Biobaku, *Egba and*

*Their Neighbors.* See also Nwabara, *Iboland,* 50; Ayandele, *Educated Elite,* 11–12; Ayandele, *Ijebu,* 8.

13. Ayandele, *Ijebu,* 12–15; Mann, "New African Elite," 51–59. See the lists of such groups in Ayandele, *Educated Elite,* 37–40; Kopytoff, *Preface,* 113, 195–96; Brown, "People of Lagos," 192–93.

14. Blackett, "Return to the Motherland," 384; *Anglo-African,* 14 Jan. 1865. Ellis describes the merry-go-round in *Land of Fetish,* 82–83. Their Victorian attributes have been colorfully detailed, for example, by Brown, "People of Lagos," 242–47, 254–70, or more recently by Echeruo, *Victorian Lagos,* both sources for my account.

15. On bookshops and libraries, see H. Thomas, *Bookshops,* 1–2; Brown, "People of Lagos," 232–53, 278–81; Lagos Institute, *Proceedings,* 1. On presses, see Ajayi, *Missions,* 158–59; Omu, *Press,* 106, 252.

16. Kopytoff, *Preface,* 127. On social habits, see Mann, *Marrying Well,* 110–27; Euba, "Dress and Status," 153–54; Brown, "People of Lagos," 153–65; Agiri, "Architecture," 341–50. On alliances with the interior, see Oroge, "Slave Question."

17. Tukur, "Critical Evaluation," 81; Isichei, *Ibo People,* 179. This transitional model dominated the literature on the African educated elite that proliferated at the time of independence, for example, in these international symposia: International Institute of Differing Civilizations, *Middle Class;* UNESCO, "Symposium"; Lloyd, *New Elites;* see also Smythe and Smythe, *Elite.*

18. Baker, *Urbanization,* 27.

19. Euba, "Dress and Status," 150–51.

20. T. Buxton, *African Slave Trade.* Wilson, *Origins,* 121–52, reprints statements of Venn and similar missionary thinkers. See also Ajayi, "Henry Venn"; Lynch, "Native Pastorate." For European views of Africa generally, see Hammond and Jablow, *Myth of Africa;* Curtin, *Image of Africa;* Comaroff, *Revelation,* 49–85.

21. Grey, *Colonial Policy* 2:287.

22. See, for example, Delany, *Niger Valley,* 110; Crummell, "Progress of Civilization." For African-American ideas, see Magubane, *Ties That Bind;* Moses, *Crummell.*

23. *African Times,* 23 May 1863, 1 July 1880.

24. Crowther, *Charge,* 7; Crowther, "Charge at Lokoja" (1869), quoted in Wilson, *Origins,* 150; Rev. Dove to Missionary Secretary, 1 June 1841, quoted in Ajayi, "Nineteenth Century Origins," 518; Horton, *West African Countries,* 175.

25. Horton, "African Products"; Crowther's journals, quoted in July, *Origins,* 185; *Lagos Observer,* 19 June 1886. For economic ideas in West Africa more widely, see Fyfe, *Horton,* 140–45; Olukoju, "Politics of Free Trade"; July, *Origins,* 93–100, 130–54. For economic activities in Lagos, see Brown, "People of Lagos," 127–52.

26. Prospectus of the *Lagos Times and Gold Coast Colony Advertiser,* in *Lagos Times,* 10 Nov. 1888; *Lagos Observer,* 3 July 1886; *Lagos Times,* 9 Mar. 1881. See also Horton, *Political Condition;* Horton, *West African Countries.* On the movement of government seats, see Kopytoff, *Preface,* 219–24.

27. Nair, *Politics and Society,* 68, 86, 167–75; Ayandele, *Missionary Impact,* 26, 74–75, 86; Noah, "Old Calabar," 54–58.

28. Crowther, "Charge at Lokoja" (1869), quoted in Ajayi, *Missions,* 224; Crowther and Taylor, *Gospel,* 227–39. See also Crowther, *Yoruba Language,* i–vii; Crowther, *Niger and Tshadda Rivers,* 62–63; and the bibliography of early missionary writing in Ajayi, *Missions,* 285–89.

29. See Pallinder-Law, "Abeokuta," 51–52, 94, 179; Pallinder-Law, "Aborted Modernization"; July, *Origins,* 196–207.

30. S. Johnson, *Yorubas,* 16–25; Ayandele, *Ijebu,* 15–19. On Johnson, see Falola, *Pioneer.*

31. S. Johnson, *Yorubas,* 126, 130; Crowther, *Charge,* 29–30. Views on pawnship and the context for them are discussed in R. Campbell, *Pilgrimage,* 56–65; Crowther's letter in Hutchinson, *Impressions,* 276–77; Oroge, "Iwofa," 79–80; Zachernuk, "Johnson." For nineteenth-century attitudes toward slavery, see Oroge, "Slave Question"; Oroge, "Slave Crisis"; Agiri, "Slavery in Yoruba Society." On marriage, see H. A. Caulrick, in Keyinde Okoro, ed., *Views of Some Native Christians of West Africa on the Subject of Polygamy* (Lagos, 1887), 12–13, quoted in Kopytoff, *Preface,* 252. On *babalawo,* see Peel, "Pastor and the *Babalawo.*" J. O. George later acknowledged Meffre's help concerning Ifa and other issues in his own work on the Yoruba (*Historical Notes,* 4, 58). Samuel Johnson finished his manuscript of *Yorubas* in 1897, but his research and writing began in the 1870s (Doortmont, "Samuel Johnson," 176).

32. *Lagos Times,* 14 Feb. 1891; prospectus of the *Miscellany,* in the *Eagle and Lagos Critic,* 28 Apr. 1883, quoted in Echeruo, *Victorian Lagos,* 7.

33. George Nicol to J. Warburton, 12 Apr. 1844, CMS CAI/0614, quoted in Wilson, *Origins,* 129; Henry Robbin to Henry Venn (1857), CMS CA 2/080, quoted in Kopytoff, *Preface,* 97.

34. *Anglo African,* 14 Nov. 1863; Echeruo, *Victorian Lagos,* 99–100; see also Omu, "Anglo-African."

35. John Craig, quoted in Echeruo, *Victorian Lagos,* 35; J. A. O. Payne, in Keyinde Okoro, ed., *Views of Some Native Christians of West Africa on the Subject of Polygamy* (Lagos, 1887), 5, quoted in Kopytoff, *Preface,* 252; Crowther, "Charge at Lokoja" (1869), quoted in Wilson, *Origins,* 150. Delany's vision is expressed in *Niger Valley,* 121. Kopytoff carefully delineates various positions in *Preface,* 272–78.

## 3. "The Sphinx Must Solve Her Own Riddle": New Imperialism and New Imperatives, 1880s–1920

1. On the economy at the end of the century, see Flint, "Colonial Experience"; Nwabughuogu, "Entrepreneurs"; Hopkins, "Economic History of Lagos." For general treatments of this period, see Osuntokun, *First World War;* Tamuno, *Evolution;* Anene, *Transition.* See also chap. 2, note 3.

2. J. Campbell, *Observations,* 22. See Hopkins, "Property Rights," 791–93; Morrill, "Two Urban Cultures," 209–11. For a detailed account of an African merchant's success, see Hopkins, "Thomas."

3. F. Coker, *Abayomi,* 13; Mann, *Marrying Well,* 23–34; see also Mann, "New African Elite," 37, 51–61, 94; Ogunlade, "Education and Politics," 345.

4. Ayandele, *Ijebu,* 38, 228; Isichei, *Ibo People,* 144–57, 177. Abernethy explores the multiple pressures for education growth from the 1840s (*Dilemma,* 25–151). The population data for 1921 in this chapter are from Talbot, *Southern Nigeria,* esp. 4:124–27, 131, 152, 178, 185–86. Although grouped in categories more appropriate to our needs than earlier statistics, data for and after 1921 must still be viewed as approximate, especially for rural populations. The figures have been rounded and roughly adjusted to account for such things as the Europeans counted among the educated population.

5. See appendixes A and B. This sketch draws details from many studies beyond those already mentioned, including Afigbo, "Education Code"; Coleman, *Nigeria,* 134; Fafanwa, *History of Education,* 99, 112, 245; Mann, *Marrying Well,* 18; Nduka, *Western Education,* 74. An education ordinance in 1882 first established conditions for government support in Lagos Colony. Unassisted schools had a reputation in official eyes for providing inferior education but flourished nevertheless. Coleman provides a comparison of southern and northern figures from 1906 to 1957 (*Nigeria,* 134, 139).

6. *Payne's Lagos and West African Almanack and Diary* (1881), quoted in Omolewa, "London University Examinations," 655.

7. J. Campbell, *Observations,* 15–16. On early professionals, see Mann, *Marrying Well,* 20; Mann, "New African Elite," 96; Adewoye, "Self-Taught Attorneys"; Adewoye, *Judicial System,* 117–18, 128; Adeloye, "Pioneer Doctors"; Coleman, *Nigeria,* 143. A common notion that about half of the approximately 1,000 Fourah Bay students enrolled between 1900 and 1949 were Nigerian is supported by Hair, "Fourah Bay," 155–57, and by Adewoye, "Antecedents," 5, 15. For elite women and women's education, see F. Coker, *Abayomi,* 20–28; Mba, *Women Mobilized,* 61–66, and passim; C. Johnson, "Nigerian Women"; Johnson-Odim, "Abayomi"; Denzer, "Women in Government," 3–4; Olusanya, "Obasa."

8. Adewoye, "Self-Taught Attorneys," 62. Coleman provides a more complete discussion of the size, distribution, and makeup of the educated community (*Nigeria,* 141–45).

9. Lagos Institute, *Proceedings.* The Institute apparently lasted at least until it issued *Lagos Water Rate Scheme* in 1916. For sketch biographies of prominent Lagosians of this era, see Gwam, *Great Nigerians;* see also Zachernuk, "Intellectual Life," 431–48; Brown, "People of Lagos," 248–52; Omu, *Press,* 26–55, 83. Omu's appendixes are also very useful for the early press. On libraries, see Payne, *Almanack,* 57.

10. On popular contacts, see Baker, *Urbanization,* 77–78; Mann, "New African Elite," 62–64, 111–22; Mann, *Marrying Well,* 27–28; Dixon-Fyle, "Saro," 126–30; Berry, "Christianity." On European contacts, see Omu, *Press,* 45, 164, 215; Ayandele, *Agbebi,* 5; Gwam, *Great Nigerians,* 10, 18.

11. Ayandele, *Educated Elite,* 30; see also Omu, *Press,* 31–33; Mann, *Marrying Well,* 31–33; Mann, "New African Elite," 7.

12. Lagos Institute, *Proceedings,* 11; Payne, *Principal Events,* 5.

13. See the discussion by various elite members in Lagos Institute, *Proceedings,* 21–33; Agbebi, *Inaugural Sermon,* 14; Folarin, *England and the English,* 45.

14. J. H. Samuel [later Adegboyega Edun] to J. D. Sutcliffe (1902), quoted in Pallinder-Law, "Abeokuta," 92; Esin, *Cause and Effect,* foreword; G. W. Johnson in 1873, quoted in Ajayi, *Missions,* 267; *LWR,* 27 July, 4 Aug. 1918; see also July, *Origins,* 288. On Agbebi, see R. Okonkwo, *Heroes,* 12; Akiwowo, "Agbebi," 123.

15. Reade, *Savage Africa,* 30, 33; Kingsley, *Travels,* 559–60. The new mood in Nigeria is captured by Ayandele, "Colonial Church Question"; Ayandele, *Holy Johnson,* 136–56; Brown, "People of Lagos," 210–30. See also Hopkins, "Chamber of Commerce"; Anyanwu, "Port Harcourt," 19–20. For evidence of racial tension, see *LWR,* 21–28 Aug. 1897; *LS,* 25 Aug., 1 Sept. 1897. On ideas in England, see Lorimer, *Colour, Class,* 201–11; Adi, *Africans in Britain,* 6–19. Reade and Burton were early heralds of the late nineteenth-century orthodoxy. For general treatments of these changing ideas, see Bolt, *Victorian Attitudes;* Kiernan, *Lords of Human Kind;* Stocking, *Victorian Anthropology;* Stepan, *Race in Science.*

16. *LWR,* 25 Apr. 1908; *Lagos Observer,* 2–16 Apr. 1887; *LS,* 11 Mar. 1896; Agbebi [then D. B. Vincent] in *SLWN,* 5 Mar. 1892. Ayandele argues that retreat was popular (*Educated Elite,* 55–69).

17. *LWR,* 9 July 1892; *LS,* 6 Oct. 1897. See also *Lagos Times,* 26 Apr. 1882; *Lagos Observer,* 26 Jan. 1881, 17–24 July 1886. On this theme generally, see Omu, *Press,* 115–29.

18. Omoniyi, *Ethiopian Movement,* 30; Omu, *Press,* 149. The most complete treatment is Adi, "Omoniyi."

19. Blyden's 1898 speech in Liverpool is in Holden, *Blyden,* 682–87; Ademola quoted in Folarin, *Life of the Egbas,* 69. Obadiah Johnson, prefiguring later fears of neocolonial control, feared dependence on foreign capital would allow foreign investors to drain Nigeria of funds for growth (Lagos Institute, *Proceedings,* 25–26).

20. Ajayi, *Missions*, 269; C. Johnson, "Nigerian Women," 101–3; Pallinder-Law, "Abeokuta," 178 n. 3. Various scholars have treated this movement. See notably P. Cole, *Elites*, 75–89; Echeruo, *Victorian Lagos*, 35–49; Ayandele, *Educated Elite*, 9–52. On medical writing, see Adeloye, *Nigerian Pioneers*, 123; on divination, see A. Cole, "Ifa"; J. Abayomi Cole, *Astrological Geomancy in Africa* (London, 1898); James Johnson, *Yoruba Heathenism* (Exeter, 1899). I have only seen the latter two in long passages reproduced in Dennett, *Black Man's Mind*, 244–71.

21. George thanked Agbebi, E. M. Lijadu, P. J. Meffre, E. H. Oke, and E. G. Vincent (*Historical Notes*, 63, 4). O. Johnson, *Lagos Past*; S. Johnson, *Yorubas*; see also Losi's 1914 *Lagos*, E. Moore, *Abeokuta*. Historical works produced with administrative problems in mind include "Native of Yoruba," "Native System of Government"; Hopkins, "Report on the Yoruba"; and, in Ghana, Sarbah, *National Constitution;* Hayford, *Native Institutions*. See also Law, "Yoruba Historiography"; July, *Origins*, 254–78.

22. United African Church minutes (1891), quoted in Webster, *Churches*, 68; *Lagos Weekly Times*, 20 Sept. 1890; Agbebi [then D. B. Vincent] in *SLWN*, 12 Nov. 1892. Webster develops this distinction between mere control and content (*Churches*, 118–35).

23. Gbadamosi and Ajayi, "Islam and Christianity in Nigeria," 360–61; Ayandele, *Educated Elite*, 90–91. For writing on theology and church policy, see Fadumah, "Religious Beliefs"; J. K. Coker, *Polygamy Defended;* S. A. Coker, *Rights of Africans;* Webster, "Attitudes and Policies." On the dominance of churchmen, see Webster, *Churches*, 48, 204–7.

24. *LWR*, 8 Sept. 1894; Agebebi to Buxton (1913), quoted in Adewoye, "Sapara Williams," 63. See also Ayandele, *Ijebu*, 46–53. On protection of indigenous rights in the 1890s, see Omu, *Press*, 137–47; P. Cole, *Elites*, 89–104.

25. Kingsley, quoted by Green, "Kingsley," 9; Kingsley, *Studies*, xviii. The best complete study is Frank, *Voyager Out*. See also Flint, "Kingsley." The merging of these threads is traced in B. Porter, *Critics of Empire*, 28–43, 146–55, 240–90; Rich, *Race and Empire*, 29–43. For Morel, see his *Affairs of West Africa* and *Nigeria*. See also Frobenius, *Voice of Africa* 1:98, 146–48, 319–49; Kuper, *Anthropologists*, 36.

26. Du Bois, *Conservation of Races*, 181, 178; Wahle, "Crummell"; Moses, *Crummell*. Blyden was an early influence on Du Bois, among many others. See Berghahn, *Images of Africa*, 69–87. Toll, *Resurgence of Race* usefully compares African and African American thinking; also Meier, *Negro Thought*. For the parallel conditions, see Geiss, *Pan-African Movement*, 163–75; Stein, *Marcus Garvey*, 7–23; Akiwowo, "Racialism." To compare the francophone Black Atlantic context, see Manchuelle, "Antillais."

27. Blyden, *African Society*, 13; Blyden, *Before Europe*, 130; Kingsley, *Studies*, xix. See also Holden, *Blyden*, 724–35; Blyden to Morel, 15 Sept. 1902, Morel Papers, F9, file B, f. 103; and the endorsement of the African Society in *LWR*, 15 Dec. 1900.

28. Blyden, *African Life*, 7–8. Blyden mentioned in this connection Shaw, *Tropical Dependency;* Dennett, *Black Man's Mind;* Kidd, *Essential Kafir;* Kidd, *Kafir Socialism;* Olivier, *White Capital;* and Finot's *Race Prejudice* (1906), among other works.

29. R. Okonkwo, "Garvey Movement in Nigeria," 100–103; Akiwowo, "Agbebi," 137. Backers of Dusé's publishing efforts included Lagosians O. Sapara and Rotimi Alade. On the people in London, see Geiss, *Pan-African Movement*, 176–98, 223; Mathurin, *Williams*, 41–85, 165–69. For Pan-Africanists in British literary and socialist circles, respectively, see Duffield, "Afro-Asian Solidarity," 125–27; Adi, "Omoniyi."

30. Henriksen, "Intellectual Influences," 284; Sarbah, *National Constitution*, vii; see also Locke, *New Negro*, 421–25, 438–43. Dennett also cites a series of historical articles in the *Nigerian Chronicle* (*Nigerian Studies*, vii–viii). Sarbah, a leading Ghanaian intellectual of the time, held a certain admiration for Kingsley which was reciprocated. See her letters in his *National Constitution*, 259–60.

31. Kingsley, *Studies*, 323, xvii; Morel, *Nigeria*, xx. See also Dennett, *Nigerian Studies*, vii–viii; Morel's eulogy to Blyden in Holden, *Blyden*, 876; *Journal of the African Society* 3 (1904): 357–59.

32. Echeruo, *Victorian Lagos*, 109; Blyden, *Christianity*, 140.

33. Webster, *Churches*, 78; Shepperson, "African Diaspora," 52; James Johnson quoted in Geiss, *Pan-African Movement*, 185; *LS*, 17 Oct. 1900; Blyden, *Christianity*, x; Hayford to Washington (1912), quoted in Harlan, "Washington," 465–66.

34. Hayford to Washington (1904), quoted in Harlan, "Washington," 462; Azikiwe, *Liberia*, 350.

35. J. Campbell, *West African Governors*, 30; Blyden and Carter, *Lagos Training College*, 21. Lynch sees him as "the unrivalled intellectual focus of English-speaking West Africa" in the late nineteenth century ("Pioneer," 385).

36. Gwam, *Great Nigerians*, 34.

37. Agbebi, "West African Problem," 343–44; Blyden, *Christianity*, 89–90; Johnson quoted in J. George, *Historical Notes*, 48; Agbebi [then D. B. Vincent] in *SLWN*, 5 Mar. 1892. Blyden has received the closest attention in Lynch, *Blyden;* Livingston, *Education and Race.* Ayandele's *Agbebi* is the most complete study; see also Akiwowo, "Agbebi"; R. Okonkwo, *Heroes*, 10–24; Ayandele, *Holy Johnson;* Omu, "Journalism."

38. Blyden, *African Problem*, 24; Blyden, *African Life*, 66; *LWR*, 25 Jan. 1902; Agbebi [then D. B. Vincent] in *SLWN*, 5 Mar. 1892.

39. Letter from Adeyimi, *Lagos Times*, 9 Aug. 1882; J. Campbell, *Election Question*, 18–19; Morel, *Nigeria*, 76–77.

40. Irele, "Negritude," 94; Ayandele, *Holy Johnson*, 286–87; see also Baker, *Urbanization*, 54.

41. Hammond and Jablow, *Myth of Africa*, 8, 183, 122.

42. Frank, *Voyager Out*, 94; P. A. Talbot, "Foreign Influences," 184; Barnes, *Duty of Empire*, 97–99; MacGregor, in Lagos Institute, *Proceedings*, 5. Morel's

program is explained in his *Affairs of West Africa*, 20–34. Kingsley and Morel also projected a West African who was "above all, and to the marrow of his bones, a trader" and thus the ideal partner for British merchants (Morel, *Nigeria*, xxi; see also Flint, "Kingsley"). Hetherington notes traits similar to Barnes's in many of Africa's interwar defenders (*Paternalism*, 54, 68).

43. Schomburg, "Negro Digs Up His Past"; Berghahn, *Images of Africa*, 93, 121, 137; Appiah, *Father's House*, 28–46. These qualities are clear in some principal works of the time: Washington, *Story of the Negro* 1:3–81; Du Bois, *Black Folk*; Hansberry, "Ancient Nigeria." A large body of literature touches on American and African-American attitudes to Africa. Berghahn, *Images of Africa*, 1–32, is a convenient entry; see also Thorpe, *Black Historians*; Magubane, *Ties That Bind*, 15–88; W. L. Williams, "Black Journalism's Opinions." On the American content of this image of Africa, see Huggins, *Harlem Renaissance*, 84–136.

44. Blyden, *Christianity*, 96, 85–87; J. E. Casely Hayford, "Introduction" to Blyden, *Before Europe*, i; Johnson (1904) quoted in Ayandele, *Holy Johnson*, 299. See also *LWR*, 22 Feb. 1902. Blyden's notion of Africa's spirituality is developed in "The Origins and Purpose of African Colonisation" and "Ethiopia Stretching Out Her hands unto God," both in *Christianity*.

45. Blyden, *African Life*, 9; Ukpabio, *African Eyes*, 62; see also *LWR*, 25 Jan. 1902, 21 May 1904. This was also taken up by Dusé Mohamed Ali's *African Times and Orient Review* (Duffield, "Dusé," 248).

46. Sekyi (1917), quoted in Langley, "Modernization," 46–47; Maye, *Back to the Land*, 7; Folarin, *Life of the Egbas*, 137–38.

47. *LWR*, 5 June 1897; Blyden, *African Life*, 10, 36–37; Azikiwe, *Liberia*, 395–96.

48. *LWR*, 3 June 1905.

49. Ibid., 27 Aug. 1904.

50. Ibid., 25 Apr. 1908; "African Doctor," "Admixture."

51. Alakija's election campaign literature, quoted in Ayandele, *Educated Elite*, 82.

52. A. Cole, "Ifa"; J. K. Coker, *Polygamy Defended*.

## 4. "Unity, Self-Help, and Co-operation": Pragmatic Prescriptions, 1920–1940

1. *Wasu* editorial, 6 (Jan. 1937): 2.

2. For overviews of the interwar economy, see Coleman, *Nigeria*, 63–230 passim; Hopkins, *West Africa*, 172–86, 237–67; Ekundare, *Economic History*, 103–222; Osuntokun, *First World War*, 21–63. On business people in particular, see Harneit–Sievers, "African Business"; Deutsch, *Middlemen*, 13–42; Ekejiuba, "Omu Okwei"; Nwabughuogu, "Entrepreneurs"; A. Macmillan, *Red Book*, 62–125.

3. Ojike, *My Africa*, 74. For biographical illustrations, see, e.g., F. Coker, *Abayomi*; Osuntokun, *Akintola*; Fatayi-Williams, *Faces*; Nwangoro, *My Destiny*, 4–6.

4. Abernethy, *Dilemma*, 37; Nduka, *Western Education*, 73–75; Coleman, *Nigeria*, 124, 134, 139, 239–42, 246; Ralston, "Middle Passage," 4, 12–25. See N. Okafor, *Universities*, 66–82, for the history of Yaba. On women, see Mba, *Women Mobilized*, 208; Denzer, "Women in Government," 2–6, 15–18; Denzer, "Yoruba Women," 19–20.

5. Anirare, *Early Life*, 45–46; Fadipe, *Sociology*, 322–24; Mbanefo, "African Looks." These careers and others are illustrated in many biographies and autobiographies, e.g., R. Okonkwo, *Heroes*; Ikime, *Member for Warri*; Longe, *Rare Breed*; F. Coker, *Ademola*, 25–27, 38–39; Awolowo, *Awo*, 80–112; Davies, *Memoirs*, 1–59; K. Moore, "Story"; see also Davies interview and note 2 above. Tamuno analyzes Legislative Council members in *Representation*, 62.

6. Nicolson, *Administration*, 241–42; Oldham, "Nigerian Education: Notes of Discussion in London," JHOP, 9/3, f. 139; Milewski, "Depression," 13–14n.

7. Davies, "Youth Movement"; NYM, "Unemployment." This comparison looks at the executive committees and notable members of these groups. Of the thirty-two names shared between the three groups of the 1920s, I was able to compile sufficient information on thirty to make observations. For the NYM, I obtained at least partial information on twenty-one. These data suggest patterns but are not conclusive.

8. Adeniyi-Jones, *Address*, 17–19; Davies, "Our Secretary's Letter Bag," *Daily Service*, 17 Oct. 1938; NYM, *Charter*, 2–3. On the foreigner issue, see Wyse, *Krio*, 139–40; Ikoli, "Vaughan"; *Daily Service*, 21 Oct. 1938.

9. Omu, *Press*, 260–64; on libraries, "Kofo" [K. A. Moore] to Perham, 29 June 1938, MPP 396/1, f. 3.

10. Carr, quoted in P. Cole, *Elites*, 113; Macaulay, *Transfer*. On Nigerian Garveyites, see R. Okonkwo, "Garvey Movement in Nigeria"; R. Okonkwo, "Garvey Movement in British West Africa"; Langley, "Garveyism"; Olusanya, "Garvey and Nigeria"; G. Williams, "Garveyism"; Gershoni, "Nationalist Rhetoric." On the NCBWA, see Olusanya, "Lagos Branch"; Eluwa, "Congress"; Langley, *Pan Africanism*. On interwar Lagos society and politics, see Omu, *Press*; July, "Sierra Leone Legacy"; Lipede, "Macaulay"; Duffield, "Dusé," 771–83; Baker, *Urbanization*; see also F. Coker, *Abayomi*, 64–94; Mba, *Rosiji*, 1–21; Awolowo interview; Davies interview; Adebo interview; Adebo, *Unforgettable Years*, 22–37; Davies, *Memoirs*, 87–117. The most detailed account of the NYM is F. Okafor, *Youth Movement*, which argues that ideological rather than ethnic differences split the movement.

11. Mba, *Women Mobilized*, 226, 64–65; see also C. Johnson, "Nigerian Women," 106–17; Ananaba, *Trade Union*, 10–15; Harneit-Sievers, "African Business."

12. Onyia, *My Role*, 11–18. On pay scales, see Osuntokun, "Administrative Problems," 39. On earlier times, see Delano, *Notes*, 11–12; Geary, *British Rule*, 9–14; Geary, "Loyalty"; Niven, *Kaleidoscope*, 1–21, 135–48, 191–96. On Stuart-Young, see Azikiwe, *Odyssey*, 235; Ojike, *My Africa*, 144. See also Pearce, *Bourdillon*, 195–248; Pearce, "Violet Bourdillon."

13. Okafor-Omali, *Villager*, 111; see also L. H. E. Onwudia to Macaulay, 10 July 1935, HMP 29/3. On provincial educated life, see Plotnicov, "Elite of Jos"; Leith-Ross, *Conversation*, 26, 46–56; Afigbo, "Azikiwe," 9–13; Adewoye, *Judicial System*, 188–97; Anyanwu, "Port Harcourt," 29–31; Wolpe, *Urban Politics*; Dixon-Fyle, "Saro"; Morrill, "Two Urban Cultures," 436–38; Hair, "Enugu," 154–55; Schwab, "Oshogbo"; Ottenberg, "Nigerian Township." On provincial study circles, see Akinsanya to Macaulay, 20 Mar. 1928, HMP 18/8; *Nigerian Daily Telegraph*, 20 Mar. 1932; *Nigerian Daily Times*, 15 Feb. 1938; Azikiwe, *Political Parties*, 8–9. On the provincial press, see I. Coker, *Seventy Years*, 25–28; I. Coker, "Nigerian Press," 77.

14. Essien, *Archibong*, 2; F. Coker, *Ademola*, 46.

15. Okafor-Omali, *Villager*, 108; Leith-Ross, *Stepping-Stones*, 103–4; Igbafe, "Benin Water Rate."

16. W. Moore, *Itsekiri*, 211.

17. On progress unions, see Okafor-Omali, *Villager*, 134–52; Otite, *Autonomy*, 124–29; Ottenberg, "Improvement"; Jones, "Changing Leadership"; Garigue, "Leadership"; Little, *Urbanization*, 103–17; Smock, *Ibo Politics*, 50–59.

18. Akpabio, "Ibibio Union"; Azikiwe, *Odyssey*, 31–190; Davies, *Memoirs*, 58–59; Mba, *Rosiji*, 25; Yoloye, "Reminiscences," 57; Awolowo interview; Davies interview. Sadly, all four Efik law students died in the early 1930s (Aye, *Old Calabar*, 157).

19. To enter the vast literature on interwar Pan-Africanism, see Geiss, *Pan-African Movement*, 283–408; Esedebe, *Pan-Africanism*. On the general context of blacks in interwar Britain, see Banton, *Coloured Quarter*, 67–72; Scobie, *Black Britannia*, 141–51; Macdonald, "Moody"; Macdonald, "Wisers"; Macdonald, "Introduction"; Robinson, "Black Intellectuals." The most studious account of West African students is Adi, *Africans in Britain*; see also Adi, "Students in Britain"; Olusanya, *Students' Union*; Garigue, "Students' Union"; Davies, *Memoirs*, 60–86.

20. Solanke, *United*, 67; *LDN* editorial, 20 Apr. 1934. An example of an antiracist editorial is *West Africa*, 22 Sept. 1934, 1047. On shared interests, see Amachree, "Colonial Students," and the various meetings reported in *West Africa*, 7 Apr. 1934, 373–74, 19 May 1934, 540, 2 June 1934, 587–88. Low's cartoon appeared in *Keys* 3 (Jan.–Mar. 1936): 33.

21. Solanke, *United*, 50; Solanke to editor, *West Africa*, 6 Oct. 1934, 1110; Adeniyi Williams to Perham, 24 Mar. 1934, MPP 24/1, ff. 5–12; Anon., "This Business of Trusteeship," *WAR* 7 (Aug. 1936): 13; Davies, *Memoirs*, 85–86. On

paternalism in the Anti-Slavery Society, see Rich, *Race and Empire,* 37–43. Hetherington judges that only Marxists escaped this (*Paternalism,* 45–60).

22. See IAIP, consignment 2, box 3/2, "File Summary—Rockefeller Fellowships: Mr Benjamin Nnamdi Azikiwe," esp. D. Westermann to Lugard, 3 July 1933, Oldham to Lugard, 13 July 1933; see also Oldham to Malinowski, 18 May 1933, BMP, Africa 1/13; Perham to Oldham, 21 Oct. 1934, in JHOP, ff. 4–5; Ulansky, "Azikiwe," 107 n. 46.

23. Solanke, *United,* 58; Ademola, "Solidarity," 609.

24. *Keys* editorial, 4 (Oct.–Dec. 1936): 16; *Keys* 2 (July–Sept. 1934): 16; Davies, *Memoirs,* 68.

25. Logan, "View of Africa," 217; Ojike, *Two Countries,* 203, 16. See the ambivalent views of America in Taylor, "American Impressions"; Fafunwa, "Adventures." On the attractions of America, see Ulansky, "Azikiwe." On the Native African Union, see *Africa* [New York] 1 (June 1928): 20. On the student experience in America both before and after WWII, see Ralston, "Middle Passage"; Sofola, *Dynamism,* 18–39; Weisbord, *Ebony Friendship,* 181–85; Edunam, "Ambassadors"; Ulansky and Ojiaku, "Nigerian Response."

26. *LWR* editorial, 27 Nov. 1920; *Nigerian Observer,* 4 Jan. 1930, quoted in Wolpe, *Urban Politics,* 85; *WAP,* 23 May 1940, quoted in Olusanya, "Garvey and Nigeria," 149.

27. Garvey, quoted in Stein, *Garvey,* 109; *LWR,* 2 July 1904; similarly, Hayford, *Ethiopia,* 172. Similar assumptions are evident in Washington, *Story of the Negro* 1:35; Du Bois, *Conservation,* 181, 183.

28. Sekyi, *The Parting of the Ways* [1925?], 23–27, quoted in Langley, "Garveyism"; *Times of Nigeria,* 24 May 1920, quoted in Olusanya, "Garvey and Nigeria," 140.

29. *LWR,* 2 May 1925, quoted in Omu, *Press,* 226; Campbell, *Observations,* 43. For samples of manifestos, see the *LWR* editorial series, 1–29 Mar. 1919, or 14 June 1919; NNDP, *Objections;* NCBWA, *Resolutions;* and the assorted NNDP election material, HMP 61/6. For discussions of "bourgeois" qualities, see Ebo, "Zikism," 1–22; Langley, *Pan Africanism,* 195–220; Ayandele, *Educated Elite,* 55–93.

30. Adeniyi-Jones, *Problems,* 39; *West African Nationhood* editorial, 18 Oct. 1930, quoted in Langley, *Pan Africanism,* 185; Stein, *Garvey,* 114.

31. Kingsley, *Studies,* 436; Lugard, *Dual Mandate,* 87; Lugard, *Report on the Amalgamation of Northern and Southern Nigeria,* Cmd. 968 (1920), 19, quoted in Wheare, *Legislative Council,* 33; Clifford to Nigerian Council, 29 Dec. 1920, quoted in Eluwa, "Congress," 131–32; Memorandum on Supreme Court, n.d., (from Nigerian Chief Secretary's Office), quoted in Adewoye, *Judicial System,* 159. Kingsley was ambiguous over whether the African was "inferior in kind" or merely different. Compare *Travels,* 659, 669; see also *Studies,* 441–42.

32. NCBWA to Milner, 31 Jan. 1921, in HMP 18/3; W. Moore, *Itsekiri,* 205.

For the reforms and response, see Adewoye, *Judicial System,* 137–69; Osuntokun, *First World War,* 3–20, 64–99; Eluwa, "Congress," 65–156.

33. *LWR* editorial, 21–28 July 1917.

34. Nigerian Reform Association, *Petition,* 4; J. Campbell, *Election Question,* 8–9.

35. E. Smith, *Aggrey,* 118; Akiwumi, "West Africa and the World," 14. For the wider context of youth movements, see Spitzer and Denzer, "Wallace-Johnson"; D. Apter, *Ghana,* 127–29; Olusanya, "Ojo-Cole."

36. Padmore, *Gold Coast,* 56; [Nwangoro] "S. O. N.," "Crossroads."

37. Taiwo, *Carr,* 166. See also Taylor, "Italy and Abyssinia"; Savage, "Western Civilisation."

38. See, e.g., Cutcliffe-Hyne, "Back to the Coast," 69; Ward, "Dr. Moody"; or Lord Leverhulme's speech, *West Africa,* 26 July 1924, 745.

39. Barzun, *Race;* Fortes, "Anthropologist's Point of View," 219; Mayhew, *Education,* 13; Secretary of State [Lord Moyne], "Constitutional Future of the Colonial Empire" (1941), quoted in Pearce, *Turning Point,* 21; Perham, *Africans and British Rule,* 20–25. See also Boas, "Fallacies"; Fraser, "Future of the African"; more generally Stepan, *Idea of Race,* 140–89; Rich, *Race and Empire,* 92–119.

40. Locke, "Afro-Americans"; U. Lee, "ASNLH," 411–12.

41. Cookson, "Colour Complex"; Cameron, reported in *WAR* 5 (June 1934): 29. Examples of reformist thought include Perham, "Restatement"; Murray, "Education"; C. Buxton, "African Friends"; W. Macmillan, "Educated African."

42. Davies, "Youth Movement"; Azikiwe, *Renascent Africa,* 19, 21.

43. Orizu, *Without Bitterness,* 294.

44. "A. B. L.," "Youth Movement," 10–11; Lijadu, "Altruism"; A. Williams, "Young Democrats"; Akintola, "Tragedy."

45. Ita, "West African Pilot"; Azikiwe, "Ethics of Colonial Imperialism," 308; Azikiwe, *Liberia,* 217; Solanke, *Special Lecture,* 2; *Wasu* editorial, 4 (Nov. 1935). This is much like the position of Du Bois in 1939 (*Black Folk,* 1).

46. "De Rem," "Negro's Position"; letter to ed., *WAR* 6 (Nov. 1935): 35; Alakija, "Western Education"; A. George, "Colour Problem."

47. Igbakan, "Nigerian Affairs"; F. Okafor, *Youth Movement,* 32. Compare Azikiwe, *Liberia,* e.g., 241–46, with his *Economic Reconstruction, Taxation,* or *Political Blueprint;* or Ita's "West African Pilot" with his *Revolt* or *Two Vital Fronts.* Azikiwe's very early pieces on Onitsha, "Political Institutions" and "Fragments," were designed in part to make broad points about Africa in general to an American audience.

48. Davies, "Our Secretary's Letter Bag," *Daily Service,* 13 Oct. 1938; Ariori, "British Empire."

49. Davies, "Our Secretary's Letter Bag," *Daily Service,* 4 July 1938, 5 July 1940; Davies, "Opportunities." See also NYM, *Charter;* NYM, "Cocoa Problem"; Odunsi, "Rational Nationalism"; Azikiwe's passage in *Renascent Africa,*

"Towards Mental Emancipation," 134–40, and Ebo's discussion of it, "Zikism," 93–103.

50. Azikiwe, *Renascent Africa*, 17; Awolowo, "Ayes Have It!"

51. Abayomi, "Modern Womanhood"; Awolowo, "Economic Programme," 5–6; Azikiwe, *Renascent Africa*, 126–27; Azikiwe, *Zik*, 23.

52. Azikiwe, *Renascent Africa*, 32.

53. *Africa and Orient Review*, Dec. 1920, quoted in Duffield, "Business Activities," 597–98; R. Cole, "West Africa in Evolution"; *LDN* editorials, 6 Feb., 6 Mar. 1934. Protests were diverse and often vitriolic. See Davies, "What I Think of the Pool"; "Cocoa Farmer," "Farmers Organize"; Tete-Ansa, "Iniquities." On the growing awareness of the economic crisis, see Langley, *Pan Africanism*, 107–15, 195–240; Osuntokun, *First World War*, 21–63; Hopkins, "Economic Aspects." For a fuller treatment of economic thought in the 1930s and 1940s, see Zachernuk, "Nigerian Critics."

54. Otemade, "Economic Independence"; *Daily Service* editorial, 28 Oct. 1940. For British support, see Burns, *British Imperialism*, 23–35; Stuart Young to West African Co-operative Producers, 11 Mar. 1930, HMP 29/2.

55. Tete-Ansa, "Ottawa Conference," 3; *LDN* editorial, 1 Feb. 1934; *Service* editorial, 14 Sept. 1935.

56. *Africa and Orient Review*, May 1920, quoted in Langley, *Pan Africanism*, 127; advertisement for National Bank of Nigeria, *Daily Service*, 12 Oct. 1940; Solanke to Macaulay, 16 Mar. 1925, HMP 18/7; Azikiwe, *Renascent Africa*, 131–32; Awolowo, "Economic Programme," 2–4. The aggressive qualities of this program are evident in Martins, "Collectivism"; advertisement for the Nigerian Mercantile Bank, *LDN*, 8 Feb. 1932; Nigerian Mercantile Bank, *Prospectus*.

57. Meier, *Negro Thought*, 121–57. On Garvey's economic ideas, see Fierce, "Economic Aspects."

58. Strickland, *Report*, 1–2; Frederick Lugard, "Introduction" to Strickland, *Co-operation*, vi, ix.

59. Lewis, "Economic Problems," 30. See also Ita, *Reconstructing*, 3–8. For early cooperatives from both Nigerian and government inspiration, see Beer, *Peasant Groups*, 19–31. For sample industrial visions, see the *West African Pilot*'s "Business Notes" series in May 1938; the *Daily Service*'s "African Enterprise" series in June 1940; or the "Trade and Industry" articles in *Wasu* 1 (Dec. 1932) and 2 (Jan. 1933). Compare Tete-Ansa, "What Does West Africa Want?" 258–59.

60. Ojo-Cole, "Glimpse"; Solanke, "Lifting the Veil," in *Wasu* 1 (Mar. 1926): 14, quoted in Olusanya, *Students' Union*, 19. Solanke's works in *Wasu* include "Ogboni," "Customary Constitution," and "Constitutional Law." See also Ojo-Cole, *Thoughts*; Akin-Awosefaju, "Ojo-Cole"; Olusanya, "Ojo-Cole."

61. Temietan, "Marriage"; Delano, *Soul*.

62. Folarin, *Life of the Egbas*, 1; W. Moore, *Itsekiri*, 11; Omoneukanrin, *Itsekiri Law*, 7; Iweka-Nuno, *Obosi*, preface; Folarin, *Native Laws*; Egharevba, *Short His-*

*tory,* viii. Solanke produced three major works on Abeokuta: *Yoruba Problems, Special Lecture,* and *Centenary.* Ajisafe produced four: *Laws and Customs, Abeokuta Centenary, History of Abeokuta* (in at least three editions), *Errors and Defeat.*

63. *Nigeria* editorial, 9 (Jan. 1937): 5. See, e.g., Ezekwe, "Native Art"; Udo-Ema, "Ekpe Society"; Udo-Ema, "Fattening Girls"; Edoka, "Ojowu Juju." On Duckworth, see Zachernuk, "Imperial Culture"; Crowder, "Outsider."

64. *Nigeria Daily Times,* 3 Feb. 1938; *African Messenger* editorial, 31 July 1927; S. Banjo, "Teaching of Yoruba"; Ibeziako, *Founder;* Azikiwe, "Political Institutions"; Azikiwe, "Fragments"; Egharevba, *Short History.* Amangala seems to have researched and written his *History of Ijaw* in the 1930s. See also Law, "Yoruba Historiography"; Eisenhofer, "Benin Kingship"; Peel, "Ethnogenesis."

65. A. Apter, *Black Critics,* esp. 13–34; Peel, "Making History." Compare, e.g, the subtle differences in Johnson's account of the Egba in his Oyo-centric *Yorubas,* 7, 17–8, with accounts by Egba: Losi, *Abeokuta,* 2–4; Ajisafe, *History of Abeokuta,* 3d ed., 9–11. See also the various studies of Johnson's impact on Yoruba historiography in Falola, *Pioneer.*

66. Essien, *Archibong,* 17; *African Messenger,* 7 Aug. 1927; Ojo-Cole, "Whole Race at School." Deniga's *African Leaders* appeared in 1915 and 1919, his *Who's Who* in 1919, 1920, 1921, and 1934.

67. Ayandele, *Educated Elite,* 142; Echeruo, "Azikiwe."

68. M. Lee, "Education," 21; Ndem, "Western Civilization." For examples of self-criticisms, see Ojo-Cole to Solanke, 14 June 1933, quoted in Olusanya, "Ojo-Cole," 99; Morgan, "Public Enemies."

## 5. "Who Are the Nigerians?": Nationalism and the Future, 1940–1960

1. On the postwar economy generally, see Hopkins, *West Africa,* 267–92; Helleiner, *Peasant Agriculture,* 24–43, 300–331; Ekundare, *Economic History,* 225–382; more recently, Hinds, "Sterling"; Deutsch, *Middlemen.* This change of colonial policy has been treated by many scholars; see Pearce, *Turning Point;* Pearce, "Governors"; Flint, "Planned Decolonization." The early works on this political history remain useful and the most detailed: Coleman, *Nigeria;* Sklar, *Political Parties;* see also Olusanya, *Second World War;* Ikime, *Groundwork.* Anyiam, *Men and Matters,* is a contemporary political narrative.

2. These statistics on education are derived from a wide variety of sources which often do not exactly agree, although all support the broad trends illustrated. On literacy rates, see Royal Institute of International Affairs, *Nigeria,* 25; Mabogunje, *Urbanization,* 130, 219; Morrill, "Two Urban Cultures," 33–36, 222; Nigeria, *Digest,* 3. On primary, secondary, and teacher training, see Nduka, *Western Education,* 72–75, 127; Nigeria, *Annual Abstract* (1960), 74; ibid.

(1963), 23, 161, 169, 175, 193; Abernethy, *Dilemma,* 20–21, 37, 128–29, 195–96; *Nigeria Year Book 1958,* 125.

3. On tertiary education statistics for Britain, see Coleman, *Nigeria,* 74, 124, 134–35, 139, 144–45, 193, 239–42; Adewoye, "Antecedents," 16; Ulansky and Ojiaku, "Nigerian Response," 381; N. Okafor, *Universities,* 95, 103, 119; Lloyd, *New Elites,* 6; Banton, *Coloured Quarter,* 44–56. For America, see Chukwuemeka, *African Dependencies,* 163 n. 1; Chukwuemeka, *Industrialization,* 49; Gordon, "Student Movement," 122; Ralston, "Middle Passage," 231–32; C. Ikoku, *Science Education,* 22; Phelps-Stokes Fund, *Survey,* 78. For Nigeria, see Ajayi and Tamuno, *Ibadan,* 282–83; Denzer, "Women in Government," 2–6; Mba, *Women Mobilized,* 61–66; Smythe, "Marginal Men," 268n; Tamuno, "Formative Years," 38–39; Fafunwa, *Education,* 245; O. Awe, "Ibadan"; Yoloye, "Reminiscences." On scholarships, see Olusanya, *Civil Service,* 132; Carey, *Colonial Students,* 29–36.

4. Jokparoba, *Urhobo People,* 4; Lasky, "Africa for Beginners" (pt. 1), 47. On book sales, see H. Thomas, *Bookshops,* 36; letter, Chukwura to Ottenberg (1954), enclosed with his book in CAMP 3874, reel 8; Uzo, *Pathfinder,* 12. On the postwar press, see I. Coker, "Nigerian Press," 79, 119–24. On libraries, see C. Thomas, "Propaganda," 74–76, 88–90, 300–302; Perry, "Libraries"; Adam to Jeffries, 11 Oct. 1946, CO 323/1883/3. For generally positive assessments of the intelligentsia, see Smythe and Smythe, *Elite,* 148–52; Nicol, "Formation." Bretton stresses their weaknesses (*Power and Stability,* 46–47).

5. Smythe and Smythe, *Elite,* 61–63.

6. Wolpe, *Urban Politics,* 174–75; *Eastern States Express* editorial, 3 May 1951.

7. *WAP,* 24 Mar. 1955. On government propaganda efforts from the war years, see C. Thomas, "Propaganda"; Clarke, *West Africans;* Smyth, "British Propaganda." On ethnic politics, see O. Awe, "Ibadan," 76–77.

8. Lloyd, "Introduction," and Mann, *Marrying Well,* 2–5, summarize this search well. My account draws from a more scattered and extensive literature than can be listed here. On the African elite in general, see International Institute of Differing Civilizations, *Middle Class;* UNESCO, "Symposium"; Lloyd, *New Elites;* Little, "African Elite"; Little, *Urbanization;* Shils, "African Intellectuals"; Lasky, "Africa for Beginners." On Nigeria in particular, see citations below plus Lloyd, "Class Consciousness"; O'Connell, "Political Class"; Leith-Ross, "New Elite"; Leith-Ross, "Middle Class." For the strengths of the concept of elites, see Nadel, "Social Elites."

9. Class analyses were, of course, part of a general trend in African studies in the early postcolonial decades. For later analyses, see, e.g., Forrest, "State Capital"; Osoba, "Deepening Crisis"; Falola and Adebayo, "Political Economy." But for the colonial period, Onimode, for example, clarifies little by characterizing the upper strata of the colonial "petty bourgeoisie" as "professionals, merchants, educators, senior civil servants and the like, who were

joined by less progressive elements such as chiefs, traders, local government functionaries etc." (*Imperialism*, 128–29).

10. Ojike, *My Africa*, 126; Amosu, "New Nigeria." On income gaps, see Baker, *Urbanization*, 40–43; Lloyd, "Introduction," 11; I. Coker, "Nigerian Press," 107.

11. Elias, "Towards Nationhood," 7; Coleman, *Nigeria*, 141.

12. Mann, *Marrying Well*, 108–9; Fatayi-Williams, *Faces*, 31.

13. Lloyd, "Elite," 134–35, Lloyd, "Introduction," 25. On UCI, see Varney, "Religion," 7; Smythe and Smythe, *Elite*, 79–80, 165–66.

14. Smythe and Smythe, *Elite*, 79. On the civil service, see Olusanya, *Civil Service*, 28–29, 38, 84; Coleman, *Nigeria*, 440 n. 47. On new lawyers, see "The Law List," *Nigerian Bar Journal* 5 (1965): 9–22. On later periods, see, e.g., Beckman, "Imperialism."

15. Plotnicov, "Elite of Jos," 281, 295–96; Smythe and Smythe, *Elite*, 64, 91–92; Adebayo, *White Man*, 1–10, 50–54.

16. Ojike, *My Africa*, 125–26; Awolowo, *Path*, 63, 31–32 (cf. 26–27, 48).

17. Buowari Brown in Nigeria, *Proceedings of the General Conference*, 165; Ita, *Two Vital Fronts*, 5; Post and Vickers, *Structure and Conflict*, 6.

18. See, e.g., Brady, "Sartorial Sidelights"; or fictional accounts: V. Ike, *Toads*, T. Aluko, *Majesty*.

19. *Occasional Papers on Nigerian Affairs* 1 (Oct. 1954): 3; Awolowo interview; *New Nigerian* 1 (Aug. 1965): vii; Solarin interview. The Citizens' Committee for Independence had two 1957 publications: *Forward to Freedom* and *Case for More States*. On the British-American split, see Smythe, "National Leadership," 223–24. See also Benson, *Black Orpheus*; Lindfors, "Popular Literature"; Lindfors, *Nigerian Literature*.

20. Adelabu, *Ebullition*; see also Post and Jenkins, *Price of Liberty*, 122–40. For estimates, see Coleman, *Nigeria*, 141; Harbison, "Human Resources," 204–5.

21. On outsiders as radicals, see A. Callaway, "School Leavers"; Smythe, "Marginal Men"; Smythe, "Young Elite." See also the caricature of young "progressive" university graduates in P. Enahoro, *How to Be a Nigerian*, 57–63. A more extensive bibliography of this and the outermost group's writing is in Zachernuk, "Intellectual Life."

22. On the Economic Society, see Akintola Williams to Macaulay, 23 Oct. 1942, HMP 33/5; Akintola Williams to Chief Secretary, 1 Mar. 1943, NNAI, Chief Secretary's Office 26/5/40867. On the Fabians, see Iyalla, "Nigerian Fabian Society"; Terence Young to Rita Hinden, 11 Mar. 1947, Marjorie Nicholson to Rita Hinden, 25 May 1949, FCP 82/2 ff. 54–56, 93. The Olympians are described in Uzo, *Political Evolution*. The New Era Bureau published *Dr Zik Goes East* and *History and Analysis*.

23. A. Callaway, "School Leavers"; Abernethy, *Dilemma*, 64; Obiechina, *Onitsha Market*, 3–30. See also Omo-Amanigie, *Imoudu*, 4. Data on these authors are scanty, but what is available supports this generalization. See Mezu,

"Cradles"; Nitecki, *Onitsha Publications.* Significant authors include B. F. A. Adinlewa, J. O. Akanu, A. D. Ike, J. U. Isuman, R. E. Jokparoba, S. M. Juwe, and A. N. Mbah. See also Clark, *Ogunde,* 79–91; and Lasekan's numerous collections: *Cartoons, 1945, Zik,* and *Joker;* see also K. Balogun, *Interpreting.*

24. Alan MacDermott to Perham, 11 Feb. 1957, MPP 396/2 f. 47. On racial attitudes in Britain, the Colonial Office, and the Nigerian government, see Flint, "Scandal"; Little, "African Elite," 275–77; C. Thomas, "Propaganda," 150–52, 186–249. British officials' hopes and fears regarding relations with the intelligentsia are well evidenced in discussions about Perham's plan for interracial "cultural centres" from 1938 to 1940; see MPP 691/1; CO 847/12/8; CO 847/15/4/47077; CO 847/19/4/47077. On elite clubs, see Fatayi-Williams, *Faces,* 26–30; Davies, *Memoirs,* 115–16; Leith-Ross, *Stepping-Stones,* 130, 138; Brook, *One-eyed Man,* 90, 165. On new social rules, see Smythe, "Intermarriage"; K. Balogun, *Village Boy,* 63–65. H. Callaway relates the dinner story in *Gender,* 51.

25. Davies, "Colonial Peoples."

26. Ajuluchuku to Nicholson, 2 July 1954, FCP 84/4 f. 65. On wartime and postwar student and political life in Britain, see chap. 4, note 18; see also Carey, *Colonial Students;* Animashawun, "African Students in Britain"; Little, *Negroes in Britain;* Political and Economic Planning, *Colonial Students.* My account also builds on interviews with S. Aluko, Awolowo, and Davies; Awolowo's correspondence with Margery Perham, OAP 1347; Fatayi-Williams, *Faces,* 11–20; Osadebay, *Building a Nation,* 21–25; Biobaku, *When We Were Young,* 109–34; Mba, *Rosiji,* 22–45. For FCB contacts at the organizational and political level, see, e.g., E. E. Esua, NUT General Secretary, to Hinden, 30 Sept. 1943, FCP 82/2 f. 12; correspondence of Aminu Kano with Hilda Selwyn-Clarke in 1956–57, FCP 84/4 ff. 81–86. On personal contacts, see the late 1940s letters between Davies and Hinden in FCP 82/2 f. 40 forward, and between Ita and Nicholson in the early 1950s in FCP 82/2 f. 120 forward. For the flavor of official visits, see "West Africa Goes Abroad," *WAR* 26 (Dec. 1955): 1137–52.

27. *Wasu* 12 (summer 1948): 31. Arikpo's correspondence with the FCB through the mid-1950s reveals this reversal (FCP 82/2 ff. 129–31 and 84/4 ff. 39–50), as do FCB attempts to establish contacts with Arthur Prest in 1953 and Mbonu Ojike in 1954 (FCP 84/4 ff. 38, 62–64). Ayo Ogunsheye's review of Joan Wheare's *Nigerian Legislative Council* in *African Affairs* 49 (July 1950): 259–60, and F. I. Ibiam's corrections to Nicholson's *West African Ferment* in 1950 (FCP 5/4 ff. 1–5) have the air of peer evaluation.

28. Margery Perham to Awolowo, 8 Feb. 1946, OAP 1347; Perham, "Foreword" to Awolowo, *Path,* 12; W. Miller, *Have We Failed,* 69, also 32, 44; Hinden, "Enigma."

29. Ojike, reviewing Omo-Amangie's *Etsakor,* in *African Echo,* 18 June 1949; Adelabu, *Ebullition,* 62.

30. Ojike, *Two Countries,* 107. On Nigerian students in America, see Phelps-

Stokes Fund, *Survey*, 16, 52–75; Gordon, "Student Movement"; Lynch, "Mbadiwe"; Edunam, "Ambassadors"; Sofola, *Dynamism*; Ralston, "Middle Passage"; Fafunwa, "Adventures." On postwar black and white American conceptions of Africa, see Staniland, *American Intellectuals*, 19–98.

31. Hailey, "New Philosophy," 163. The new colonial discourse is conveniently summarized in J. Huxley and Deane, *Future of the Colonies*, where they quote Colonial Secretary Stanley (41). To enter the large literature on the new colonial policies of the 1930s and the process of decolonization emerging from them, see Hargreaves, *Decolonization*; Flint, "Planned Decolonization"; Pearce, *Turning Point*. For early colonial rethinking, see W. Macmillan, *Warning*; W. Macmillan, *Africa Emergent*; Perham, "Restatement"; Coupland, *Empire in These Days*. For Hailey's ideas, see his *African Survey* or, more conveniently, his *Britain and Her Dependencies*. Hailey's suspicions about the abilities of blacks are clear in his "Some Problems." Compare Barnes, "Uprising of Colonial Peoples." On Britain's general acceptance of the Labour Party, see Addison, *Road to 1945*. On imperial propaganda, see Clarke, *West Africans*, esp. 60–78; Olusanya, *Second World War*, 41–71.

32. *WAR* 13 (Aug. 1942): 9; Davies, "Colonial Peoples"; Carr in Legislative Council, 7 Mar. 1940, quoted in Taiwo, *Carr*, 144; [Nwangoro], "Gist of It."

33. J. Campbell, "British Imperialism"; Udoma, *Lion*; Awolowo, *Path*, esp. 17–37; Ojike, *My Africa*; K. Mbadiwe, *Axis Aims*; Orizu, *Without Bitterness*; Azikiwe, *Political Blueprint*.

34. NYM, quoted in Awolowo, *Awo*, 124–25, and in Azikiwe, *Economic Reconstruction*, 33.

35. Ojike, *My Africa*, 114–15; S. Coker in *Nigerian Worker* 1 (Oct. 1943): 2; Azikiwe, "Post War Nigerian Economics." Awolowo's comment was to Colonial Secretary Stanley in Lagos (*Nigerian Worker* 1 [Oct. 1943]). For limited demands before 1942, see, e.g., *African Mirror* editorial, 27 June 1940; WASU, "West African Problems" (1941); ibid. (1942); memoranda by the Oni of Ife and the Olowo of Owo, in [Chiefs], "Sixth Conference of Chiefs of the Western Provinces of Nigeria," 43–44. For later years, see esp. Azikiwe, *Economic Reconstruction*; Olumayiwa, "Towards Post War Economic Reconstruction." On industrialization, see Iyalla to Rita Hinden, 23 Dec. 1943, FCP 82/1A f.32; Yaba Club, *Industrial Development Fund*; Phillips, "Industries in Post-War Nigeria"; Dina, "Problems of Industrialisation." The wide consensus on planning among both core and more peripheral writers, respectively, can be seen in Orizu, *Without Bitterness*, 213–53, and Adinlewa, *Akure District*, 29–31. Cf. Hinden, *Plan*.

36. Azikiwe, "United Nation"; Azikiwe, *Economic Reconstruction*, 5; "CODE," "Nigerian Freedom" (22 Sept.); Ejimofor, *Troubled World*, 9. Compare Azikiwe's rhetoric two years later, in a police report of an NCNC meeting, 24 Mar. 1945, CO 537/286/30453/49; see also "African," "Saving Wage." On the dollar crisis, see Hinds, "Sterling."

37. Azikiwe's Presidential Address to the NCNC, *WAP,* 9 Apr. 1948. The wartime mood in Britain is expressed in Padmore and Cunard, *White Mans' Duty.* On this florescence of radical Pan-Africanism, see Sherwood, "Nkrumah"; Geiss, *Pan-African Movement,* 385–418; Esedebe, *Pan-Africanism,* 161–85. On more radical activities in America, see Sherwood, "No New Deal"; Lynch, *Radicals;* Lynch, "Pan African Responses."

38. J. Balogun, *Virtual Monopoly,* 7–8; Ransome-Kuti, in NCNC, "Whither Nigeria?" 52; Obiahwu, "Bigger Plan"; Rosiji, "Colonial Development Corporation."

39. Macmillan, "Freedom for Colonial Peoples," 84–85; Hancock, *Argument of Empire,* 117; Hinden, "Socialism and the Colonial World," 13–14; Creech Jones, "Labour's Colonial Policy." See also Colonel Stanley's exposition of "Conservative Colonial Policy."

40. Orizu, *Without Bitterness,* 260; K. Mbadiwe, *British and Axis Aims,* 65; Ojike, *My Africa,* 241; *Labour Champion* editorial, 28 Feb. 1950. Ajibola was a lonely voice suggesting British control was compatible with economic development (*Economic Development,* 34–35).

41. Hinden, *Socialists and the Empire,* 18–19, 26; FCB to Akintola, 10 Apr. 1945, FCP 82/2 f. 19.

42. *WAP* editorial, 1 July 1948. On socialist slogans, see *WAP* editorials, 27 May, 30 May, 10 June, 5 July 1944; Azikiwe, *Ideology,* 91–92.

43. *WAP* editorials, 8, 30 Jan. 1948; Mallam Dipcharima and Chief Essien, in NCNC, "Whither Nigeria?" 55–56, 45.

44. N. Eze, "Discourse on Violence"; *African Echo,* 5 Mar. 1949; [Zikists], "Call to Action." The most extended study is Iweriebor, "Radical Nationalism"; see also Olusanya, "Zikist Movement"; Nzimiro, "Zikism and Social Thought." For examples of Zikist extremism, see "Zikist Secretary," "Era of Revolution"; Agwuna, "Call for Revolution." On the National Socialists, see Azikiwe, *Ideology,* 91–92. Many scholars locate the roots of Nigerian radicalism in the late 1940s, for example, Abdulraheem and Olukoshi, "Struggle for Socialism," 64–68; Babatope, *Socialist Alternative,* 43–46.

45. On American alumni, see, e.g., A. Enahoro, *Azikiwe,* 25–27; Tugbiyele, *Emergence,* 23, 56. On Zikist membership, see Iweriebor, "Radical Nationalism," 53–109; Wolpe, *Urban Politics,* 124–25, for Port Harcourt; Okoye interview for Onitsha.

46. *Nigerian Eastern Mail,* 3 July 1948; "CODE," "Nigerian Freedom" (24 Sept.); Ogunsheye, "Nigerian Nationalism," 123; Azikiwe, *Choose Independence,* 10–12; see also Azikiwe, *Zik,* 90. Awolowo found occasion for some harsh attacks in the early 1950s, for example, "Imperialist Agents."

47. Compare the lists in *Wasu* 5 (Sept. 1927): 3–4 and 12, 5 (summer 1948): 29–30. On Nigeria's leadership, see, e.g., Akinyede, *Constitutional Problems,* 55–61.

48. Obio-Offiong, *Nsit History,* 18; Orizu, *Without Bitterness,* 149; Akinsuroju,

*Theatre*, 20; Ita, *Sterile Truths*, 31. For universal models of African history, see Dike, "History and African Nationalism"; Elias, *Customary Law*, 5–6, 301; Epelle, *Promise*, esp. 30–65; see also D. Okonkwo, *History of Nigeria*, esp. 173–346. For a more elaborate Marxist example, see A. Okafor, *Political Ideologies*; for a less elaborate one, Chukwura, *Eastern Motor Transport Union*. On the industrial future, see Achogbuo, *Economic Problems*, 43; Chukwuemeka, *Industrialization*, 20–21.

49. Hans Vischer to Greenridge, Secretary of the Anti-Slavery Society, 1941, quoted in Rich, *Race and Empire*, 157; Hinden to Hugh Foot, 25 Mar. 1949, M. Nicholson to Eyo Ita, 19 Sept. 1950, FCP 82/2, ff. 69, 109; Ita, *Liberal Spirit*, 12. See also W. Miller, *Have We Failed*. On agreements on plan details, see Adebo interview; Dean, *Plan Implementation*, 12–18; Stolper, *Planning without Facts*; Adebo, *Unforgettable Years*; Falola, *Development Planning*, e.g., 137–39. On the charges of insanity, see Tignor, "Political Corruption," 180–82.

50. *Nigerian Freedom* editorial, 24 Nov. 1951.

51. Mbanefo, "Unity and Cooperation," 32; Oluwasanmi, "Minorities," 5–6; Arikpo, *Who Are the Nigerians?* 32; Awolowo, "Nigerian Nation." On the need to connect Nigerians, see Martins, "Spirit of Collectivism"; Dynamic Party, *1956 Constitutional Conference;* Offonry's series on Nigerian cultures, including "Ibo People" and "Hausas." For presentations of the nation's historical roots, see Akinyede, *Constitutional Problems*, 62–69; Tugbiyele, *Emergence*, esp. 17–32; Epelle, *Promise*, esp. 14–29.

52. Fidelis Ogunsheye, foreword to Uzo, *Pathfinder*, ii. Some of the more notable works on politics aside from government and political party material include Uzo's *Political Evolution;* Onyia, *Review of the Constitution;* S. A. Aluko, *Problems of Self-Government;* Elias, "Towards Nationhood"; Akinsuroju, *London Constitutional Conference;* Akintoye, *Self-Government.*

53. Chukwuemeka, *African Dependencies*, 97, 140; Azikiwe, *Economic Reconstruction*, 13; Ogunsheye, "Economic Problem"; Awolowo, "Street Beggar Economy," 41. On enduring fears, see also *African Echo* editorial, 7 June 1949; Nwachuku, "Why 'African' Business Enterprises Fail"; Uwanaka, *New Nigeria*, 5–8.

54. Ojike, "Economic Philosophy"; Awolowo, "Re-Statement of Economic Policy," 5. On the accommodation between African and foreign business interests, see Harneit-Sievers, "African Business," 108–17. On the shift of British priorities, see Hargreaves, "Toward the Transfer." On ideas for state action, see Dina, "Problems of Industrialisation," 11–13; Meniru, "Economic Prosperity"; Asabia, "Progress in Underdeveloped Countries." For a sample industrial scheme, see Ajibola, *Economic Development*, 22–26. On American links, see Ojike, *My Africa*, 277–92; Chukwuemeka, *African Dependencies*, 127–35, 178–87.

55. Oluwasanmi, "Economic Reconstruction," 26–27.

56. Awolowo, *Some Aspects*, 1; K. Mbadiwe, "New Commonwealth"; Daramola, "What Is Commerce," 12; *WAP*, 21 Feb. 1955. See also NCNC, "Pol-

icy for a Free Nigeria," 5–7. Chief Okorodudu's "Nigeria" speech at the 1955 Royal Empire Summer School is a good example of the new cordial atmosphere. Epelle, *Promise*, 165–97, usefully reproduces many government and party economic programs on the eve of independence.

57. NCNC, "Policy for a Free Nigeria," 2. For some sample pronouncements, see AG, *Democratic Socialism*; Awolowo, "Approach to the Economic Development of Nigeria." For commentary on Nigerian socialism, see Lewis, *Politics in West Africa*, 38–39; Nwala, "Ideological Dependency"; Zachernuk, "Awolowo's Economic Thought."

58. Alafe-Aluko, "Sober Reflection," 36; Akinadewo, *Political Nigeria*, 17; Oji, *Bribery*, 14; Akak, *Bribery*, 9.

59. I. Olorun-Nimbe, "Introduction" to G. I. Mbadiwe, *Golden Dawn*; Awolowo, "Nigerian Nation," 27; Solarin, *Self-Government*, 79–83.

60. A. Enahoro, *Azikiwe*, 45; Ita, *Liberal Spirit*, 15; Phillips, *Political Nigeria*, 3–5; Ita, *Reconstructing*, 9; Onipede, "African Nationalism," 278. See also A. Ikoku, "Impression of New Zealand." On late colonial corruption, see Tignor, "Political Corruption."

61. Akinsuroju, *Theatre*, 4.

62. Ogbalu, preface to Azikiwe, *Choose Independence*, 6; *New Africa* editorial, 25 Mar. 1950; "Stormy Corner by 'Goodie,'" *Nigerian Statesman*, 11 June 1955; Protest Committee of Nigerian Youths, *Politics without Bitterness*, 11.

63. Akinsuroju, *Theatre*, 27; Mgbako, *Truth and Falsehood*, 8.

64. Oji, *Bribery*, 7–8; Juwe, *Zik and the Freedom of Nigeria*, 40, 49; *Nigerian Daily Record* editorial, 25 Oct. 1951. This sense of foreboding was shared by many British observers, e.g., Nicholson, *West African Ferment*; E. Huxley, "West Africa in Transition."

65. Onipede, "African Nationalism," 285; A. Enahoro quoted *Pan Africa* in *Azikiwe*, preface; Ita, *Liberal Spirit*, 27–28. For appeals to liberal ideals, Tugbiyele, *Emergence*, and Onyia, *Review of the Constitution*, are good examples among many.

66. See Mba, *Women Mobilized*, 166–223, 282; C. Johnson, "Nigerian Women," 166–98, 228–30; see also Whitaker, "Western Region," 26; Obi, *Our Struggle*; Johnson-Odim, "Ransome-Kuti"; Johnson-Odim, "Abayomi"; Mba, "Ransome-Kuti"; Olusanya, "Oluwole."

67. On the National Church, see Furlong, "Azikiwe"; Onyioha, *National Church*. On millenarianism, see Clarke, *West Africans*, 88–102. On the need for faith, see Ejimofor, *Troubled World*; Bishop Odutola's speech in *Eastern States Express*, 21 Apr. 1959; Ilogu, "Nationalism and the Church." On the need to transcend faith, see, e.g., J. Banjo, "Morality"; Solarin, *Self-Government*, 68–70.

68. Orizu, *Without Bitterness*, 150; Afikpo Youth Welfare League, "Constitution," 1; Adelabu, *Ebullition*, 94; *Eastern States Express* editorial, 2 May 1951. The literature on local cultures can only be touched on here; it deserves more careful study. On Yoruba culture and history, see Egbe Omo Oduduwa, *Sym-*

*posium;* Adekanmbi, *Yoruba Way.* The Yoruba Historical Research Company published several books by E. A. Kenyo, including *Progenitor* and *Founder.* There was much activity regarding Igbo language and culture, e.g.: Akanu, *Edda;* A. Ike, *Origin;* A. Ike, *Great Men;* Orakwue, *Onitsha Custom;* K. C. Eze, *Ibo Native Laws;* Olisah, *Ibo Native Law.* Concerted efforts to establish a written literature evoked a debate on orthography examined by Afigbo, *Ropes of Sand,* 355–86. See also Ogbalu, *New Igbo Orthography;* Utchay, *Igbo Orthography.* Egharevba wrote prolifically while also establishing the Benin Museum. See his *Concise Lives; Laws and Customs; Stories of Ancient Benin;* see also Usuanlele and Falola, "Jacob Egharevba." There were many other local historians producing accomplished work, for example, Okojie, *Ishan Native Laws.*

69. Ajayi, "Possibilities"; Oduche, *Akamelu,* 3; Idigo, *Aguleri,* 113. Similar themes are apparent in Obio-Offiong, *Nsit History,* 38–44; Ekeghe, *Abiriba;* Adegbamigbe, *Ile-Oluji;* Aluto, *Nnewi;* Ogali, *Item;* Ijoma, *Osomari People.* Ajayi's comments were augmented by Dike, "History and Self-Government." Although these early contributions to nationalist historiography are largely missed in Neale's *Writing "Independent" History,* her basic critique of the genre applies.

70. Idigo, *Aguleri,* 113; Isuman, *Need for More States,* "Dedication." Many local authors identify local and national leaders rather than the British as antagonists. Good examples are Umo, *Umuahia Today;* Numa, *Urhobo Nation;* Juwe, *Western Ibo People;* Adinlewa, *Akure District.*

71. The cartoon ran in the *Labour Champion* in February and March 1950. On radical parties and later Zikist careers, see Okoye interview; Okoye, *Letter;* Sklar, *Political Parties,* 81, 270–71; *People,* 13, 18, 22, 27 May 1950; *Daily Service,* 9 Nov. 1953. On the enduring nationalist premise, see A. Okafor's *Nigeria* and *Political Ideologies;* Nigerian Peoples Party, *New Nigeria,* 3–5.

72. See, e.g., *Labour Champion* editorials, 2 Mar., 9 June 1950; Agwuna, *Go with the Masses* 1:4; Socialist Workers and Farmers Party, *Manifesto,* 13. On AG tactical radicalism, see Osoba, "Ideological Trends."

73. Adelabu, *Ebullition,* 80–81, 112–13; Orizu, *Without Bitterness,* 287–93; Juwe, *National Church,* 11; Akak, *Bribery,* 113; Utchay, *Principles and Methods;* G. I. Mbadiwe, *Golden Dawn,* 15. For typical criticisms of action but not policy, see, e.g., Nigerian Youth Congress, *Way Forward,* 4–7.

## 6. Colonial Subjects in Context

1. Crowder, "Whose Dream," 23. On postcolonial social criticism, see, e.g., Achebe, *Trouble;* Nwala, "Ideological Dependency"; Nwanko, *Power Dynamics;* Soyinka, *Open Sore.*

2. JanMohamed, "Manichean Allegory."

3. Bhabha, *Location of Culture.* Continuities between colonial and postcolonial thought in Nigeria are not hard to see, even if they remain poorly ana-

lyzed. Early professional historians at the University of Ibadan in the 1960s looked back to the nineteenth-century intelligentsia to help found their sense of Nigerian identity, partly it seems in reaction to the absence of historical consciousness of the 1950s. See Ajayi, *Missions;* Ayandele, *Missionary Impact;* Ayandele, *Holy Johnson.* The political philosophies developed by both Azikiwe and Awolowo in their later careers look back to the interwar period as a relevant starting point. See, e.g., Azikiwe, *Ideology;* Awolowo, *Problems of Africa.* Contemporary historians remain interested in Samuel Johnson's work on the Yoruba as a foundation for their own work; see, e.g., Falola, *Pioneer.*

4. For work on Yoruba thought, see, e.g., Peel, "Olaju"; on women, see Bolanle, *Nigerian Women.* On history writing in colonial Nigeria, see Barber, "I Could Speak"; Neale, *Writing "Independent" History;* Law, "Yoruba Historiography": Zachernuk, "Origins"; Zachernuk, "Imperial Culture." On where gendered questions might take this study, see McClintock, *Imperial Leather.*

# Bibliography

## Archival Sources

Awolowo, Obafemi. Papers. Sopolu Library, Ikenne, Nigeria.
Colonial Office Records. Public Record Office, Kew.
Fabian Colonial Bureau. Papers. Rhodes House, Oxford.
International African Institute. Papers. London School of Economics.
Macaulay, Herbert. Papers. Africana Collection, University of Ibadan.
Malinowski, Bronislaw. Papers. London School of Economics.
Morel, E. D. Papers. London School of Economics.
Nigerian National Archives, Ibadan.
Oldham, J. H. Papers. Rhodes House, Oxford.
Perham, Margery. Papers. Rhodes House, Oxford.
Royal Commonwealth Society Collection, Cambridge University Library.

## Interviews

Chief S. O. Adebo, Abeokuta, 6 Aug. 1986.
Professor S. A. Aluko, Akure, 11 Aug. 1986.
Chief Obafemi Awolowo, Ikenne, 8 Aug. 1986.
Chief H. O. Davies, Lagos, 8 July 1986.
Mokwugo Okoye, Enugu, 13 Aug. 1986.
Tai Solarin, Ikenne, 5 July 1986.

## Newspapers and Journals

| | |
|---:|---|
| *Africa* | New York |
| *Africa: Today and Tommorrow* | New York |
| *Africana* | London |
| *African Echo* | Ebute Metta |
| *African Interpreter* | New York |

| | |
|---|---|
| *African Messenger* | Lagos |
| *African Mirror* | Lagos |
| *African Public Opinion* | [Lagos?] |
| *African Times* | London |
| *Anglo-African* | Lagos |
| *Beacon* | Ibadan |
| *Comet* | Lagos |
| *Daily Service* | Lagos |
| *Eastern States Express* | Aba |
| *Elder Dempster Review* | Liverpool |
| *Empire* | London |
| *Ibadan* | Ibadan |
| *The Keys* | London |
| *Labour Champion* | Lagos |
| *Lagos Daily News* | Lagos |
| *Lagos Observer* | Lagos |
| *Lagos Standard* | Lagos |
| *Lagos Times* | Lagos |
| *Lagos Weekly Record* | Lagos |
| *New Africa* | Enugu |
| *New Nigerian* | Ibadan |
| *Nigeria Magazine* | Lagos |
| *Nigerian Daily Record* | Enugu |
| *Nigerian Daily Times* | Lagos |
| *Nigerian Eastern Mail* | Calabar |
| *Nigerian Freedom* | Calabar |
| *Nigerian Statesman* | Lagos |
| *Nigerian Tribune* | Ibadan |
| *Nigerian Worker* | Lagos |
| *People* | Port Harcourt |
| *Service* | Lagos |
| *Sierra Leone Weekly News* | Freetown |
| *University Herald* | Ibadan |
| *Wasu* | London |
| *West Africa* | London |
| *West African Pilot* | Lagos |
| *West African Review* | Liverpool |

## Articles, Books, Pamphlets, and Unpublished Works

Abayomi, Oyinkan M. "Modern Womanhood." *Service*, Dec. 1935, p. 14.

Abdulraheem, Tajudeen, and Adebayo Olukoshi. "The Left in Nigerian Politics and the Struggle for Socialism, 1945–1985." *ROAPE* 37 (1986): 64–80.

Abernethy, David. *Political Dilemma of Popular Education.* Stanford, Calif.: Stanford Univ. Press, 1969.

"A.B.L." "Nigerian Youth Movement Today and Tomorrow." *Service,* Sept. 1936, pp. 9–11.

Achebe, Chinua. *The Trouble with Nigeria.* London: Heinemann, 1983.

Achogbuo, Onogbo. *Democratic Socialism, Being the Manifesto of the Action Group of Nigeria for an Independent Nigeria.* Lagos: AG Bureau of Information, 1960.

———. *Economic Problems in Independent Nigeria: A Call to Release the Productive Forces of the Nigerian People.* Enugu: n.p., [1960].

Addison, Paul. *The Road to 1945: British Politics in the Second World War.* London: Cape, 1975.

Adebayo, Augustus. *White Man in Black Skin.* Ibadan: Spectrum, 1981.

Adebo, Simeon O. *Our Unforgettable Years.* Yaba and Ibadan: Macmillan Nigeria, 1984.

Adefuye, Ade, Babatunde Agiri, and Jide Osuntokun, eds. *Peoples of Lagos State.* Lagos: Lantern Books, 1987.

Adegbamigbe, A. A. *History, Laws, and Customs of Ile-Oluji.* Ile-Oluji: the author, 1962.

Adekanmbi, Sola. *The Yoruba Way: A Handbook of Yoruba Customs.* Lagos: the author, 1955.

Adelabu, Adegoke. *Africa in Ebullition.* Ibadan: the author, [1952].

Adeloye, Adelola. "Nigerian Pioneer Doctors and Early West African Politics." *Nigeria Magazine* 121 (1976): 2–24.

———. *Nigerian Pioneers of Modern Medicine: Selected Writings.* Ibadan: I.U.P.: 1977.

Ademola, A. Ade. "The Solidarity of the African Race." In *Negro Anthology,* ed. Nancy Cunard. 1934. Rpt. New York: Negro University Press, 1969.

Adeniyi-Jones, Curtis C. *Political and Administrative Problems of Nigeria.* London: Bonner, 1928.

———. *Address Given by Honorable Dr. C. C. Adeniyi-Jones, M.B., B.S. etc., President of the Nigerian National Democratic Party at a Mass Meeting Held at Glover Memorial Hall, Lagos, on 1rst October 1938.* N.p., [1938?].

Adewoye, Omoniyi. "Self-Taught Attorneys in Lagos, 1865–1913." *JHSN* 5 (1969): 47–65.

———. "Sapara Williams: The Lawyer and the Public Servant." *JHSN* 6 (1971): 47–65.

———. "The Antecedents." In *Ibadan,* ed. Ajayi and Tamuno.

———. *The Judicial System in Southern Nigeria, 1854–1954: Law and Justice in a Dependency.* London: Longman, 1978.

Adi, Hakim. "Bandele Omoniyi—A Neglected Nigerian Nationalist." *African Affairs* 90 (1991): 581–65.

———. "West African Students in Britain, 1900–1960: The Politics of Exile." *Immigrants and Minorities* 12 (1993): 107–28.

———. *West Africans in Britain, 1900–1960: Nationalism, Pan-Africanism, and Communism.* London: Lawrence and Wishart, 1998.

Adinlewa, Benjamin F. A. *Akure District: Progress, Problems, and Possibilities.* Ikare: the author, 1952.

Afigbo, A. E. "The Background to the Southern Nigerian Education Code of 1903." *JHSN* 4 (1968): 197–226.

———. *Ropes of Sand: Studies in Igbo History and Culture.* Ibadan: I.U.P., 1981.

———. "Nnamdi Azikiwe: His Cultural and Historial Roots." In *Azikiwe and the African Revolution,* ed. M. S. O. Olisa and O. M. Ikejiani-Clark. Onitsha: Africana-FEP, 1989.

Afikpo Youth Welfare League. *Constitution of the Afikpo Youth Welfare League.* Calabar: [Henshaw Press], [1946?].

"African." "Africans Demand a Saving Wage." *WAR* 14 (Sept. 1943): 19–20.

"African Doctor." "The Admixture of Black and White." *WAR* 6 (Feb. 1933): 50.

Agbebi, Mojola. *Inaugural Sermon Delivered at the Celebration of the First Anniversary of the "African Church," Lagos, West Africa, December 21, 1902.* New York: Edgar Howorth, 1903.

———. "The West African Problem." In *Inter-racial Problems,* ed. G. Spiller. London: P. S. King, 1911.

Agiri, Babatunde. "Slavery in Yoruba Society in the Nineteenth Century." In *The Ideology of Slavery in Africa,* ed. Paul Lovejoy. Beverly Hills, Calif.: Sage, 1981.

———. "Architecture as a Source of History: The Lagos Example." In *Peoples of Lagos State,* ed. Adefuye et al.

Agwuna, Osita Christopher. "A Call for Revolution, Speech for the Zikist Movement Given on 27 October 1948 in Tom Jones Memorial Hall, Lagos." In CO 537/3557.

———. *Go with the Masses: Studies in Essential Tactics in National and Colonial Struggles*. Vol. 1. Enugu: [Progress Printing Works], [1953].

Ajayi, J. F. Ade. "The Possibilities of the Development of Nigerian History." *University Herald* 1 (Apr. 1948): 13–15.

———. "Henry Venn and the Policy of Development." *JHSN* 1 (1959): 331–42.

———. "Nineteenth Century Origins of Nigerian Nationalism." *JHSN* 2 (1961): 196–210.

———. *Christian Missions in Nigeria, 1841–1891: The Making of a New Elite*. London: Longman, 1966.

Ajayi, J. F. A., and Tekena N. Tamuno, eds. *The University of Ibadan, 1948–1973: A History of the First Twenty-Five Years*. Ibadan: I.U.P., 1973.

Ajibola, J. O. *Economic Development of West Africa*. London: the author, [1949].

Ajisafe, Ajayi Kolawole. *The Laws and Customs of the Yoruba People*. London: Routledge; Lagos: CMS Bookshops, 1924.

———. *Abeokuta Centenary and Its Celebrations*. N.p., [1931].

———. *The Errors and Defeat of Ladipo Solanke, M.A., B.C.L., LL.B.* Lagos: [Hope Rising Press], 1931.

———. *History of Abeokuta with Illustrations and a Short Biography with Important Events during the Reign of Oba Alaiyeluwa Ademola II Alake of Abeokuta*. 3d ed. Lagos: [Kash and Klare Bookshop], 1948.

Akak, Eyo Okon. *Bribery and Corruption in Nigeria*. Ibadan: n.p., 1953.

Akanu, Jonathon Okorie. *The History of Edda*. Ekoli Edda, Afikpo: the author, 1956.

Akere, Funso. "Linguistic Assimilation in Socio-Historical Dimensions in Urban and Sub-Urban Lagos." In *Peoples of Lagos State*, ed. Adefuye et al.

Akinadewo, Samuel Ade-Kahunsi. *Political Nigeria on the Eve of Self-Government*. Ibadan: [Adeyemi Printing Works], 1957.

Akin-Awosefaju, H. T. "The Late Mr. Julius Ojo-Cole, a Tribute." *Nigerian Daily Times*, 22 Feb. 1938.

Akinsuroju, Olurunayomi. *Nigerian Political Theatre (1923–53)*. Lagos: City Publishing Association, 1953.

———. *London Constitutional Conference: A Review*. Lagos: [Pacific Printing Works], 1957.

Akintola, S. L. "The Tragedy of Western Civilization." *Comet*, 13 Sept. 1939.

Akintoye, O. A. *Self-Government for Nigeria*. Lagos: the author, 1956.

Akinyede, G. B. A. *The Political and Constitutional Problems of Nigeria.* Lagos: Nigerian Printing and Publishing, 1957.

Akiwowo, Akinsola. "The Place of Mojola Agbebi in the African Nationalist Movements, 1890–1917." *Phylon* 26 (1965): 122–39.

———. "Racialism and Shifts in the Mental Orientation of Black People in West Africa and the Americas, 1856 to 1956." *Phylon* 31 (1970): 256–64.

Akiwumi, Abiola. "West Africa and the World." *Wasu* 1 (Dec. 1926): 14–16.

Akpabio, Ibanga Udo. "The Romance of the Ibibio Union." *African Interpreter* 1 (1943): 14, 20.

Alafe-Aluko, M. Ola. "A Time for Sober Reflection." *University Herald* 1 (July 1948): 36.

Alakija, O. A. "The African Must Have Western Education." *Elders Review* 9 (July 1930): 94–95.

Aluko, S. A. *The Problems of Self-Government for Nigeria: A Critical Analysis.* Devon: Arthur H. Stockwell, [1955].

Aluko, T. M. *His Worshipful Majesty.* London: Heinemann, 1973.

Aluto, John O. *A Groundwork of Nnewi History (from the Earliest Times to 1955 Inclusive).* Nnewi: the author, 1963.

Amachree, G. K. J. "Why Colonial Students Supported Labour at the Last Election: A Summary of West African Students' Opinions." *Wasu* 12 (Mar. 1946): 19–21.

Amangala, G. I. *Short History of Ijaw.* Port Harcourt: [Ikiess Press], 1954 (introduction dated 1939).

Amosu, Nunasu. "The New Nigeria." *Beacon* 2 (Christmas 1960): 34–35.

Ananaba, Wogu. *The Trade Union Movement in Nigeria.* London: Hurst, 1969.

Anene, J. C. *Southern Nigeria in Transition, 1885–1906: Theory and Practice in a Colonial Protectorate.* Cambridge: C.U.P., 1966.

Animashawun, G. K. "African Students in Britain." *Race* 5 (1963): 38–47.

Anirare, Daniel [Aladesanmi II, the Ewi of Ado-Ekiti]. *My Early Life.* N.p., 1977.

Anyanwu, C. N. "The Growth of Port Harcourt, 1912–1960." In *The City of Port Harcourt: A Symposium on Its Growth and Development,* ed. W. Ogionwo. Ibadan: Heinemann Educational, 1979.

Anyiam, Fred. *Men and Matters in Nigerian Politics (1934–58).* N.p.: Yaba, 1959.

Appiah, Kwame Anthony. *In My Father's House: Africa in the Philosophy of Culture.* New York: O.U.P., 1992.

Apter, Andrew. *Black Critics and Kings: The Hermeneutics of Power in Yoruba Society.* Chicago: Univ. of Chicago Press, 1992.

Apter, David E. *Ghana in Transition.* 2d ed. Princeton, N.J.: Princeton Univ. Press, 1972.

Arikpo, Okoi. *Who Are the Nigerians?* Lagos: Ministry of Information, [1957?].

Ariori, A. T. "Nigeria in the British Empire." *Service,* Sept. 1935, pp. 18–19.

Asabia, S. O. "Thoughts on the Probable Course of Economic Progress in Underdeveloped Countries with Particular Reference to Nigeria." *New Nigerian* 1 (Dec. 1962): 20–24.

Asad, Talal. "Afterword: From the History of Colonial Anthropology to the Anthropology of Western Hegemony." In *Colonial Situations,* ed. George W. Stocking, Jr. Madison: Univ. of Wisconsin Press, 1991.

Ashcroft, Bill, Gareth Griffiths, and Helen Tiffin. *The Empire Writes Back: Theory and Practice in Post-Colonial Literatures.* New York: Routledge, 1989.

Awe, Bolanle, ed. *Nigerian Women in Perspective.* Lagos: Sankore and Ibadan: Bookcraft, 1992.

Awe, Olumuyiwa. "Ibadan: Recollections and Reflections." In *Ibadan,* ed. Ajayi and Tamuno.

Awolowo, Obafemi. "Economic Programme Submitted to the Nigerian Youth Movement, Ibadan Branch, 18 June 1940." OAP, MS.

———. "The Ayes Have It!" *Daily Service,* 6 Apr. 1943.

———. "There Is No Such Thing as a Nigerian Nation." *WAR* 16 (Aug. 1945): 26–27.

———. *Path to Nigerian Freedom.* London: Faber, 1947.

———. "Street Beggar Economy (1952)." In *Voice of Reason: Selected Speeches of Chief Obafemi Awolowo.* Akure: Fagbamigbe, 1981.

———. "Re-statement of Economic Policy, Being an Address Delivered by Chief the Hon. Obafemi Awolowo to the Central Committee of the Action Group in May 1954." OAP.

———. "Imperialist Agents in Dependent Countries." In *Action Group Summer School Lectures 1955,* ed. Action Group. [Ibadan]: AG Bureau of Information, [1955].

———. *Some Aspects of Our Economic Problems: An Address Delivered to the Lagos Chamber of Commerce.* Lagos: Government Printer, 1955.

———. *Awo: The Autobiography of Chief Obafemi Awolowo.* Cambridge: C.U.P., 1960.

———. "Approach to the Economic Problem of Nigeria: An Address at the University of Nsukka, 30 January, 1961." Typescript. OAP.

———. *The Problems of Africa.* London: Macmillan Education, 1977.

Ayandele, E. A. *The Missionary Impact on Modern Nigeria, 1842–1914: A Social and Political Analysis.* London: Longmans, 1966.

———. "The Colonial Church Question in Lagos Politics, 1905–1911." *Odu* 4 (1968): 53–73.

———. *Holy Johnson: Pioneer of African Nationalism, 1836–1917.* London: Cass, 1970.

———. *A Visionary of the African Church: Mojola Agbebi, 1860–1917.* Nairobi: East Africa Publishing House, 1971.

———. *The Educated Elite in the Nigerian Society.* Ibadan: I.U.P., 1974.

———. *The Ijebu of Yorubaland, 1850–1950: Politics, Economy, and Society.* Ibadan: Heinemann Educational Books Nigeria, 1992.

Aye, Effiong U. *Old Calabar through the Centuries.* Calabar: Hope Waddell Press, 1967.

Azikiwe, Nnamdi. "Nigerian Political Institutions." *JNH* 14 (1929): 328–40.

———. "Fragments of Onitsha History." *JNH* 15 (1930): 474–97.

———. "Ethics of Colonial Imperialism." *JNH* 16 (1931): 287–308.

———. *Liberia in World Politics.* 1934. Rpt. Westport, Conn.: Negro Univ. Press, 1970.

———. *Renascent Africa.* 1937. Rpt. London: Frank Cass, 1968.

———. "Post War Nigerian Economics." *WAP*, 11 June 1943.

———. "Let Us Build a United Nation." *Comet*, 20 Oct. 1943.

———. *Economic Reconstruction of Nigeria.* Lagos: African Book Co., 1943.

———. *Political Blueprint of Nigeria.* Lagos: African Book Co., [1943].

———. *Taxation in Nigeria.* Lagos: African Book Co., [1943].

———. *The Development of Political Parties in Nigeria.* London: Office of the Commissioner in the United Kingdom for the Eastern Region of Nigeria, 1957.

———. *Choose Independence or More States: A National Challenge by Dr. Nnamdi Azikiwe.* Onitsha: Varsity, [1958].

———. *Zik: A Selection from the Speeches of Nnamdi Azikiwe.* Cambridge: C.U.P., 1961.

———. *My Odyssey: An Autobiography.* London: C. Hurst, 1970.

———. *Ideology for Nigeria: Capitalism, Socialism, or Welfarism?* Lagos: Macmillan Nigeria, 1980.

Babatope, E. *Nigeria: A Socialist Alternative.* Benin City: Jodah Publications, 1986.

Baker, Pauline H. *Urbanization and Political Change: The Politics of Lagos, 1917–1967.* Los Angeles: Univ. of California Press, 1974.

Balogun, Joseph Okanlawon. *The Existence of Virtual Monopoly in the British Colony of Nigeria.* Lagos: [Ife-Olu Printing Works], 1944.

Balogun, Kola. *Interpreting "Nigeria in Cartoons": An Appreciation of the Book.* Lagos: [Ijaiye Press], 1944.

———. *Village Boy: My Own Story*. Ibadan: Africanus, 1969.

Banjo, J. A. "The New Morality." *University Herald* 1 (July 1948): 20–21.

Banjo, S. Ayodele. "The Teaching of Yoruba in the Secondary Schools of Nigeria." *Nigeria* 13 (Mar. 1938): 59–69.

Banton, M. P. *The Coloured Quarter*. London: Cape, 1955.

Barber, Karin. "Discursive Strategies in the Texts of Ifa and in the 'Holy Book of Odu of the African Church of Orunmila.'" In *Self-Assertion*, ed. Barber and Moraes Farias.

———. *I Could Speak until Tomorrow: Oriki, Women, and the Past in a Yoruba Town*. Washington, D.C.: Smithsonian Institution Press, 1991.

———. "African-Language Literature and Postcolonial Criticism." *Research in African Literatures* 26 (1995): 3–30.

Barber, Karin, and P. F. de Moraes Farias, eds. *Self-Assertion and Brokerage: Early Cultural Nationalism in West Africa*. Birmingham: Birmingham Univ. Centre of African Studies, 1990.

Barnes, Leonard. *Duty of Empire*. London: Gollancz, 1935.

———. "The Uprising of Colonial Peoples." In *Where Stands Democracy? A Collection of Essays by Members of the Fabian Society*. London: Macmillan, 1940.

Barzun, J. *Race: A Study in Modern Superstition*. New York: Harcourt-Brace, 1937.

Bassin, Mark. "Inventing Siberia." *American Historical Review* 96 (1991): 763–94.

Bastian, Misty L. "'Bloodhounds Who Have No Friends': Witchcraft and Locality in the Nigerian Popular Press." In *Modernity and Its Malcontents: Ritual and Power in Postcolonial Africa*, ed. Jean Comaroff and John Comaroff. Chicago: Univ. of Chicago Press, 1993.

Beckman, Bjorn. "Imperialism and the 'National Bourgeoisie.'" *ROAPE* 22 (1981): 5–19.

Beer, C. E. F. *The Politics of Peasant Groups in Western Nigeria*. Ibadan: I.U.P., 1976.

Benson, Peter. *"Black Orpheus," "Transition," and Modern Cultural Awakening in Africa*. Berkeley and Los Angeles: Univ. of California Press, 1986.

Berghahn, Marion. *Images of Africa in Black American Literature*. London: Macmillan, 1977.

Berry, Sara. "Christianity and the Rise of Cocoa-Growing in Ibadan and Ondo." *JHSN* 4 (1968): 439–51.

Bhabha, Homi. *The Location of Culture*. London: Routledge, 1994.

Biobaku, Saburi O. *Egba and Their Neighbors, 1842–1872*. Oxford: Clarendon, 1957.

————. *When We Were Young*. Ibadan: Univ. Press, 1992.

Blackett, R. J. M. "Return to the Motherland: Robert Campbell, a Jamaican in Early Colonial Lagos." *Phylon* 40 (1979): 375–86.

Blyden, Edward Wilmot. *Christianity, Islam, and the Negro Race*. 2d ed. London: W. B. Whittingham, 1888.

————. *The African Problem and the Method of Its Solution . . . Delivered at the Seventy-third Anniversary of the American Colonization Society*. Washington, D.C.: [Gibson Bros.], 1890.

————. *The African Society and Miss Mary H. Kingsley*. London: West Africa, 1901.

————. *West Africa before Europe and Other Addresses*. London: C. M. Phillips, 1905.

————. *African Life and Customs*. 1908. Rpt. London: African Publication Society, 1969.

Blyden, E. W., and Sir Gilbert Carter. *The Lagos Training College and Industrial Institute*. Lagos: Lagos Standard, 1896.

Boadi-Siaw, S. Y. "Brazilian Returnees of West Africa." In *Global Dimensions*, ed. Harris.

Boas, Franz. "Fallacies of Racial Inferiority." *Current History* 25 (Feb. 1927): 676–82.

Bolt, Christine. *Victorian Attitudes to Race*. Toronto: Univ. of Toronto Press, 1971.

Brady, M. "Sartorial Sidelights in West Africa." *WAR* 26 (Dec. 1955): 1120–24.

Bretton, Henry L. *Power and Stability in Nigeria: The Politics of Decolonization*. New York: Praeger, 1962.

Brook, Ian [Ian Brinkworth]. *The One-Eyed Man Is King*. London: Cassell, 1966.

Brown, Spencer Hunter. "A History of the People of Lagos, 1852–1886." Ph.D. diss., Northwestern University, 1964.

————. "Public Health in Lagos, 1850–1900: Perceptions, Patterns, and Perspectives." *IJAHS* 25 (1992): 337–60.

Burns, Elinor. *British Imperialism in West Africa*. [London]: Labour Research Department, 1927.

Buxton, Charles R. "Some African Friends." *Service*, May 1935, pp. 13–15.

Buxton, Thomas Fowell. *The African Slave Trade and Its Remedy*. 2d ed. 1840. Rpt. London: Dawsons, 1968.

Callaway, Archibald. "School Leavers and the Developing Economy of Nigeria." In *Nigerian Political Scene*, ed. Tilman and Cole.

Callaway, Helen. *Gender, Culture, and Empire: European Women in Colonial Nigeria*. Basingstoke: Macmillan, 1987.

Campbell, J. G. *Observations on Some Topics in Nigeria during the Adminis-tration of His Excellency Sir Frederick Lugard G.C.M.G., First Governor General of Nigeria.* Lagos: the author, [1918].

———. *Our West African Governors: The Congress Movement and Herbert Macaulay.* Lagos: [Bosero Press], 1921.

———. *Lagos: Awake on the Election Question.* Lagos: n.p., 1923.

———. "British Imperialism and Self Government." Typescript, [1945]. CAMP mf 929.

Campbell, Robert. *A Pilgrimage to My Motherland.* New York: Thomas Hamilton, 1861.

Carey, Alexander T. *Colonial Students: A Study of the Social Adaptation of Colonial Students in London.* London: Secker and Warburg, 1956.

Chakrabarty, Dipesh. "Postcoloniality and the Artifice of History: Who Speaks for the 'Indian' Pasts?" *Representations* 37 (winter 1992): 1–26.

Chatterjee, Partha. *Nationalist Thought and the Colonial World: A Derivative Discourse?* London: Zed, 1986.

[Chiefs]. "Sixth Conference of Chiefs of the Western Provinces of Nigeria: Record of Proceedings." Mimeo, [1942].

Chinweizu, Onwuchekwa Jemie, and Ihechukwu Madubuike. *Toward the Decolonization of African Literature.* Vol 1. Enugu: Fourth Dimension, 1980.

Chukwuemeka, Nwanko. *African Dependencies: A Challenge to Western Democracy.* New York: William-Frederick Press, 1950.

———. *Industrialization of Nigeria.* New York: William-Frederick Press, 1951.

Chukwura, Christopher Okobie. *A Short History of Eastern Motor Transport Union, Nigeria.* Aba: [International Press], 1951.

Citizens' Committee for Independence. *Forward to Freedom: Constitutional Proposals for a United Nigeria.* Lagos: the Committee, 1957.

———. *The Case for More States: Memorandum Submitted to the Minorities Commission.* Ibadan: the Committee, 1957.

Clark, Ebun. *Herbert Ogunde: The Making of Nigerian Theatre.* London: O.U.P., 1982.

Clarke, Peter B. *West Africans at War, 1914–18, 1939–45: Colonial Propaganda and Its Cultural Aftermath.* London: Ethnographica, 1986.

Clifford, James. *The Predicament of Culture: Twentieth Century Ethnography, Literature, and Art.* Cambridge: Harvard Univ. Press, 1988.

"A Cocoa Farmer." "West African Farmers Organize." *Africa* (New York) 1 (1928): 24.

"CODE." "Nigerian Freedom: Evolution or Revolution." 10-part series in *The People*, 18 Sept.–3 Oct. 1951.

Coker, Folarin. *The Right Honourable Sir Adetokunbo Ademola, C.F.R., K.B.E., P.C.* 2d ed. Lagos: Times Press, 1972.

———. *A Lady: A Biography of Lady Oyinkan Abayomi.* Ibadan: Evans Brothers, 1987.

Coker, Increase H. E. *Seventy Years of the Nigerian Press.* [Lagos]: Daily Times, [1952?].

———. "The Nigerian Press." In *Report on the Press in West Africa.* Committee for Inter African Relations, mimeo, 1960.

Coker, Jacob Kanyinde. *Polygamy Defended: A Defence of Polygamy . . . against the Minute of the C.M.S. on Polygamy.* [Lagos?]: [Karaole Printing Works], [1915?].

Coker, Samuel A. *Lecture: The Rights of Africans to Organize and Establish Indigenous Churches Unattached to, and Uncontrolled by Foreign Church Organizations.* Lagos: [Tika Tore Printing Works], [1917].

Cole, Abayomi. "Ifa Viewed Theologically, Mythologically, and Scientifically." *LWR,* 15 Dec. 1900.

Cole, Patrick. *Modern and Traditional Elites in the Politics of Lagos.* London: Cambridge Univ. Press, 1975.

Cole, Robert B. "West Africa in Evolution." *Wasu* 2 (Apr. 1933): 31.

Coleman, James S. *Nigeria: Background to Nationalism.* 1958. Rpt. Benin City: Broburg and Wistrom, 1986.

Comaroff, Jean, and John Comaroff. *Of Revelation and Revolution: Christianity, Colonialism, and Consciousness in South Africa.* Vol 1. Chicago: Univ. of Chicago Press, 1991.

Cookson, C. E. "The Colour Complex." *WAR* 6 (Dec. 1935): 9–10.

Cooper, Frederick, Allen Isaacman, Florencia Mallon, William Roseberry, and Steve Stern. *Confronting Historical Paradigms: Peasants, Labor, and the Capitalist System in Africa and Latin America.* Madison: Univ. of Wisconsin Press, 1993.

Coupland, Reginald. *The Empire in These Days.* London: Macmillan, 1935.

Creech Jones, Arthur. "Labour's Colonial Policy." *West Africa,* 18 Feb. 1950, p. 125.

Crowder, Michael. "The Outsider and African Culture: The Case of E. H. Duckworth and *Nigeria Magazine.*" In *African Culture and Intellectual Leaders and the Development of the New African Nations,* ed. Robert W. July and Peter Benson. New York: Rockefeller Foundation, and Ibadan: I.U.P., 1982.

———. "Whose Dream Was It Anyway? Twenty-Five Years of African Independence." *African Affairs* 86 (Jan. 1987): 1–24.

Crowther, Samuel. *A Grammar and Vocabulary of the Yoruba Language Together with Introductory Remarks by O. E. Vidal, Bishop of Sierra Leone.* London: Seeleys, 1852.

————. *Journal of an Expedition up the Niger and Tshadda Rivers in 1854.* 1855. Rpt. London: Cass, 1970.

————. *A Charge Delivered on the Banks of the River Niger in West Africa.* London: Seeley, Jackson and Halliday, 1866.

Crowther, Samuel, and John Christopher Taylor. *The Gospel on the Banks of the Niger: Journals and Notices of the Native Missionaries Accompanying the Niger Expedition of 1857–1859.* 1859. Rpt. London: Dawsons, 1968.

Crummell, Alexander. "The Progress of Civilization along the West Coast of Africa." In *The Future of Africa, Being Addresses, Sermons, Etc., Delivered in the Republic of Liberia.* 1861. Rpt. New York: Negro Universities Press, 1969.

Curtin, Philip D. *The Image of Africa: British Ideas and Action, 1780–1850.* Madison: Univ. of Wisconsin Press, 1964.

Cutcliffe-Hyne, C. J. "Back to the Coast Again." *Elders Review* 9 (July 1930): 286–87, 305.

Daniel, John. "The Culture of Dependency and Political Education in Africa." In *Political Economy of Africa*, ed. Dennis Cohen and John Daniel. London: Longman, 1981.

Daramola, J. B. "What Is Commerce." In *Commerce and Industry in Nigeria.* Lagos: Government Printer, 1955.

Davidson, Basil. *The Black Man's Burden: Africa and the Curse of the Nation-State.* New York: Times Books, 1992.

Davies, H. O. "The Youth Movement in West Africa." *WAR* 7 (Mar. 1936): 5, 8.

————. "Opportunities for Africans." *WAP*, 25 Nov. 1937.

————. "What I Think of the Pool." *WAP*, 26 Jan. 1938.

————. "Colonial Peoples and the New Order." *Daily Service*, 6 Nov. 1940.

————. *Memoirs.* Ibadan: Evans Brothers, 1989.

Davis, J., ed. *Africa as Seen by American Negroes.* N.p.: Presence Africaine, 1958.

Dean, Edward. *Plan Implementation in Nigeria, 1962–1966.* Ibadan: O.U.P., 1972.

Delano, Isaac Oluwole. *The Soul of Nigeria.* London: T. Werner Laurie, 1937.

————. *Notes and Comments from Nigeria.* London and Redhill: United Society for Christian Literature, 1944.

Delany, Martin. *Official Report of the Niger Valley Exploring Party* (1861). Rpt. in *Search for a Place: Black Separatism and Africa, 1860*, ed. H. M. Bell. Ann Arbor: Univ. of Michigan Press, 1971.

Deniga, Adeoye. *African Leaders.* 2d ed. rev. and enl. Lagos: [African Church Printing Press], 1919.

————. *Nigerian Who's Who for 1922.* Lagos: [Awoboh Press], 1921.

————. *Nigerian Who's Who for 1934.* 4th ed. Lagos: [Awoboh Press], 1934.

Dennett, R. E. *At the Back of the Black Man's Mind: or, Notes on the Kingly Office in West Africa.* London: Macmillan, 1906.

————. *Nigerian Studies.* London: Macmillan, 1910.

Denzer, LaRay. "Women in Government Service in Colonial Nigeria, 1862–1945." Working Papers in African Studies, No. 136. Boston: African Studies Center, Boston University, 1989.

————. "Yoruba Women: A Historiographical Study." *IJAHS* 27 (1994): 1–39.

"De Rem," "Negro's Position among the Nations of the World." *LDN,* 6 Mar. 1934.

Deutsch, Jan-Georg. *Educating the Middlemen: A Political and Economic History of Statutory Cocoa Marketing in Nigeria, 1936–1947.* Berlin: Center for Modern Oriental Studies, 1995.

Dike, Kenneth Onwuka. "History and African Nationalism." Proceedings, First Annual Conference of the West African Institute of Social and Economic Research, University College Ibadan, 1952. Rpt. Ibadan: Nigerian Institute of Social and Economic Research, 1961.

————. "African History and Self-Government." *West Africa,* 28 Feb. 1953, p. 177.

————. *Trade and Politics in the Niger Delta, 1830–1885.* Oxford: Clarendon Press, 1956.

Dina, I. O. "Problems of Industrialisation." *University Herald* 1 (Dec. 1948): 9–13.

Dirks, Nicholas B., ed. *Colonialism and Culture.* Ann Arbor: Univ. of Michigan Press, 1992.

Dixon-Fyle, Mac. "The Saro in the Political Life of Early Port Harcourt, 1913–49." *JAH* 30 (1989): 125–38.

Doortmont, M. R. "Samuel Johnson (1846–1901): Missionary, Diplomat, and Historian." In *Yoruba Historiography,* ed. Falola.

Du Bois, W. E. B. *The Conservation of Races.* 1897. In *The Seventh Son: The Thought and Writings of W. E. B. Du Bois,* ed. Julius Lester. New York: Random House, 1971.

————. *Black Folk: Then and Now.* 1939. Rpt. New York: Kraus-Thomson, 1975.

Duffield, Ian. "The Business Activities of Dusé Mohamed Ali: An Example of the Economic Dimension of Pan-Africanism, 1912–1945." *JHSN* 4 (1969): 571–600.

————. "Dusé Mohamed Ali and the Development of Pan Africanism, 1866–1945." Ph.D. diss., Edinburgh University, 1971.

———. "Dusé Mohamed Ali, Afro-Asian Solidarity, and Pan-Africanism in Early Twentieth-Century London." In *Blacks in Britain*, ed. Gundara and Duffield.

———. "Skilled Workers or Marginalized Poor? The African Population of the United Kingdom, 1812–1852." *Immigrants and Minorities* 12 (1993): 49–106.

Dynamic Party. *Memorandum on 1956 Constitutional Conference.* Ibadan: Dynamic Party, 1955.

Ebo, Chukwuemeka. "The Foundations of Zikism: A Historical Analysis of the Development of the Political Ideology of Dr. Nnamdi Azikiwe, 1937–1960." Ph.D. diss., New York University, 1963.

Echeruo, Michael J. C. "Nnamdi Azikiwe and Nineteenth Century Nigerian Thought." *JMAS* 12 (1974): 245–63.

———. *Victorian Lagos: Aspects of Nineteenth Century Lagos Life.* New York: Africana; London: Macmillan, 1978.

Edoka, P. N. "Ojowu Juju Ceremony at Ugharefe." *Nigeria* 15 (Sept. 1938): 232–33.

Edunam, Efiong E. B. "Unaccredited Ambassadors: Nigerian Students as Africa's Spokesmen in the United States, 1920–1950." *Calabar Historical Journal* 3 (1985): 136–53.

Egbe Omo Oduduwa, ed. *A Yoruba Symposium Prepared in Honour of the 6th General Meeting of the Egbe Omo Oduduwa.* Ibadan: n.p., 1953.

Egharevba, Jacob Uwadiae. *Short History of Benin.* 1936. 2d ed., rev. and enl. Benin: the author, 1953.

———. *Concise Lives of the Famous Iyases of Benin.* Benin City: [Egharevba Press], 1946.

———. *Benin Laws and Customs.* 2d ed. Lagos: [Service Printers], 1947.

———. *Some Stories of Ancient Benin.* 2d ed. Lagos: [Ribway Printers], 1951.

Eisenhofer, Stefan. "The Origins of the Benin Kingship in the Works of Jacob Egharevba." *History in Africa* 22 (1995): 141–63.

Ejimofor, Emeribe. *You and Your Troubled World: A Political, Economic, and Religious Survey.* N.p.: the author, [1952?].

Ekeghe, Ogbonna O. *A Short History of Abiriba.* N.p.: [1955].

Ekejiuba, Felicia. "Omu Okwei, the Merchant Queen of Osmari: A Biographical Sketch." *JHSN* 3 (1967): 633–46.

Ekundare, R. Olufemi. *An Economic History of Nigeria, 1860–1960.* London: Methuen, 1973.

Elias, T. Olawale. "Towards Nationhood in Nigeria." In *Occasional Papers on Nigerian Affairs* 1 (1954): 5–20.

——. *The Nature of African Customary Law*. Manchester: Manchester Univ. Press, 1956.

Ellis, A. B. *The Land of Fetish*. 1883. Rpt. Westport, Conn.: Negro Universities Press, 1970.

Eluwa, Gabriel Ihie Chineuye. "The Colonial Office and the Emergence of the National Congress of British West Africa." Ph.D. diss., Michigan State University, 1967.

Emerson, Rupert. *From Empire to Nation: The Rise to Self-Assertion of Asian and African Peoples*. Boston: Beacon, 1960.

Emerson, Rupert, and Martin Kilson, eds. *The Political Awakening of Africa*. Englewood Cliffs, N.J.: Prentice-Hall, 1965.

Enahoro, Anthony. *Nnamdi Azikiwe: Saint or Sinner?* Lagos: [Ribway Press], [1949].

Enahoro, Peter. *How to Be a Nigerian*. [Lagos]: Daily Times, 1966.

Epelle, Sam. *The Promise of Nigeria*. London: Pan Books, 1960.

Esedebe, P. Olisanwuche. *Pan-Africanism: The Idea and the Movement, 1776–1963*. Washington, D.C.: Howard Univ. Press, 1982.

Esin, E. Ekanem. *Cause and Effect*. Lagos: CMS, 1915.

Essien, Nyong. *The Life of His Royal Highness the Late Prince Archibong Archibong of Calabar*. Shekinah Library Series. Lagos, 1929.

Euba, Titlola. "Dress and Status in 19th Century Lagos." In *Peoples of Lagos State*, ed. Adefuye et al.

Eze, Kingsley C. *Our Interesting Ibo Native Laws and Customs*. Fegge-Osha: Edwin Madumelu, n.d. Rpt. in *Igbo Market Literature*, comp. Mezu.

Eze, Nduka. "A Discourse on Violence and Pacifism as Instruments of Struggle for Freedom." *Labour Champion*, 13 May 1950.

Ezekwe, P. V. N. "Native Art and Industry in Awka." *Nigerian Teacher* 1 (1934): 28–33.

Fadipe, N. A. *The Sociology of the Yoruba*. Ph.D. diss., University of London, 1939. Published with an introduction by F. O. Okediji and O. O. Okediji. Ibadan: I.U.P., 1970.

Fadumah, Orishetukeh. "Religious Beliefs of the Yoruba People." In *Africa and the American Negro: Addresses and Proceedings of the Congress on Africa of Gammon Theological Seminary*. 1896. Rpt. Miami: Mnemosyne, 1969.

Fafunwa, Babs. "An African's Adventures in America." In *An African Treasury*, ed. Langston Hughes. New York: Crown, 1961.

——. *History of Education in Nigeria*. London: George Allen and Unwin, 1974.

Falola, Toyin. *The Political Economy of a Pre-Colonial State: Ibadan, 1830–1900*. Ile-Ife: Univ. of Ife Press, 1984.

——. "From Hospitality to Hostility: Ibadan and Strangers, 1830–1904." *JAH* 26 (1985): 51–68.

——. *Development Planning and Decolonization in Nigeria.* Gainesville: Univ. Press of Florida, 1996.

——, ed. *Yoruba Historiography.* Madison: Univ. of Wisconsin Press, 1991.

——, ed. *The Pioneer, Patriot, and Patriarch: Samuel Johnson and the Yoruba People.* Madison: Univ. of Wisconsin Press, 1993.

Falola, Toyin, and A. G. Adebayo. "The Context: The Political Economy of Colonial Nigeria." In *Chief Obafemi Awolowo,* ed. Oyelaran et al.

Fanon, Frantz. *The Wretched of the Earth.* Trans. C. Farrington. New York: Grove, 1968.

Fatayi-Williams, Atanda. *Faces, Cases, and Places: Memoirs by Fatayi-Williams, Nigerian Jurist.* London: Butterworths, 1983.

Fierce, Milfred C. "Economic Aspects of the Marcus Garvey Movement." In *Pan Africanism,* ed. Robert Chrisman and Nathan Hare. New York: Bobbs-Merrill, 1974.

Flint, John E. "Mary Kingsley: A Reassessment." *JAH* 4 (1963): 99–104.

——. "Nigeria: The Colonial Experience from 1880 to 1914." In *Colonialism in Africa.* Vol 1. Ed. L. H. Gann and Peter Duignan. London: C.U.P., 1969.

——. "Economic Changes in West Africa in the Nineteenth Century." In *History of West Africa.* Vol. 2. Ed. Michael Crowder and J. F. A. Ajayi. London: Longmans, 1974.

——. "Planned Decolonization and Its Failure in British Africa." *African Affairs* 82 (July 1983): 389–411.

——. "Scandal at the Bristol Hotel: Some Thoughts on Racial Discrimination in Britain and West Africa and Its Relationship to the Planning of Decolonisation, 1939–47." *JICH* 12 (1983): 74–93.

Folarin, Adebesin. *England and the English: A Stimulus for Every Ambitious African.* Lagos and London: John Taylor, [1910?].

——. *A Short Historical Review of the Life of the Egbas from 1829 to 1930.* Abeokuta: n.p., 1931.

——. *The Native Laws and Customs of Egbaland.* [Abeokuta?]: [E.N.A. Printing Press], 1939.

Forde, Daryll, ed., *Efik Traders of Old Calabar.* London: O.U.P., 1956.

Forrest, Tom. "State Capital, Capitalist Development, and Class Formation in Nigeria." In *The African Bourgeoisie: Capitalist Development in Nigeria, Kenya, and the Ivory Coast,* ed. Paul M. Lubeck. Boulder, Colo.: Lynne Reinner, 1987.

Fortes, Meyer. "An Anthropologist's Point of View." In *Fabian Colonial Essays,* ed. Rita Hinden. London: Fabian Publications and Allen and Unwin, 1945.

Frank, Katherine. *A Voyager Out: A Life of Mary Kingsley.* Boston: Houghton Mifflin, 1986.

Fraser, A. G. "The Future of the African." *Elders Review* 9 (Sept. 1930): 154–55.

Frobenius, Leo. *The Voice of Africa.* 2 vols. Trans. Rudolph Blind. 1913. Rpt. New York: Benjamin Blom, 1968.

Fryer, Peter. *Staying Power: The History of Black People in Britain.* London: Pluto, 1984.

Furlong, Patrick J. "Azikiwe and the National Church of Nigeria and the Cameroons." *African Affairs* 91 (1992): 433–52.

Fyfe, Christopher. "Peter Nichols—Old Calabar and Freetown." *JHSN* 22 (1961): 105–14.

———. *Africanus Horton, 1835–1883: West African Scientist and Patriot.* New York: O.U.P., 1972.

Garigue, Philip. "The West African Students' Union." *Africa* 23 (Jan. 1953): 55–69.

———. "Changing Political Leadership in West Africa." *Africa* 24 (Jan. 1954): 220–32.

Gbadamosi, T. G. O., and J. F. A. Ajayi, "Islam and Christianity in Nigeria." In *Groundwork of Nigerian History,* ed. Ikime.

Geary, Willam Nevill M. *Nigeria under British Rule.* London: Methuen, 1927.

———. "Are We Straining African Loyalty?" *Elders Review* 10 (1931).

Geiss, Imanuel. *The Pan-African Movement.* Trans. Ann Keep. London: Methuen, 1974.

George, Afolabi. "The Colour Problem (As It Relates to the Negro)." *University Herald* 1 (July 1948): 15.

George, J. O. *Historical Notes on the Yoruba Country and Its Tribes.* Lagos: n.p., 1895.

Gershoni, Yekutiel. "Nationalist Rhetoric, Conservative Action: The United Negro Improvement Association in West Africa in the Early 1920s." Paper presented at the annual meeting of the African Studies Association, Orlando, Fla., 1995.

Gifford, Prosser, and W. Roger Louis, eds. *The Transfer of Power in Africa: Decolonization, 1940–1960.* New Haven and London: Yale Univ. Press, 1982.

Gilroy, Paul. *The Black Atlantic: Modernity and Double Consciousness.* Cambridge: Harvard Univ. Press, 1993.

Gordon, Jacob U. "The Nigerian Student Movement in the United States, 1949–1967." *Current Bibliography on African Affairs* 10 (1977/78): 119–46.

Green, Alice Stopford. "Mary Kingsley." *Journal of the African Society* 1 (Oct. 1901): 1–16.

Grey, Henry George (Earl). *The Colonial Policy of Lord John Russell's Administration.* 2d ed. 2 vols. London: Richard Bentley, 1853.

Gundara, J. S., and I. Duffield, eds. *Essays on the History of Blacks in Britain.* Aldershot: Avebury, 1992.

Gwam, L. C. *Great Nigerians.* Lagos: Daily Times, n.d.

Hailey, Malcolm (Lord). *An African Survey: A Study of Problems Arising in Africa South of the Sahara.* 1938. Rev. ed. London: O.U.P., 1945.

———. "Some Problems Dealt With in the 'African Survey.'" *International Affairs* 18 (Mar.–Apr. 1939): 196–210.

———. "A New Philosophy of Colonial Rule." *United Empire* 32 (Nov.–Dec. 1941): 163–69.

———. *Britain and Her Dependencies.* London: Longmans, Green, 1943.

Hair, Paul E. H. "An Industrial and Urban Community in East Nigeria: Enugu, 1914–1953." Proceedings, Conference of the West African Institute of Social and Economic Research (Sociological section). Ibadan, 1953.

———. "An Analysis of the Register of Fourah Bay College, 1827–1950." *Sierra Leone Studies* 7 (1956): 155–60.

———. "Africanism: The Freetown Contribution." *JMAS* 5 (1967): 521–39.

Hammond, Dorothy, and Alta Jablow. *The Myth of Africa.* 2d ed. New York: Library of Social Sciences, 1977.

Hancock, W. K. *Argument of Empire.* Harmondsworth: Penguin, 1943.

Hansberry, William L. "The Material Culture of Ancient Nigeria." *JNH* 6 (1921): 261–95.

Harbison, F. "Human Resources and Economic Development in Nigeria." In *Nigerian Political Scene,* ed. Tilman and Cole.

Hargreaves, John D. *A Life of Sir Samuel Lewis.* London: O.U.P., 1958.

———. "Toward the Transfer of Power in British West Africa." In *Transfer of Power,* ed. Gifford and Louis.

———. *Decolonization in Africa.* London and New York: Longman, 1988.

Harlan, Louis R. "Booker T. Washington and the White Man's Burden." *American Historical Review* 71 (1966): 441–67.

Harneit-Sievers, Axel. "African Business, 'Economic Nationalism,' and British Colonial Policy: Southern Nigeria, 1935–1954." *African Economic History* 23 (1995): 79–128.

Harris, Joseph, ed. *Global Dimensions of the African Diaspora.* Washington, D.C.: Howard Univ. Press, 1982.

Harunah, Hakeem B. "Lagos-Abeokuta Relations in 19th Century Yorubaland." In *Peoples of Lagos State,* ed. Adefuye et al.

Hayford, J. E. Casely. *Gold Coast Native Institutions with Thoughts upon a Healthy Imperial Policy for the Gold Coast and Ashanti.* 1903. Rpt. London: Cass, 1970.

————. *Ethiopia Unbound: Studies in Race Emancipation.* 1911. 2d ed., with an introduction by F. Nnabuenyi Ugonna. London: Cass, 1969.

Helleiner, Gerald K. *Peasant Agriculture, Government, and Economic Growth in Nigeria.* Homewood, Ill.: Richard Irwin, 1966.

Henriksen, Thomas H. "African Intellectual Influences of Black Americans: The Role of Edward W. Blyden." *Phylon* 36 (1975): 279–90.

Hetherington, Penelope. *British Paternalism and Africa, 1920–1940.* London: Cass, 1978.

Hinden, Rita. *Plan for Africa: A Report Prepared for the Colonial Bureau of the Fabian Society.* London: George Allen and Unwin, 1941.

————. *Socialists and the Empire: Five Years' Work of the Fabian Colonial Bureau.* 1946. Rpt. London: Gollancz, 1947.

————. "The Enigma of the African." *Tribune* 27 Feb. 1948, rpt. in *Wasu* 12 (summer 1948): 14–16.

————. "Socialism and the Colonial World." In *New Fabian Colonial Essays,* ed. Arthur Creech Jones. London: Hogarth, 1959.

Hinds, Allister E. "Sterling and Imperial Policy, 1945–1951." *JICH* 15 (1987): 148–169.

Hodgkin, Thomas. *African Nationalism in Colonial Africa.* London: Muller, 1956.

Holden, Edith. *Blyden of Liberia.* New York: Vantage, 1966.

Hopkins, Anthony G. "An Economic History of Lagos, 1880–1914." Ph.D. diss., University of London, 1964.

————. "The Lagos Chamber of Commerce, 1888–1903." *JHSN* 3 (1965): 241–88.

————. "Richard Beale Blaize, 1845–1904: Merchant Prince of West Africa." *Tarikh* 1 (1966): 71–79.

————. "Some Economic Aspects of Political Movements in Nigeria and the Gold Coast, 1918–1939." *JAH* 7 (1966): 133–52.

————. "A Report on the Yoruba, 1910." *JHSN* 5 (1969): 67–100.

————. *An Economic History of West Africa.* London: Longman, 1973.

————. "Property Rights and Empire Building: Britain's Annexation of Lagos, 1861." *Journal of Economic History* 40 (1980): 777–98.

————. "Peter Thomas." In *Les Africains.* Vol. 9. Ed. Charles-André Julien. Paris: Jaguar, 1990.

Horton, Africanus B. "African Products." *African Times,* 23 May 1864.

————. *West African Countries and Peoples, British and Native.* 1868. Rpt. Nendeln/Lichtenstein: Kraus, 1970.

————. *Letters on the Political Condition of the Gold Coast.* 1870. Rpt. London: Cass, 1970.

Hountondji, Paulin J. *African Philosophy: Myth and Reality.* Trans. Henri Evans. London: Hutchinson, 1983.

Huggins, Nathan I. *Harlem Renaissance.* New York: O.U.P., 1971.

Hutchinson, Thomas J. *Impressions of West Africa.* London: Longman, Brown, Green: 1858.

Huxley, Elspeth. "West Africa in Transition." *Geographical Magazine* 25 (Oct. 1952): 310–20.

Huxley, Julian, and Phyllis Deane. *The Future of the Colonies.* London: Pilot Press, 1944.

Ibeziako, M. Ogo. *Founder and Some Celebrities of Onitsha: Some Aspects of Ancient Civilization.* N.p.: 1937.

Idigo, M. C. M. *A History of Aguleri.* Yaba: Nicholas Printing and Publishing, 1955.

Igbafe, P. A. "The Benin Water Rate Agitation, 1937–1938: An Example of Social Conflict." *JHSN* 4 (1968): 355–73.

Igbakan, Eko. "Some Observations on Nigerian Affairs." *African Messenger,* 9 Oct. 1927.

Ijoma, Edmund Agha. *A Short History of Osomari People.* Onitsha: the author, 1962.

Ike, Akwaelumo D. *The Origin of the Ibos.* 2d ed. Aba: [Silent Prayer Home Press], 1951.

————. *Great Men of Ibo Land.* Aba: the author, 1952.

Ike, Vincent. *Toads for Supper.* London: Harvill, 1965.

Ikime, Obaro. *The Member for Warri Province: The Life and Times of Chief Mukoro Mowoe of Warri, 1890–1948.* Ibadan: Institute of African Studies, University of Ibadan, 1977.

————, ed. *Groundwork of Nigerian History.* Ibadan: Heinemann Educational, 1980.

Ikoku, A. "My Impression of New Zealand." *African Echo,* 19 May 1951.

Ikoku, Chimere. *Science Education in the United States: A Guide to Prospective Students.* Lagos: n.p., [1959?].

Ikoli, Ernest. "The Late Dr. J. C. Vaughan." *Service,* Apr. 1938.

Ilogu, Edmond. "Nationalism and the Church in Nigeria." *International Review of Missions* 51 (1962): 439–50.

Inden, Ronald. *Imagining India.* Oxford: Blackwell: 1990.

International Institute of Differing Civilizations, ed. *Development of a Middle Class in Tropical and Sub-Tropical Africa.* Bruxelles: International Institute of Differing Civilizations, 1956.

Irele, Abiola. "Negritude and African Personality." In *The African Experience in Literature and Ideology.* Ibadan and London: Heinemann, 1981.

Isichei, Elizabeth. *The Ibo People and the Europeans: The Genesis of a Relationship—to 1906.* London: Faber and Faber, 1973.

Isuman, Jaafaru Ushomo. *Need for More States in Nigeria, with Some Submissions for a Mid-West State.* [Sapele or Benin?]: n.p., 1957.

Ita, Eyo. "The West African Pilot." *WAP,* 8 Feb. 1938.

———. *Reconstructing towards Wider Integration: A Theory of Social Symbiosis.* Calabar: West African People's Institute Press, [1946?].

———. *The Revolt of the Liberal Spirit in Nigeria.* Calabar: West African People's Institute Press, 1949.

———. *Sterile Truths and Fertile Lies.* Calabar: West African People's Institute Press, 1949.

———. *Two Vital Fronts in Nigeria's Advancement.* Calabar: West African People's Institute Press, 1949.

Iweka-Nuno, I. E. *History of Obosi and of Ibo-Land in Brief, Partially Translated from the Ibo Copy.* N.p.: 1924.

Iweriebor, Ehiedu E. G. "Radical Nationalism in Nigeria: The Zikist Movement, 1945–50." Ph.D. diss., Columbia University, 1990.

Iyalla, Max. "Nigerian Fabian Society." *Fabian Quarterly* 42 (July 1944): 1.

JanMohamed, Abdul R. "The Economy of the Manichean Allegory: The Function of Racial Difference in Colonialist Literature." In *"Race," Writing, and Difference,* ed. Henry Louis Gates Jr. Chicago: Univ. of Chicago Press, 1986.

Johnson, Cheryl Jeffries. "Nigerian Women and British Colonialism: The Yoruba Example with Selected Biographies." Ph.D. diss., Northwestern University, 1978.

Johnson-Odim, Cheryl. "Funmilayo Ransome-Kuti and the Struggles for Nigerian Independence and Women's Equality." In *Expanding the Bounds of Women's History,* ed. Cheryl Johnson-Odim and Margaret Strobel. Bloomington and Indianapolis: Indiana Univ. Press, 1992.

———. "Lady Oyinkan Abayomi." In *Nigerian Women,* ed. B. Awe.

Johnson, Obadiah. *Lagos Past.* A paper read before the Lagos Institute, 20 Nov. 1901. Rpt. Ibadan: Special Archives, 1985.

Johnson, Samuel. *The History of the Yorubas, from Earliest Times to the Beginning of the British Protectorate,* ed. Obadiah Johnson. 1921. Rpt. London: Routledge and Kegan Paul, 1966.

Jokparoba, R. E. *The Urhobo People in Nigerian Politics.* Lagos: [Obajinmi Printing Works], [1958?].

Jones, G. I. "Changing Leadership in Eastern Nigeria: Before, during, and after the Colonial Period." In *Politics in Leadership,* ed. William A.

Shack and Percy S. Cohen. Oxford: Clarendon Press; New York: O.U.P., 1979.

July, Robert W. "Nineteenth Century Negritude: Edward Wilmot Blyden." *JAH* 5 (1964): 73–86.

———. *The Origins of Modern African Thought: Its Development in West Africa during the Nineteenth and Twentieth Centuries.* New York: Praeger, 1967.

———. "Sierra Leone Legacy in Nigeria: Herbert Macaulay and Henry Carr." In *Freetown: A Symposium,* ed. Christopher Fyfe and Eldred Jones. Freetown: Sierra Leone Univ. Press, 1968.

———. *An African Voice: The Role of the Humanities in African Independence.* Durham, N.C.: Duke Univ. Press, 1987.

Juwe, Sylve Mubundu. *Why Is the National Church of Nigeria and the Cameroons and the God of Africa.* Port Harcourt: [Goodwill Press], [1949?].

———. *The Western Ibo People and the Coming Days.* Port Harcourt: [Goodwill Press], 1953.

———. *Zik and the Freedom of Nigeria.* Port Harcourt: [Goodwill Press], 1953.

Kenyo, Elisha Alademomi. *Origin of the Progenitor of the Yoruba Race.* Lagos: Yoruba Historical Research Co., 1950.

———. *Founder of the Yoruba Nation.* Lagos: Yoruba Historical Research Co., 1959.

Kidd, Dudley. *The Essential Kafir.* London: Adam and Charles Black, 1904.

———. *Kafir Socialism.* London: Adam and Charles Black, 1908.

Kiernan, Victor. *The Lords of Human Kind.* Harmondsworth: Penguin, 1972.

Kimble, David. *A Political History of Ghana: The Rise of Gold Coast Nationalism, 1850–1928.* Oxford: Clarendon Press, 1965.

Kingsley, Mary. *Travels in West Africa: Congo Français, Corisco, and Cameroons.* 1897. 2d ed. London: Macmillan, 1900.

———. *West African Studies.* 1899. 2d ed. London: Macmillan, 1901.

Kohn, Hans, and Wallace Sokolsky, *African Nationalism in the Twentieth Century.* Princeton, N.J.: Van Nostrand, 1965.

Kopytoff, Jean Herskovits. *A Preface to Modern Nigeria: The "Sierra Leonians" in Yoruba, 1830–1890.* Madison: Univ. of Wisconsin Press, 1965.

Kuper, Adam. *Anthropologists and Anthropology: The British School, 1922–1972.* London: Allen Lane, 1973.

Lagos Institute. *Proceedings of Inaugural Meeting, October 16, 1901.* Lagos: n.p., 1901.

———. *Lagos Water Rate Scheme, Further Correspondence.* Lagos: n.p., 1916.

Langley, Jabez Ayodele. "Garveyism and African Nationalism." *Race* 11 (1969): 157–72.

———. "Modernization and Its Malcontents: Kobina Sekyi of Ghana and the Re-statement of African Political Theory." In *Political Theory and Ideology in African Society.* Edinburgh: Centre of African Studies, University of Edinburgh, 1971.

———. *Pan Africanism and Nationalism in West Africa, 1900–1945: A Study in Ideology and Social Classes.* Oxford: Clarendon, 1973.

Lasekan, Akinola. *Nigeria in Cartoons.* Lagos: African Art and Craft Studio, 1944.

———. *Nigeria in 1945.* Lagos: [Ijaiye Press], 1946.

———. *Zik of Africa.* Lagos: Zik's Press, 1947.

———. *The Nigerian Joker.* Lagos: Ribway Printing Press, 1949.

Lasky, Melvin J. "Africa for Beginners." *Encounter* [pt. 1] 17 (July 1961): 32–48; [pt. 2] 3 (Sept. 1961): 33–49.

Latham, A. J. M. *Old Calabar, 1600–1891: The Impact of the International Economy upon a Traditional Society.* Oxford: Clarendon, 1973.

Law, Robin. "Early Yoruba Historiography." In *Pioneer, Patriot,* ed. Falola.

———, ed. *From Slave Trade to "Legitimate" Commerce: The Commercial Transition in Nineteenth-Century West Africa.* Cambridge: C.U.P., 1995.

Lee, M. "Is Education Making Africans Intolerant?" *WAR* 3 (Nov. 1932): 21–23.

Lee, Ulysses. "The ASNLH, the *Journal of Negro History,* and the American Scholarly Interest in Africa." In *Africa as Seen by American Negroes,* ed. J. Davis.

Leith-Ross, Sylvia. *African Conversation Piece.* London: Hutchinson, 1944.

———. "The Development of a Middle Class in the Federation of Nigeria." In International Institute of Differing Civilizations, *Middle Class.*

———. "The Rise of a New Elite amongst the Women of Nigeria." *International Social Science Bulletin* 8 (1956): 481–88.

———. *Stepping-Stones: Memoirs of Colonial Nigeria, 1907–1960,* ed. Michael Crowder. London and Boston: Peter Owen, 1983.

Lewis, W. Arthur. "African Economic Problems." *Keys* 5 (July–Sept. 1937): 15–16, 28–30.

———. *Politics in West Africa.* Toronto and New York: O.U.P., 1965.

Lijadu, Ayodele. "The Doctrine of Altruism." *Service,* Sept. 1936, pp. 8, 10.

Lindfors, Bernth. "Popular Literature for an African Elite." *JMAS* 12 (1974): 471–86.

———. *Early Nigerian Literature.* New York and London: Africana, 1982.

Lipede, Abiola Ade. "The Political Activities of Herbert Heelas Macaulay between the Wars." M.Phil. thesis, University of London, 1981.

Little, Kenneth. *Negroes in Britain: A Study of Race Relations in English Society.* 1948. 2d ed. London: Routledge and Kegan Paul, 1972.

———. "The African Elite in British West Africa." In *Race Relations in World Perspective,* ed. Andrew W. Lind. Honolulu: Univ. of Hawaii Press, 1955.

———. *West African Urbanization: A Study of Voluntary Associations in Social Change.* Cambridge: C.U.P., 1965.

Livingston, Thomas W. *Education and Race: A Biography of Edward Wilmot Blyden.* San Francisco: Glendessary, 1975.

Lloyd, Peter C. "Class Consciousness among the Yoruba." In *New Elites,* ed. Lloyd.

———. "Introduction." In *New Elites,* ed. Lloyd.

———. "The Elite." In *The City of Ibadan,* ed. P. Lloyd, A. L. Mabogunje, and B. Awe. London: C.U.P., 1967.

———, ed. *The New Elites of Tropical Africa.* London: O.U.P., 1966.

Locke, Alain. "Afro-Americans and West Africans: A New Understanding." *Wasu* 1 (Jan. 1929): 18–24.

———, ed. *The New Negro: An Interpretation.* 1925. Rpt. New York and London: Johnson Reprint, 1968.

Logan, Rayford W. "The American Negro's View of Africa." In *Africa as Seen by American Negroes,* ed. J. Davis.

Longe, Foluso. *A Rare Breed: The Story of Chief Timothy Adeola Odutola, Ogbeni Ojoa of Ijebu-Ode.* Lagos: Manufacturers' Association of Nigeria, 1981.

Lorimer, Douglas A. *Colour, Class, and the Victorians: English Attitudes to the Negro in the Mid-Nineteenth Century.* Leicester: Leicester Univ. Press, 1978.

Losi, John B. Ogunjimi. *History of Lagos.* Lagos, 1914. Rpt. Lagos: African Education Books, 1967.

———. *History of Abekouta.* Lagos: Bosere Press, 1924.

Lugard, Frederick. *The Dual Mandate in British Tropical Africa.* 1922. Rpt. London: Cass, 1965.

Lynch, Hollis R. "The Native Pastorate Controversy and Cultural Ethnocentrism in Sierra Leone, 1871–74." *JAH* 5 (1964): 395–413.

———. "Edward W. Blyden: Pioneer West African Nationalist." *JAH* 6 (1965): 373–88.

———. *Edward Wilmot Blyden: Pan-Negro Patriot, 1832–1912.* London: O.U.P., 1967.

———. *Black American Radicals and the Liberation of Africa: The Council on African Affairs, 1937–1955.* Cornell University Africana Studies and Research Center Monograph Series. Ithaca, N.Y., 1978.

————. "K. O. Mbadiwe, 1939–1947: The American Years of a Nigerian Political Leader." *Journal of African Studies* 7 (1980–81): 184–203.

————. "Pan-African Responses in the United States to British Colonial Rule in Africa in the 1940s." In *Transfer of Power*, ed. Gifford and Louis.

Lynn, Martin. "Technology, Trade, and 'A Race of Native Capitalists': The Krio Diaspora of West Africa and the Steamship, 1852–95." *JAH* 33 (1992): 421–40.

————. *Commerce and Economic Change in West Africa: The Palm Oil Trade in the Nineteenth Century*. Cambridge: C.U.P., 1997.

Mabogunje, Akin. *Urbanization in Nigeria*. London: Univ. of London Press, 1968.

Macaulay, Herbert. *Transfer or Retirement, Henry Carr Must Go!* Lagos, 1924. 2d ed. under the title *Henry Rawlinson Carr*, ed. Abiodun Ojugbele. Ebute Metta, Nigeria: Alayande Publishing, 1983.

Macdonald, Roderick J. "Dr. Harold Moody and the League of Coloured People, 1931–1947: A Retrospective View." *Race* 14 (1973): 291–310.

————. "Introduction." *Keys*. 1933–39. Rpt. Millwood, N.Y.: Kraus-Thomson, 1976.

————. "'The Wisers Who Are Far Away': The Role of London's Black Press in the 1930s and 1940s." In *Blacks in Britain*, ed. Gundara and Duffield.

Macmillan, Allister, ed. *The Red Book of West Africa*. 1922. Rpt. London: Cass, 1968.

Macmillan, W. M. "The Importance of the Educated African." *African Affairs* 33 (Apr. 1934): 137–42.

————. *Warning from the West Indies*. 1936. Rev. ed. Harmondsworth: Penguin, 1938.

————. *Africa Emergent*. 1938. Rev. ed. Harmondsworth: Penguin, 1949.

————. "Freedom for Colonial Peoples." In *Programme for Victory: A Collection of Essays Prepared for the Fabian Society*. London: London Labour Book Service, 1941.

Magubane, Bernard Makhosezwe. *The Ties That Bind: African-American Consciousness of Africa*. Trenton, N.J.: Africa World Press, 1987.

Manchuelle, François. "Le role Antillais dans l'apparition du nationalisme culturel en Afrique noire francophone." *Cahiers d'Etudes Africaines* 32 (1992): 375–408.

Mann, Kristin. "A Social History of the New African Elite in Lagos Colony, 1880–1913." Ph.D. diss., Stanford University, 1977.

————. *Marrying Well: Marriage, Status, and Social Change among the Educated Elite in Colonial Lagos*. Cambridge: C.U.P., 1985.

Martins, Olatunji. "Spirit of Collectivism." *Service*, Dec. 1935, pp. 18–20.

Mathurin, Owen Charles. *Henry Sylvester Williams and the Origins of the Pan-African Movement, 1869–1911*. London and Westport, Conn.: Greenwood, 1976.

Maye, Ivanhoe F. *Back to the Land: A Paper Read at a Meeting Held under the Auspices of the British West African Conference, (Lagos Branch) at Ebute Metta, Nigeria, on the 18th September, 1919*. Lagos: the author, 1919.

Mayhew, Arthur. *Educational Policy in the Colonial Empire*. London: Longmans, 1938.

Mba, Nina Emma. *Nigerian Women Mobilized: Women's Political Activity in Southern Nigeria, 1900–1965*. Berkeley: Institute of International Studies, University of California, 1982.

———. "Literature as a Source of Nigerian History: Case Study of *The Water House* and the Brazilians in Lagos." In *Peoples of Lagos State*, ed. Adefuye et al.

———. *Ayo Rosiji: Man with a Vision*. Ibadan: Spectrum, 1992.

———. "Olufunmilayo Ransome-Kuti." In *Nigerian Women*, ed. B. Awe.

Mbadiwe, George Igbodebe. *Golden Dawn*. Lagos: [Ife-Olu Printing Works], 1947.

Mbadiwe, Kingsley Ozuomba. *British and Axis Aims in Africa*. New York: Wendell Malliet, 1942.

———. "Nigeria in the New Commonwealth. (An Address as Nigerian Minister of Communications and Civil Aviation, Church House, London, 28 June 1956.)" In FCP 83/2.

Mbanefo, L. "An African Looks at England and Thinks about Africa." *WAR* 7 (Dec. 1936): 99, 101, 103.

———. "Unity and Cooperation among the Paramount Chiefs of Nigeria." *Wasu* 6 (Coronation Issue 1937): 31–32.

McClintock, Anne. *Imperial Leather: Race, Gender, and Sexuality in the Colonial Contest*. New York: Routledge, 1995.

Meier, August. *Negro Thought in America, 1880–1915: Racial Ideologies in the Age of Booker T. Washington*. Ann Arbor: Univ. of Michigan Press, 1963.

Meniru, G. Udegbunem. "Economic Prosperity." *WAP*, 14 and 15 Feb. 1955.

Mezu, S. Okechukwu. "The Cradles of Modern African Writing: A Case Study of the Igbo Market Literature." In *Igbo Market Literature*, comp. Mezu.

———, comp. *Igbo Market Literature*. Buffalo: Black Academy Press, 1972.

Mgbako, Fanasi O. *Truth and Falsehood: Addresses of Welcome presented to*

*Dr. K. O. Mbadiwe and Dr. Nnamdi Azikiwe.* Osha: [New Era Press], [1958?].

Milewski, Jan J., "The Great Depression of the Early 1930's in a Colonial Country: A Case Study of Nigeria." *Africana Bulletin* 23 (1975): 7–45.

Miller, Christopher. *Theories of Africans: Francophone Literature and Anthropology in Africa.* Chicago: Univ. of Chicago Press, 1990.

Miller, Walter R. *Have We Failed in Nigeria?* London and Redhill: United Society for Christian Literature, 1947.

Mohiddin, Ahmed. "Towards Relevant Culture and Politics in Africa." *African Development* 2 (1977): 55–69.

Moore, E. O. O. [later known as A. K. Ajisafe]. *History of Abeokuta.* London: the author, 1916.

Moore, Kofoworola Aina. "The Story of Kofoworola Aina Moore, of the Yoruba Tribe, Nigeria." In *Ten Africans,* ed. Margery Perham. London: Faber and Faber, 1936.

Moore, Willam A. *History of Itsekiri.* 1936. 2d ed. London: Cass, 1970.

Morel, Edmund D. *Affairs of West Africa.* 1902. Rpt. London: Cass, 1968.

———. *Nigeria: Its Peoples and Problems.* 2d ed. London: Smith, Elder, 1912.

Morgan, N. O. Abiodun. "Nigeria's Public Enemies." *Service,* Dec. 1935, pp. 12–13.

Morrill, Warren T. "Two Urban Cultures of Calabar, Nigeria." Ph.D. diss., University of Chicago, 1961.

Moses, Wilson J. *Alexander Crummell: A Study in Civilization and Discontent.* Oxford: O.U.P., 1989.

Mudimbe, V. Y. *The Invention of Africa: Gnosis, Philosophy, and the Order of Knowledge.* Bloomington: Indiana Univ. Press, 1988.

———. *The Idea of Africa.* Bloomington: Indiana Univ. Press, 1994.

Mungazi, Dickson A. *The Mind of Black Africa.* Westport, Conn.: Praeger, 1996.

Murray, A. V. "Education under Indirect Rule." *Journal of the Royal African Society* 34 (July 1935): 227–62.

Nadel, S. F. "The Concept of Social Elites." *International Social Science Bulletin* 8 (1956): 413–24.

Nair, Kannan K. *Politics and Society in South Eastern Nigeria, 1841–1906.* London: Cass, 1972.

Nandy, Ashis. *The Intimate Enemy: Loss and Recovery of Self under Colonialism.* Delhi: O.U.P., 1983.

National Congress of British West Africa. *Resolutions of the Fourth Session of the National Congress of British West Africa Held in Lagos, January 1930.* HMP 18/2.

National Council of Nigeria and the Cameroons. "Whither Nigeria?

Anglo-Nigerian Relations in Perspective." *Pan-Africa* 1 (Oct.–Dec. 1947): 31–74.

———. "Policy for a Free Nigeria." Typescript, 1959. OAP.

"A Native of Yoruba." "Native System of Government and Land Tenure in the Yoruba Country." *African Affairs* 1 (Apr. 1902): 312–15.

Ndem, E. B. "The African in Western Civilization." *Comet*, 20 Apr. 1940.

Nduka, Otonti. *Western Education and the Nigerian Cultural Background.* Ibadan: I.U.P., 1965.

Neale, Caroline. *Writing "Independent" History: African Historiography, 1960–1980.* Westport, Conn., and London: Greenwood, 1985.

New Era Bureau. *Dr Zik Goes East: Is It the Betrayal of a Principle or an Act of Bold Realism?* Lagos: New Era Bureau, 1953.

———. *History and Analysis: The London Regionalisation Conference, Before and After.* Lagos: New Era Bureau, [1953].

Ngugi wa Thiong'o. *Moving the Centre.* London: Currey, 1993.

Nicholson, Marjorie. *West African Ferment.* London: Fabian Publications and Victor Gollancz, 1950.

Nicol, Davidson. "The Formation of a West African Intellectual Community." In *The West African Intellectual Community.* Ibadan: Published for The Congress on Cultural Freedom by I.U.P., 1962.

———, ed. *Black Nationalism in Africa, 1867: Extracts from the Political, Educational, Scientific, and Medical Writings of Africanus Horton.* New York: Africana, 1969.

Nicolson, I. F. *The British Administration in Nigeria, 1900–1960: Men, Methods, Myths.* Oxford: Clarendon, 1969.

Nigeria. *Proceedings of the General Conference on Review of the Constitution, January, 1950.* Lagos: Government Printer, 1950.

Nigeria (Federal Republic of). *Annual Abstract of Statistics.* Lagos: Federal Office of Statistics, 1960.

———. *Annual Abstract of Statistics.* Lagos: Federal Office of Statistics, 1963.

———. *Digest of Statistics* 15 (Jan. and Apr. 1966).

Nigerian Mercantile Bank. *Prospectus.* N.p., 1931. HMP 30/10.

Nigerian National Democratic Party. *Memorandum of Objections against the Enactment of the Native Courts Ordinance and Native Authority Extension Ordinance and the General Tax Ordinance.* Lagos: n.p., [1927]. HMP 33/8.

Nigerian Peoples Party. *The New Nigeria.* Yaba: Nigerian Peoples Party, 1961.

Nigerian Reform Association. *Petition against the Provincial and Native Courts Ordinances by the Nigerian Reform Association, to His Excellency,*

*Sir Frederick Lugard . . . with Altruistic Observations by Two European Barristers.* Lagos: [African Church Printing Press, 1917].

Nigerian Youth Congress. *Nigeria: The Way Forward.* Policy and Programme of the Nigerian Youth Congress. Ebute Metta: Information and Publicity Bureau of the Nigerian Youth Congress, [1961].

Nigerian Youth Movement. "Memorandum on the Question of Unemployment." *Service,* June 1936, pp. 29–32.

———. *Nigerian Youth Charter: The Official Programme of the Nigerian Youth Movement.* Typescript, [1938].

———. "Memorandum on Cocoa Problem in Nigeria Prepared by the Nigerian Youth Movement for Cocoa Commission Visiting West Africa." *Daily Service,* 26 and 27 Oct. 1938.

*Nigeria Year Book 1953.* Lagos: n.p., 1953.

Nitecki, Andre. *Onitsha Publications.* Syracuse, N.Y.: Maxwell Graduate School of Citizenship and Public Affairs Program of Eastern African Studies, 1967.

Niven, Rex. *Nigerian Kaleidoscope: Memoirs of a Colonial Servant.* London: C. Hurst, 1982.

Noah, M. Efiong. "Political History of the City States of Old Calabar, 1820–60." In *Studies in Southern Nigerian History,* ed. Boniface Obichere. London: Cass, 1982.

Northrup, David. "Nineteenth-Century Patterns of Slavery and Economic Growth in Southeastern Nigeria." *IJAHS* 12 (1979): 1–16.

Numa, Frederick Yamu. *The Pride of Urhobo Nation.* Lagos: the author, 1950.

Nwabara, S. N. *Iboland: A Century of Contact with Britain, 1860–1960.* Atlantic Highlands, N.J.: Humanities Press, 1978.

Nwabughuogu, Anthony I. "From Wealthy Entrepreneurs to Petty Traders: The Decline of African Middlemen in Eastern Nigeria, 1900–1950." *JAH* 23 (1982): 365–79.

Nwachuku, J. R. "Why 'African' Business Enterprises Fail." *People,* 15–20 Dec. 1951.

Nwala, U. "Ideological Dependency and the Problem of Autonomy in Nigeria." *Journal of Asian and African Studies* 14 (1979): 59–66.

[Nwangoro, S. O.] "S. O. N." "Africa at the Crossroads." *Africa Public Opinion,* 29 Mar. 1938.

———. "The Gist of It." *Comet,* 16 Sept. 1939.

Nwangoro, S. O. N. *My Destiny: Part I.* Aba: [Education Mission Press], 1946.

Nwanko, Arthur A. *The Power Dynamics of the Nigerian Society.* Enugu: Fourth Dimension, 1988.

Nwanunobi, C. O. "Incendiarism and Other Fires in Nineteenth-Century Lagos (1863–1888)." *Africa* 60 (1990): 111–20.

Nzimiro, Ikenna. "Zikism and Social Thought in the Nigerian Pre-Independence Period, 1944–1950." In *Themes in African Social and Political Thought*, ed. Onigu Otite. Enugu: Fourth Dimension, 1978.

Obi, Chike. *Our Struggle Part II. The Struggle for Freedom after Political Independence—The Economic Stage*. Enugu: n.p., 1962.

Obiahwu. "Bigger Plan—Worse Plight." *Wasu* 12 (summer 1947): 21–22.

Obiechina, E. N. *Onitsha Market Literature*. London and Ibadan: Heinemann, 1972.

Obio-Offiong, Udo-Ekong Etuk. *An Introduction to Nsit History: a History of Afagha Obio Offiong and a First Step to the Study of Ibibio History*. Aba: the author, 1958.

O'Connell, James. "The Political Class and Economic Growth." *Nigerian Journal of Social and Economic Studies* 8 (1966): 129–40.

Oduche, Okwudinka Nwoye. *Life History of Ogbuefi Oduche Akunwata Akamelu*. Enugu: [Escana Press], 1951.

Odunsi, Ladipo O. "The Prelude to Rational Nationalism." *Daily Service*, 16 Sept. 1940.

Offonry, Henry Kano. "The Ibo People." *WAR* 18 (Feb. 1947): 167–68.

———. "The Hausas . . . a Most Pleasant People." *WAR* 18 (Aug. 1947): 943, 945.

Ogali, Ogali Agu. *History of Item, Past and Present*. Enugu: the author, 1960.

Ogbalu, F. Chidozie. *Investigation into the New Igbo Orthography*. N.p., [1952?].

Ogunlade, F. O. "Education and Politics in Colonial Nigeria: The Case of King's College, Lagos (1906–1911)." *JHSN* 7 (1974): 325–45.

Ogunsheye, Fidelis A. "Nigeria's Economic Problem." *African Echo*, 31 Mar. 1951.

———. "Nigerian Nationalism, 1919–1952." *Nigeria Year Book 1953*. Lagos: n.p., 1953.

Ohadike, D. C. *The Ekumeku Movement: Western Igbo Resistance to the British Conquest of Nigeria, 1883–1914*. Athens: Ohio Univ. Press, 1991.

Oji, Bassey Asi. *Age of Bribery*. Aba: the author, 1953.

Ojike, Mbonu. *My Africa*. New York: John Day, 1946.

———. *I Have Two Countries*. New York: John Day, 1947.

———. "My Economic Philosophy." *African Echo*, 25 Jan. 1949.

Ojo-Cole, Julius. "A Glimpse of Yoruba Civilization." *Wasu* 3 and 4 (Mar.–June 1927): 16–19.

———. *Collection of Yoruba Thoughts*. Lagos: Nigerian Press, 1931.

———. "A Whole Race at School: Booker T. Washington." *LDN*, 6–16 Jan. 1932.

Okafor, Amanke. *Nigeria: Why We Fight for Freedom.* 2d ed. London: the author, 1950.

———. *Political Ideologies of Our Time.* London: the author, 1952.

Okafor, F. O. E. *The Nigerian Youth Movement, 1934–44: A Re-appraisal of the Historiography.* Onitsha: Etukokwu Publishers, 1989.

Okafor, Nduka. *The Development of Universities in Nigeria: A Study of the Influence of Politics and Other Factors on University Development in Nigeria.* London: Longman, 1971.

Okafor-Omali, Dilim. *A Nigerian Villager in Two Worlds.* London: Faber and Faber, 1965.

Okojie, Christopher Gbelokoto. *Ishan Native Laws and Customs.* Irrua: the author, 1960.

Okonkwo, Daniel Onuzulike. *History of Nigeria in a New Setting, from the Earliest Time to 1961.* Nnewi: the author, 1961.

Okonkwo, Rina L. "The Garvey Movement in Nigeria." *Calabar Historical Journal* 2 (1978): 98–113.

———. "The Garvey Movement in British West Africa." *JAH* 21 (1980): 105–17.

———. "The Lagos Auxiliary of the Anti-Slavery and Aborigines Rights Protection Society." *IJAHS* 15 (1982): 423–33.

———. *Heroes of West African Nationalism.* Enugu: Delta, 1985.

Okorodudu, Chief M. E. R. "Nigeria." *United Empire* 46 (1955): 227–30.

Okoth, P. G. "The Creation of a Dependent Culture: The Imperial School Curriculum in Uganda." In *The Imperial Curriculum,* ed. J. Mangan. London: Routledge, 1993.

Okoye, Mokwugo. *Letter to Dr Azikiwe: A Dissent Remembered.* 1955. Rpt. with new introduction, Enugu: Fourth Dimension, 1979.

Olisah, Okenwa. *The Ibo Native Law and Custom.* Okenwa Publications, Onitsha, 1963. Rpt. in *Igbo Market Literature,* comp. Mezu.

Olivier, Sydney. *White Capital and Coloured Labour.* London: Independent Labour Party, 1910.

Olukoju, Ayodeji. "The Politics of Free Trade between Lagos and the Hinterland, 1861–1907." In *Peoples of Lagos State,* ed. Adefuye et al.

Olumayiwa, A. B. "Towards Post War Economic Reconstruction." *WAP,* 28 and 29 May 1942.

Olusanya, Gabriel O. "The Zikist Movement: A Study of Political Radicalism." *JMAS* 4 (1966): 323–33.

———. "The Lagos Branch of the National Congress of British West Africa." *JHSN* 4 (1968): 324–33.

———. "Julius Ojo-Cole: A Neglected Nigerian Nationalist and Educationist." *JHSN* 7 (1973): 91–102.

————. *The Second World War and Politics in Nigeria, 1939–1953*. London: Evans Brothers; Lagos: University of Lagos, 1973.

————. *The Evolution of the Nigerian Civil Service, 1861–1960: The Problems of Nigerianization*. Lagos: University of Lagos, 1975.

————. *The West African Students' Union and the Politics of Decolonization, 1925–1958*. Ibadan: Daystar Press, 1982.

————. "Garvey and Nigeria." In *Garvey: Africa, Europe, the Americas*, ed. Rupert Lewis and Maureen Warner-Lewis. Kingston: Institute of Social and Economic Research, University of the West Indies, 1986.

————. "Charlotte Olajumoke Obasa." In *Nigerian Women*, ed. B. Awe.

————. "Olaniwun Adunni Oluwole." In *Nigerian Women*, ed. B. Awe.

Oluwasanmi, H. A. "The Problem of Minorities in Nigeria." *Ibadan* 2 (Feb. 1958): 5–7.

————. "The Economic Reconstruction of Nigeria." *Beacon* 2 (Christmas 1960): 17–27.

Omo-Amangie, Peter Inahourema. *A Brief History of Etsakor*. Lagos: [Ope Ife Press], 1946.

————. *A Life History of M. A. O. Imoudu*. Lagos: [Pacific Printing Works], 1957.

Omolewa, Michael. "The Promotion of London University Examinations in Nigeria, 1887–1951." *IJAHS* 13 (1980): 651–71.

Omoneukanrin, C. O. *Itsekiri Law and Custom: An Indispensable Handbook for the Study of the Itsekiri People*. Lagos: [Ife-Olu Printing Works], 1942.

Omoniyi, Bandele. *A Defense of the Ethiopian Movement*. London: St. James Press, 1908.

Omu, Fred I. A. "The Anglo-African, 1863–65." *Nigeria Magazine* 90 (Sept. 1966): 206–12.

————. "Journalism and the Rise of Nigerian Nationalism: John Payne Jackson, 1848–1915." *JHSN* 7 (1974): 521–39.

————. *Press and Politics in Nigeria, 1880–1937*. London: Longman, 1978.

Onimode, Bade. *Imperialism and Underdevelopment in Nigeria*. London: Zed Press, 1972.

Onipede, F. Oladipo. "African Nationalism: A Critical Portrait." *Dissent* 3 (summer 1956): 276–85.

Onyia, J. I. G. *Review of the Constitution of Nigeria for 1950*. Aba: the author, 1949.

————. *My Role in Nationalism*. Asaba: the author, 1986.

Onyioha, K. O. K. *The National Church of Nigeria: Its Catechism and Credo*. Ebute Metta: The National Church, 1950.

Orakwue, Jerry I. *Onitsha Custom of Title Taking.* Onitsha: [Renascent Africa Press], [1953?].

Oriji, John. "A Re-assessment of the Organization and Benefits of the Slave Trade and Palm Produce Trade amongst the Ngwa-Igbo." *CJAS* 16 (1982): 523–48.

Orizu, A. A. Nwafor. *Without Bitterness: Western Nations in Post-War Africa.* New York: Creative Age Press, 1944.

Oroge, E. Adeniyi. "The Fugitive Slave Question in Anglo-Egba Relations, 1861–1881." *JHSN* 8 (1975): 61–80.

———. "The Fugitive Slave Crisis of 1859: A Factor in the Growth of Anti-British Feelings among the Yoruba." *Odu,* n.s., 12 (1975): 40–54.

———. "Iwofa: An Historical Survey of the Yoruba Institution." *African Economic History* 14 (1985): 75–106.

Osadebay, Dennis C. *Building a Nation (An Autobiography).* Yaba: Macmillan Nigeria, 1978.

Osaghae, Eghosa E. "Colonialism and African Political Thought." *Ufahamu* 19 (1991): 22–38.

Osoba, Segun. "Ideological Trends in the Nigerian National Liberation Movement and the Problems of National Identity, Solidarity, and Motivation, 1934–1965: A Preliminary Assessment." *Ibadan,* Oct. 1969, 26–38.

———. "The Deepening Crisis of the Nigerian National Bourgeoisie." *ROAPE* 13 (1978): 63–77.

Osuntokun, Akinjide. "Post-First World War Economic and Administrative Problems in Nigeria and the Response of the Clifford Administration." *JHSN* 7 (1973): 35–48.

———. *Nigeria in the First World War.* London: Longman, 1979.

———. *Chief S. L. Akintola: His Life and Times.* London: Cass, 1984.

———. "Introduction of Christianity and Islam in Lagos State." In *Peoples of Lagos State,* ed. Adefuye et al.

Otemade, Fuwape. "Economic Independence." *Daily Service,* 3 Oct. 1938.

Otite, Onigu. *Autonomy and Independence: The Urhobo Kingdom of Okpe in Modern Nigeria.* London: Hurst, 1973.

Ottenberg, Simon. "Improvement Associations among the Afikpo Igbo." *Africa* 25 (1955): 1–28.

———. "The Social and Administrative History of a Nigerian Township." *International Journal of Comparative Sociology* 7 (1966): 174–96.

Oyelaran, Olasope, Toyin Falola, Mokwugo Okoye, and Adewale Thompson, eds. *Chief Obafemi Awolowo: The End of an Era?* Ife-Ife: Obafemi Awolowo Univ. Press, 1988.

Paden, John N. *Ahmadu Bello: Sardauna of Sokoto.* Toronto: Hodder and Stoughton, 1986.

Padmore, George. *The Gold Coast Revolution.* London: Dobson, 1953.

Padmore, George, and Nancy Cunard. *The White Man's Duty: An Analysis of the Colonial Question in the Light of the Atlantic Charter.* London: W. H. Allen, 1942.

Page, Jesse. *Samuel Crowther: The Slave Boy Who Became Bishop of the Niger.* London: Partridge, [1888].

Pallinder-Law, Agenta. "Government in Abeokuta, 1830–1914, with Special Reference to Egba United Government." Ph.D. diss., Uppsala University, 1973.

———. "Aborted Modernization in West Africa? The Case of Abeokuta." *JAH* 15 (1974): 65–82.

Payne, J. A. *Payne's Lagos and West African Almanack and Diary for 1882.* London: n.p., 1881.

———. *Table of Principal Events in Yoruba History, with Certain Other Matters of General Interest, Compiled Principally for Use in the Courts within the British Colony of Lagos, West Africa.* Lagos: n.p., 1893.

Pearce, R. D. "Governors, Nationalists, and Constitutions in Nigeria, 1935–1951." *JICH* 9 (1981): 289–307.

———. *The Turning Point in Africa: British Colonial Policy, 1938–48.* London: Cass, 1982.

———. "Violet Bourdillon." *African Affairs* 82 (Apr. 1983): 267–77.

———. *Sir Bernard Bourdillon: The Biography of a Twentieth-Century Colonialist.* Oxford: Kensal Press, 1987.

Peel, J. D. Y. "Olaju: A Yoruba Concept of Development." *Journal of Development Studies* 14 (1978): 139–65.

———. *Ijeshas and Nigerians: The Incorporation of a Yoruba Kingdom, 1890s–1970s.* Cambridge: C.U.P., 1983.

———. "Making History: The Past in the Ijesha Present." *Man,* n.s., 19 (1984): 111–32.

———. "The Pastor and the *Babalawo:* Interaction of Religions in Nineteenth-Century Yorubaland." *Africa* 60 (1990): 338–69.

———. "The Cultural Work of Yoruba Ethnogenesis." In *Pioneer, Patriot,* ed. Falola.

Perham, Margery. "Restatement of Indirect Rule." *Africa* 7 (1934): 321–34.

———. *Africans and British Rule.* London: O.U.P., 1941.

Perry, Ruth. "Libraries in West Africa." *WAR* 26 (Sept. 1955): 827, 829, 831.

Phelps-Stokes Fund. *A Survey of African Students Studying in the United States.* New York: Phelps-Stokes Fund, 1949.

Phillips, Samuel Charles. "Industries in Post-War Nigeria." *Comet*, 12 Jan. 1944.

———. *Political Nigeria: Some Suggestions*. Oshogbo: the author, [1958].

Plotnicov, Leonard. "The Modern African Elite of Jos." In *Social Stratification in Africa*, ed. Plotnicov and A. Tuden. New York: Free Press, 1970.

Political and Economic Planning. *Colonial Students in Britain: A Report by P.E.P.* London: P.E.P., 1955.

Porter, A. T. *Creoledom: A Study of the Development of Freetown Society*. London: O.U.P., 1963.

Porter, Bernard. *Critics of Empire: British Radical Attitudes to Colonialism in Africa, 1895–1915*. London: Macmillan, 1968.

Post, Kenneth, and George Jenkins. *The Price of Liberty*. Cambridge: C.U.P., 1973.

Post, Kenneth, and Michael Vickers. *Structure and Conflict in Nigeria, 1960–1966*. London: Heinemann, 1973.

Prah, K. K. *Essays on African Society and History*. Accra: Ghana Universities Press, 1976.

Prakash, Gyan. "Writing Post-Orientalist Histories of the Third World: Indian Historiography Is Good to Think." In *Colonialism and Culture*, ed. Nicholas B. Dirks. Ann Arbor: Univ. of Michigan Press, 1992.

Priestley, Margaret. *West African Trade and Coast Society: A Family Study*. London: O.U.P., 1969.

Protest Committee of Nigerian Youths. *Politics without Bitterness*. Umuahia Ibeku: n.p., [1955].

Ralston, Richard D. "The Return of Brazilian Freedmen to West Africa in the 18th and 19th Centuries." *CJAS* 3 (1970): 577–92.

———. "A Second Middle Passage: African Student Sojourns in the United States and Their Influence upon the Character of African Leadership." Ph.D. diss., University of California, Los Angeles, 1972.

Ranger, Terence. "The Invention of Tradition in Colonial Africa." In *The Invention of Tradition*, ed. T. Ranger and E. Hobsbawm. Cambridge: Cambridge Univ. Press, 1983.

———. "The Invention of Tradition Revisited: The Case of Colonial Africa." In *Legitimacy*, ed. Ranger and Vaughan.

Ranger, Terence, and Olufemi Vaughan, eds. *Legitimacy and the State in Twentieth-Century Africa*. London: Macmillan, 1993.

Reade, Winwood. *Savage Africa*. 1864. Rpt. New York: Johnson Reprint, 1967.

Rich, Paul B. *Race and Empire in British Politics*. Cambridge: C.U.P., 1986.

Robinson, Cedric J. "Black Intellectuals at the British Core, 1920s-1940s." In *Blacks in Britain,* ed. Gundara and Duffield.

Rosiji, Ayo. "Colonial Development Corporation: What an African Thinks." *WAR* 18 (Sept. 1947): 1034.

Royal Institute of International Affairs. *Nigeria: The Political and Economic Background.* London: O.U.P., 1960.

Said, Edward W. *Orientalism.* New York: Vintage, 1978.

———. *Culture and Imperialism.* New York: Knopf, 1993.

Sarbah, John Mensah. *Fanti National Constitution: A Short Treatise on the Constitution and Government of the Fanti, Asanti, and Other Akan Tribes of West Africa.* 1906. 2d ed., with new introduction by H. R. Lynch. London: Cass, 1968.

Savage, V. Akinbomi. "Western Civilisation and War." *Service,* Dec. 1935, pp. 15–17.

Schomburg, Arthur. "The Negro Digs Up His Past." In *New Negro,* ed. Locke.

Schwab, William B. "Oshogbo — An Urban Community?" In *Urbanization and Migration in West Africa,* ed. Hilda Kuper. Berkeley and Los Angeles: Univ. of California Press, 1965.

Scobie, Edward. *Black Britannia: A History of Blacks in Britain.* Chicago: Johnson, 1972.

Shaw, Flora L. *A Tropical Dependency.* London: James Nisbet, 1905.

Shepherd, George. W. *The Politics of African Nationalism.* New York: Praeger, 1962.

Shepperson, George. "African Diaspora: Concept and Context." In *Global Dimensions,* ed. Harris.

Sherwood, Marika. "Kwame Nkrumah: The London Years, 1945–47." *Immigrants and Minorities* 12 (1993): 165–94.

———. "'There Is No New Deal for the Blackman in San Francisco': African Attempts to Influence the Founding Conference of the United Nations, April–July 1945." *IJAHS* 29 (1996): 71–94.

Shils, Edward. "The African Intellectuals." In *Christianity and African Education,* ed. R. P. Beaver. Grand Rapids, Mich.: W. B. Erdmans, 1966.

Sklar, Richard. *Nigerian Political Parties: Power in an Emergent African Nation.* Princeton, N.J.: Princeton Univ. Press, 1963.

Smith, Edwin W. *Aggrey of Africa: A Study in Black and White.* London: Student Christian Movement Press, 1929.

Smock, Audrey C. *Ibo Politics: The Role of Ethnic Unions in Eastern Nigeria.* Cambridge: Harvard Univ. Press, 1971.

Smyth, Rosaleen. "Britain's African Colonies and British Propaganda during the Second World War." *JICH* 14 (1985): 65–82.

Smythe, Hugh H. "Intermarriage in West Africa." *Sociology and Social Research* 42 (1958): 353–57.

———. "Human Relations in Nigeria: The Young Elite." *Journal of Human Relations* 6 (1958): 54–72.

———. "Nigeria's Marginal Men." *Phylon* 19 (1958): 268–76.

———. "The Problem of National Leadership in Nigeria." *Social Research* 25 (1958): 215–27.

Smythe, Hugh H., and Mabel M. Smythe. *The New Nigerian Elite*. Stanford, Calif.: Stanford Univ. Press, 1960.

Socialist Workers and Farmers Party of Nigeria. *Manifesto*. Lagos: [Ribway Printers], 1965.

Sofola, J. A. *Dynamism in African Leadership: The American Influence*. Ibadan: Daystar, 1982.

Solanke, Ladipo. "The Ogboni Institution in Yoruba." *Wasu* 1 (Dec. 1926): 28–34.

———. "The Customary Constitution of the Yoruba or Aku Commonwealth." *Wasu* 1 (Mar.–June 1927): 30–36.

———. *United West Africa (or Africa) at the Bar of the Family of Nations*. 1927. Rpt. London: African Publication Society, 1969.

———. *Lectures Delivered at the Abeokuta Centenary Celebrations on the Egba-Yoruba Constitutional Law and Its Historical Development*. Lagos: [Asaoku Printing Works], 1931.

———. *A Special Lecture Addressed to Mr. A. K. Ajisafe . . . on Egba Yoruba Constitutional Law and Its Historical Development*. Lagos: [Ife-Olu Printing Works], 1931.

———. *Yoruba Problems and How to Solve Them*. Ibadan: [Lisabi Press], 1931.

———. "Yoruba (or Aku) Constitutional Law and Its Historical Developments." *Wasu* 1 (Dec. 1932): 21–25; 2 (Jan. 1933): 28–38; 2 (Apr.–June 1933): 35–38; 3 (1934): 24–25.

Solarin, Tai. *Towards Nigeria's Moral Self-Government*. Ikenne: the author, 1959.

Soyinka, Wole. *Ake: The Years of Childhood*. London: Rex Collings, 1981.

———. *Isara: A Voyage around Essay*. New York: Random House, 1989.

———. *The Open Sore of a Continent*. New York: O.U.P., 1996.

Soyode, I. J. Oluwole. *Easy Reference Almanack for A.D. 1921*. Lagos: [Awoboh Printing Press], 1921.

Spitzer, Leo. *The Creoles of Sierra Leone: Responses to Colonialism, 1870–1945*. Madison: Univ. of Wisconsin Press, 1974.

Spitzer, Leo, and LaRay Denzer. "I. T. A. Wallace-Johnson and the West African Youth League." *IJAHS* 6 (1973): 413–52, 565–601.

Staniland, Martin. *American Intellectuals and African Nationalists, 1955–1970*. New Haven and London: Yale Univ. Press, 1991.

Stanley, Oliver. "Conservative Colonial Policy." *West Africa*, 4 Feb. 1950, 81.

Stein, Judith. *The World of Marcus Garvey: Race and Class in Modern Society*. Baton Rouge and London: Louisiana State Univ. Press, 1986.

Stepan, Nancy. *The Idea of Race in Science: Great Britain, 1800–1960*. London: Macmillan, 1982.

Stocking, George W., Jr. *Victorian Anthropology*. New York: Free Press, 1987.

Stolper, W. F. *Planning without Facts: Lessons in Resource Allocation from Nigeria's Development*. Cambridge: Harvard Univ. Press, 1966.

Strickland, C. F. *Co-operation for Africa*. London: O.U.P., 1933.

———. *Report on the Introduction of Co-operative Societies into Nigeria*. Lagos: Government Printer, 1934.

Taiwo, C. O. *Henry Carr: An African Contribution to Education*. Ibadan: O.U.P., 1975.

Talbot, P. A. "Some Foreign Influences on Nigeria." *Journal of the African Society* 24 (1925): 178–201.

———. *Peoples of Southern Nigeria*, 4 vols. London: O.U.P., 1926.

Tamuno, Takena N. *Nigeria and Elective Representation, 1923–1947*. London: Heinemann, 1966.

———. *The Evolution of the Nigerian State: The Southern Phase, 1898–1914*. London: Longman, 1972.

———. "The Formative Years, 1947–56." In *Ibadan*, ed. Ajayi and Tamuno.

Taylor, Ayodele. "Italy and Abyssinia." *Service*, Sept. 1936, p. 32.

———. "American Impressions." *Keys* 5 (Jan.–Mar. 1938): 70.

Temietan, S. O. "Marriage amongst the Jekri Tribes as Contrasted with That amongst the Hausa Tribes." *Nigeria* 13 (Mar. 1938): 75–78.

Tete-Ansa, W. "What Does West Africa Want?" *Empire Review* 44 (Sept. 1926): 253–59.

———. "The Iniquities of the West African Trade Monopolies." Typescript, 1931. HMP 31/10.

———. "The Ottawa Conference and British West Africa." Typescript, [1932]. HMP 29/4.

Thomas, Clare. "Colonial Propaganda and Public Relations and the Administration of Nigeria, 1939–1951." Ph.D. diss., Cambridge University, 1986.

Thomas, H. B. *History of Nigeria Bookshops*. Typescript, 1969. Royal Commonwealth Society.

Thomas, N. *Colonialism's Culture: Anthropology, Travel, and Government*. Cambridge: Polity, 1994.

Thornton, A. P. *The Imperial Idea and Its Enemies: A Study in British Power.* 2d ed. London: Macmillan, 1985.

Thorpe, Earl E. *Black Historians: A Critique.* New York: Morrow, 1971.

Tignor, Robert. "Political Corruption in Nigeria before Independence." *JMAS* 31 (1993): 175–202.

Tilman, R. O., and T. Cole, eds. *The Nigerian Political Scene.* Durham, N.C.: Duke Univ. Press, 1962.

Toll, William. *The Resurgence of Race: Black Social Theory from Reconstruction to the Pan-African Conferences.* Philadelphia: Temple Univ. Press, 1979.

Trotter, David. "Colonial Subjects." *Critical Quarterly* 32 (1990): 3–20.

Tugbiyele, Emmanuel Akande. *The Emergence of Nationalism and Federalism in Nigeria.* Agbor: the author, [1956].

Tukur, Mahmud, "A Critical Evaluation of Professor Ayandele's Book, *The Educated Elite in the Nigerian Society.*" In *The Essential Mahmud: Selected Writings of Mahmud Modibbo Tukur,* ed. Tanimu Abubakar. Zaria: n.p., 1990.

Turner, Lorenzo D. "Some Contacts of Brazilian Ex-Slaves with Nigeria, West Africa." *JNH* 27 (1942): 55–67.

Uchendu, Victor C. "Slaves and Slavery in Igboland, Nigeria." In *Slavery in Africa,* ed. S. Miers and I. Kopytoff. Madison: Univ. of Wisconsin Press, 1977.

Udo-Ema, A. J. "The Ekpe Society." *Nigeria* 16 (1938): 314–16.

———. "Fattening Girls in Oron, Calabar." *Nigeria* 21 (1940): 386–89.

Udoma, E. Udo. *The Lion and the Oil Palm.* Dublin: Univ. Press, 1943.

Ukpabio, Essien Essien Ukoh [written under pseudonym of Reverend Esiere]. *As Seen through African Eyes.* London: Stockwell, n.d.

Ulansky, Gene. "Nnamdi Azikiwe and the Myth of America." Ph.D. diss., University of California, Berkeley, 1980.

Ulansky, Gene, and M. O. Ojiaku. "Early Nigerian Response to American Education." *Phylon* 33 (winter 1972): 380–88.

Umo, R. Kano. *History of Aro Settlements.* Yaba: Mbonu Ojike, [1950?].

———. *Umuahia Today.* Information Series No. 2. Umuahia: Language Academy, 1955.

UNESCO, "Symposium on African Elites." *International Social Science Bulletin* 8 (1956): 413–98.

Usuanlele, U., and T. Falola, "The Scholarship of Jacob Egharevba of Benin." *History in Africa* 21 (1994): 303–18.

Utchay, Thomas Kanu. *Principles and Methods of Right Thinking Book I, Being an Introductory Book to KNODUBI System: A Readable Philosophy for Every Body.* Aba: [Education Mission Press], 1952.

————. *The Problems of the Igbo Orthography, Being the Solution to the Igbo Orthography Question.* N.p., [1952].

Uwanaka, Charles U. *New Nigeria.* Lagos: Pacific Printing and Publishing, 1953.

Uzo, Timothy Moka. *The Nigerian Political Evolution: A Stock-taking of the National Possibilities.* Lagos: Olympian Publishing Bureau, 1949.

————. *The Pathfinder: A Test of Political Ideals and an Interaction of Facts, Politics, and Common Sense in Nigeria.* Lagos: Olympian Publishing Bureau, 1953.

Varney, Peter D. "Religion in a West African University." *Journal of Religion in Africa* 2 (1969): 1–42.

Wahle, Kathleen O'Mara. "Alexander Crummell: Black Evangelist and Pan-Negro Nationalist." *Phylon* 29 (1968): 388–95.

Walvin, James. *Black and White: The Negro and English Society, 1555–1945.* London: Allen Lane, The Penguin Press, 1973.

Ward, E. D. "Dr. Moody Tilts a Lance." *WAR* 13 (Feb. 1942): 14–15.

Washington, Booker T. *The Story of the Negro.* 1909. 2 vols. Rpt. Gloucester, Mass.: Peter Smith, 1969.

Webster, James B. "The Bible and the Plough." *JHSN* 2 (1963): 418–34.

————. *The African Churches among the Yoruba, 1888–1922.* Oxford: Clarendon, 1964.

————. "Attitudes and Policies of the Yoruba African Churches towards Polygamy." In *Christianity in Tropical Africa*, ed. C. G. Baeta. London: O.U.P., 1966.

Weisbord, Robert G. *Ebony Friendship: Africa, Africans, and the Afro-American.* London and Westport, Conn.: Greenwood, 1973.

West African Students' Union. "Resolutions of the Conference on West African Problems, 29 and 30 August, 1941." CO 554/130/92946.

————. "W.A.S.U. Conference on West African Problems, 29 and 30 August, l942." *Wasu* 10 (May 1943): 1–41.

Wheare, Joan. *The Nigerian Legislative Council.* London: Faber and Faber, 1949.

Whitaker, Philip. "The Western Region of Nigeria, May 1956." In *Five Elections in Africa*, ed. W. J. M. Mackenzie and Kenneth Robinson. Oxford: Clarendon Press, 1960.

Williams, Ayodele. "The Policy of the Nigerian Young Democrats." Typescript, [1938]. HMP 73/6.

Williams, Gavin. "Nigeria: A Political Economy." In *Nigeria Economy and Society*, ed. Gavin Williams. London: Rex Collings, 1976.

————. "Garveyism, Akinpelu Obiesan, and His Contemporaries: Ibadan, 1920–22." In *Legitimacy*, ed. Ranger and Vaughan.

Williams, Patrick, and Laura Chrisman, "Colonial Discourse and Post-Colonial Theory: An Introduction." In *Colonial Discourse and Post-Colonial Theory: A Reader,* ed. P. Williams and L. Chrisman. New York: Columbia Univ. Press, 1994.

Williams, Walter L. "Black Journalism's Opinions about Africa during the Late Nineteenth Century." *Phylon* 34 (1973): 224–35.

Wilson, Henry S., ed. *Origins of West African Nationalism.* London: Macmillan, 1969.

Wolpe, Howard. *Urban Politics in Nigeria: A Study of Port Harcourt.* Los Angeles, Berkeley, London: Univ. of California Press, 1974.

Wyse, Akintola. "On Misunderstandings Arising from the Use of the Term *Creole* in the Literature on Sierra Leone: A Rejoinder." *Africa* 49 (1979): 408–17.

———. *The Krio of Sierra Leone: An Interpretive History.* Freetown: Okrafo-Smart, in association with the Sierra Leone Academy, 1989.

Yaba Club. *Appeal for Industrial Development Fund for Southern Nigeria.* Ibadan: [Smiles and Service Press], 1943.

Yoloye, E. A. "Reminiscences of an Ibadan Alumnus." In *Ibadan Voices: Ibadan University in Transition,* ed. Tekena N. Tamuno. Ibadan: I.U.P., 1981.

Zachernuk, P. S. "Nigerian Critics of Empire: Political and Economic Ideas among the Nigerian Educated Elite, 1920–1950." M.A. thesis, Dalhousie, 1983.

———. "Awolowo's Economic Thought in Historical Perspective." In *Chief Obafemi Awolowo,* ed. Oyelaran et al.

———. "Intellectual Life in a Colonial Context: The Southern Nigerian Intelligentsia, 1860–1960." Ph.D. diss., University of Toronto, 1991.

———. "The Lagos Elite and the Idea of Progress." In *Yoruba Historiography,* ed. Falola.

———. "Johnson and the Victorian Image of the Yoruba." In *Pioneer, Patriot,* ed. Falola.

———. "Of Origins and Colonial Order: Southern Nigerian Historians and the 'Hamitic Hypothesis' c. 1870–1970." *JAH* 35 (1994): 427–55.

———. "African History and Imperial Culture in Colonial Nigerian Schools." *Africa* 68 (1998): 484–505.

[Zikists], "Call to Action." 11 Nov. 1948. In CO 537/3557.

"Zikist Secretary." "In an Era of Revolution." *African Echo,* 8, 9 Mar. 1949.

# Index